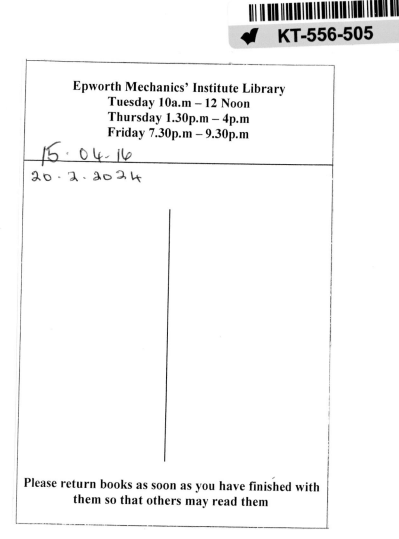

Epworth Mechanics' Institute Library
Tuesday 10a.m – 12 Noon
Thursday 1.30p.m – 4p.m
Friday 7.30p.m – 9.30p.m

15 · 04 · 16

20 · 2 · 2024

Please return books as soon as you have finished with them so that others may read them

ANYONE
CAN DO IT

ANYONE CAN DO IT

The Autobiography

Duncan Bannatyne

The right of Duncan Bannatyne to be identified as the author
of this work has been asserted by him in accordance with
the Copyright, Designs and Patents Act 1988.

First published in hardback in Great Britain in 2006 by
Orion Books
an imprint of the Orion Publishing Group Ltd
Orion House, 5 Upper St Martin's Lane,
London WC2H 9EA

3 5 7 9 10 8 6 4 2

A CIP catalogue record for this book is
available from the British Library.

ISBN-13: 978 0 75287 563 7
ISBN-10: 0 75287 563 9

Printed in Great Britain by
Clays Ltd, St Ives plc

The Orion Publishing Group's policy is to use papers that
are natural, renewable and recyclable and made from wood
grown in sustainable forests. The logging and manufacturing
processes are expected to conform to the environmental
regulations of the country of origin.

Every effort has been made to fulfil requirements with
regard to reproducing copyright material. The author and publisher
will be glad to rectify any omissions at the earliest opportunity.

www.orionbooks.co.uk

Contents

To my children: Abigail, Hollie, Jennifer, Eve, Emily and Tom.
Remember I love you more …

Acknowledgements

First and foremost, a big thank you to all my family and friends who have assisted me throughout the last fifty or so years of my life, as well as to all employees and professionals who have helped me in my business career.

I would also like to thank Jo Monroe for her help with the writing of this book, my agent David Smith at Annette Green Authors' Agency, as well as my publisher Ian Marshall, his assistant Lorraine Baxter and all at Orion. Thank you to my assistant, Kim Crowther, whose help with this book has been invaluable. Thank you all.

Introduction

Anyone can do it.

'Making £100 million is so easy anyone can do it. Few people believe me when I say that, but with this book I hope to show that it's true. Even people with no family connections, no money and no education can do it: I know because I did. I had an incredibly poor childhood, I left school without a single qualification and spent my twenties doing a string of dead-end jobs. It wasn't until I hit thirty that I took my career seriously and by thirty-five I was seriously rich.

Contrary to the advice in any business book I've ever read, I made my money without sector expertise, contacts or capital. I never had a USP, never had "first mover advantage" or invented anything, and I didn't even do anything unique or that someone else couldn't have done. What I did have was a *Yellow Pages* and some determination – and that's all it takes.'

Duncan Bannatyne

ONE

Meet the Bannatynes
1949–60

*When I am determined to do
something, I usually do it.*

People often ask me if I think entrepreneurs are born or made
because they want to know if there's something in my childhood
that singled me out for success. I don't know, to be honest, but I do
know that if you had a childhood like mine, you'll never get bored
of using private jets, owning luxury villas or staying in the best
hotels.

I was born on Wednesday, 2 February 1949 at Springfield House
in Dalmuir to the west of Glasgow, the second child of Bill and Jean
Bannatyne. They named me Duncan Walker after my father's uncle.

Springfield House was a large six-bedroom house, the type
normally occupied by wealthy families, but we were far from
wealthy. Springfield was a 'requisition house', one of several
properties taken over by the council to provide families with
accommodation while a massive rebuilding programme replaced
houses that had been lost during the Second World War. We shared
it with six other families and each family had just one room. The
toilet was communal, but as there was no bathroom, bath time at
Springfield meant boiling the kettle on the stove and filling the tin

bath in front of the coal fire. I remember that although my mum was gentler at towelling us dry, I always wanted my dad to do it: he may have been rougher, but he was also quicker, and it was bloody cold in that flat!

Our family grew fast: there was just eighteen months between myself and my older sister, Helen, and only fifty weeks between me and my younger brother George. Eventually there would be seven of us: after George came Anne, then William, and Campbell. My youngest brother Sandy was born on my dad's fifty-first birthday, which was after I had left home and joined the Royal Navy. When George was born, the council rehoused us for a short time in a prefab, then into a small semi-detached house on Canberra Avenue, and when we outgrew that, we moved into another council property, a 'four-in-a-block' (a bit like a semi, but with two flats on each side) on Dickens Avenue, where I shared a bed with my brothers in a room heated by a coal fire. By the time my father came home from the pub, the embers would be dying down and he'd often come into our room and put his big winter coat over the three of us.

My mum was born Jean McGovan Holmes in Paisley on 26 October 1925, the seventh of seven children. During the war, she worked at a munitions factory in Glasgow packing 25lb shells with cordite. She married my father in May 1946 and dedicated her life to bringing up us kids in an era with no washing machines, Hoovers or any of today's labour-saving devices. I have memories of my mum wringing our clothes dry on the mangle, and when I look back I can't believe how hard my parents worked just raising a family, especially my mum.

During the war my father served with the Argyll and Sutherland Highlanders regiment. He and his good friend Robert King were part of the thin red line during the Second World War and, after the fall of Singapore, both were captured by the Japanese. The Japanese transporter they were on was bombed by the Americans and both crew and prisoners had to abandon ship. My father watched helpless as many of his companions and fellow soldiers drowned. He always said that if he hadn't been a strong swimmer he wouldn't have survived. After several hours in the water, he was rescued from the sea, not by the Americans, but by the Japanese again. What a choice: drown or face life in a prison camp. I can't imagine what an experience like that does to you.

After a spell of hard labour on the notorious Burma railway he and Robert were taken to Nagasaki, where they worked in a mine near where the Americans dropped the atomic bomb. Somehow he survived brutal treatment that amounted to slave labour, and was forced to work in appalling conditions that killed many of his captured comrades. At the end of the war the liberators described my dad – who was 6ft tall but weighed under 7 stone – and his companions as 'the living dead', men who were so starved they should have died. When my father came home from the war, his mother was dead and his father was too sick to take care of him, and although he was entitled to double rations to help build him up again, it took the love and care of his wonderful Auntie Maisy and her husband Duncan, after whom I was named, to nurse him back to health. Auntie Maisy had an unusual way of lifting his spirits: she introduced him to my mother Jean. My father was ten years older than my mother, which was pretty scandalous in those days, and Jean's parents disapproved of their relationship. As far as I know, my mother's parents never spoke to my father and I've always thought they must have really loved each other to have married against her family's wishes.

My father wasn't the kind of man who talked about his experiences in the POW camp, and I wasn't the kind of kid who asked too many questions, but over the years and usually after a few pints of beer, I pieced together little snippets of information about his traumatic experience during the war. I didn't understand the full horror, however, until I reached my twenties when my father broke down after a family funeral and told me that the crematorium had brought back terrible memories of his years in the POW camp. He said it had reminded him of the times when he'd had to pile up the bodies of his dead comrades and set light to them. 'I will never forget the putrid smell of burning flesh,' he wept. He also told me a story of a time when he and his comrades, who were close to starvation, were driven to catch and eat a large rat, and how delicious that rat had tasted. In many ways my dad was just an ordinary man, but in other ways he was utterly remarkable.

The main thing I think I inherited from him was his unswerving determination. After all he had been through, he was adamant that he would get fit, get a job, get married, have children, bring up a family and contribute to the rebuilding of the country he had fought for. He succeeded, and it can't have been easy. When I'm determined to do something, like him, I usually do it, too.

We were a big, boisterous family and there were endless squabbles between us, but never any major fallings out. I am old enough to remember life before television, and before we got our first TV in the sixties, long after everyone else in the street had got one, most of my memories are of playing outside, kicking cans around or going to the local baths for a swim, where I began my life-long affinity with water. After my father's experience in the war, he made sure that all his children could swim, and we also spent a lot of time with him in the garden and allotment, growing vegetables which my mum would use in a stew. Dad also kept rabbits and chickens, which again ended up in my mum's kitchen where all us kids were made to do our fair share of the chores.

On Saturdays we would often go to the pictures and watch a cowboy movie at the Regal cinema. Usually two of us would pay to go in, and then we'd go into the toilets and pull the others in through the window. We'd then spend their ticket money on sweets. Once we had the TV, I would watch shows like *Watch With Mother* with my younger siblings, and my sisters and I seldom missed an episode of *I Love Lucy*. But there wasn't much to do, and once – in a desperate bid for excitement – I got into trouble with a couple of pals when we nicked some turnips from the local allotment! On another occasion, the local copper rounded up a few of us for throwing stones at swans. I don't remember if we actually threw any stones, what I do remember is that I'd been told to look after my little sister Anne, and when the police took us away they hadn't realised Anne was in her pram and had been left behind all on her own!

I think I always wanted life to be more exciting than it was. I was terrible at being bored and so took myself off to the library to read cowboy books and adventure stories. One day I picked up a book on magic and taught myself to do some tricks. It entertained my friends and I was asked to put on a show for the Boys' Brigade. I liked the attention, and looking back I can see there was a bit of a show-off inside who wouldn't come to the fore again until I started a TV career in my fifties.

Although my mum's dad still refused to talk to my father, the rest of mum's family were close. Her sister Margaret and my cousins David and Sheila lived locally, and we often spent time at Auntie Margaret's. She was a complete Trojan, a hardworking woman who wouldn't take any lip from any of us, and if we tried anything, she'd threaten us with her carpet beater, though she never actually used it. My cousins on my dad's side of the family also figured pretty heavily in my childhood, so we were devastated when two of them died within a couple of years of each other. One succumbed to leukaemia, and the family was only just coming to terms with that when her younger brother Alex ran out of the school gates and was hit by a bus. They managed to jack the bus off him, but just when it looked like he would make it, the jack collapsed and the bus crushed him, killing him instantly. A few years later their older brother died of a heart attack – it's no wonder both parents became alcoholics and didn't live long into their forties. The crematorium in Clydebank wasn't far from our street, and it loomed large over our young lives, a grim reminder that life could always get worse.

In one sense, most people in Clydebank were the same: a lot of us lived in a council house and supported either Rangers or Celtic, most people's mothers stayed at home and most people's dads worked at the Singer sewing machine factory. It was a huge factory – the largest in the world when it was built in 1884 – and at its peak in 1960, it employed more than 6,000 people. My dad worked in the foundry, pouring liquid metal into the moulds that made the sewing machines. Like everyone else, when the bell rang at the end of the working day, he headed straight for the pub and often wouldn't come home until closing time.

In another sense, though, I knew we were different. Other kids had bikes and got ice creams when the ice cream van came round, and some of their parents had cars and televisions and other things to be envious of. There was a kid next door who was an only child and he had so many toys that it just emphasised how few we had.

Often when I asked for something like an ice cream, I was told I couldn't have it. And when I asked why, I always got the same answer: because we were poor. I heard that phrase so often that I grew to hate it. I know there were times when my parents could buy ice creams, and there were occasions when my grandma gave me enough money for a treat, but my overriding memory is that more often than not we went without. I didn't understand why we were poor, because as far as I could see we were as good as anyone else. It felt like we were being punished when we'd done nothing wrong, so I promised myself that when I grew up I would not be poor. That's a completely different thing to saying I was going to be wealthy – there was no way I'd have dared to dream I would become rich – I just wanted to have enough money to buy my whole family an ice cream. And I was determined that when I grew up I would have a car and that my children would have bikes and as many ice creams as they wanted.

My memory is that my brothers and sisters were much happier with our lot than I was. At some point, I remember having a day out to see the Queen, who was visiting Glasgow. Everyone was getting very excited and saying what a special day it was, but the crowd was fifty deep and I couldn't see a thing. I didn't see the point of it: I wanted to meet her properly and have a cup of tea with her! I remember being dissatisfied a lot of the time and rarely happy. My brothers and sisters always got excited when we took the bus to Saltcoats on the west coast for our summer holiday, but I couldn't see what all the fuss was about and found it boring. It was almost as if I was enduring my childhood while I waited for something bigger and better to come along.

School wasn't any different from home life in that I was often unhappy. I think it must have been because I got into trouble a lot and found it hard to pay attention to things I didn't see the point of. I went to Dalmuir Primary School and the one subject where I showed some natural ability was maths, but even my maths teacher didn't have much time for me because I was unable to show my workings out. I could calculate quite complicated sums in my head, but I couldn't explain how I worked the answers out. It's obviously an ability that's served me well in later life as I can instantly tell in negotiations if someone's trying to swindle me, but at school it just made me seem like a cocky troublemaker.

Nevertheless, I could see that the kids who went to high school – what in England would be called a grammar school – had better toys than me, and so I made it my mission to do as well as I could at school so I would pass my 11 Plus and get into what we called the 'posh school'. My sister Helen had already failed her 11 Plus, so no one held out much hope for me, but I knuckled down anyway, staying in and reading while my brothers were out playing, and studying really hard.

When I passed – I was the only one in the family who did – my parents were incredibly proud of me. I remember my dad saying, 'My son's going to be a doctor, my son's going to make something of himself,' and of course it felt terrific, it's a moment I remember with pride.

However, when I started school, it was immediately obvious that I was going to find it tough. There were 600 children at that school, and on the day I started 598 of them had a school uniform. I was one of the other two. Uniforms were expensive and my mum had had trouble getting the right clothes. I think she'd borrowed a blazer and made some trousers herself, but it wasn't a proper uniform like the other kids had. She told me to tell the teachers that I would have my proper uniform for the second week of term, but in that first week the damage was done: everybody knew I was poor and they either teased me about it or shied away from me. Not only was I different from the kids at school, at home I was also seen as different because I went to a posh school. Wherever I went, I felt like a misfit.

TWO

An entrepreneur in the making

1960–64

You have to make your own chances.

I noticed that most of the kids at the high school had bikes and, as the only kid without one, I felt incredibly left out. I had been asking my dad almost all my life for a bike, but now I began asking him every day. Of course, his answer was still the same – we were still poor – so I decided that if he couldn't buy me a bike then I'd have to buy one myself. I knew a couple of kids at school had paper rounds, so I thought I'd get one and save up.

The local paper shop was in Duntocher Road, not far from our place on Dickens Avenue. It was always known as Jenny's News-agents, after its owner. I went in and asked for a paper round, but Jenny looked down her nose at me and said, 'There's none available.' I didn't believe her and instinctively knew that she thought I was a scruffy urchin who couldn't be trusted. I also knew there were people in Clydebank who wanted a paper delivered because my mum was one of them.

So I told Jenny, 'My mother wants a paper delivered but no one delivers in our street.'

'Well you can't create a paper round for just one house,' she replied.

'How many houses do you need?' I asked.

Jenny looked me up and down, and thought for a second about a number that would put me off. 'One hundred,' she said. And that was it. I made up my mind that I was going to find a hundred households that wanted a paper delivery. From that moment on I was small boy on a mission to buy his first bike and I rushed back home to get a pencil and paper. I wrote my mum's name at the top of the list and then started knocking on doors, asking if anyone wanted a paper delivery.

I started with the neighbours who all knew me, and when they said 'yes' I grew in confidence and carried on knocking on doors until the evening. I ended up in streets I didn't really know, cold-calling complete strangers, not that I knew it was called cold-calling in those days, of course. I had to knock on about 150 doors to get my 100 names, but by the time it was getting dark I had them. Knowing that I was late, and knowing that my parents would be worried, I decided to take what I thought was a short cut home and ended up getting lost. By the time I got home it was completely dark and my parents were frantic. Earlier, I'd anticipated praise from my dad for showing initiative, but all I got was a clip round the ear for worrying my mother.

That night, with the list of names tucked under my pillow for safe keeping, I dreamt of the bike I would buy, and as soon as I woke up I went straight back to Jenny and asked again for a paper round. This time she had no option but to say yes. It was my first taste of entrepreneurialism, and looking back, I can see that it was also my first mistake in business: I now realise that my list of names was very valuable to Jenny and I should have sold it to her rather than giving it away. Still, we live and learn.

I don't know why I was the kind of kid that got off his backside and didn't take no for an answer. I think I just knew that the other kids who had paper rounds were no better than me, so perhaps it was a sense of injustice that drove me to prove I was as good as them? I can't be sure, but I do see getting that paper round as the first clue as to what I would achieve in business when I grew up. I guess I learned early that business and opportunity aren't handed to you on a plate and that you have to make your own chances.

I was so determined to get a bike that I was never tempted to spend any of the money I made on sweets; I just put it all away, and after about three months I think I'd saved enough money to buy a second-hand bike on HP. I was so happy – it was the most fantastic feeling because it wasn't just a bike, it was a reward for hard work, dedication and having a bit of know-how. Oddly, I have absolutely no memory of learning to ride, I can't even think who would have taught me, but I do remember that having a bike wasn't enough to make me popular with the other kids and that I was still finding school hard. A few months later, though, I managed to make another dream come true: in the summer, when the ice-cream van came round again, I had enough money from my paper round to go out and buy ice creams for my whole family. Ice cream had never tasted so good.

As I grew up, I would occasionally find myself getting into fisticuffs with the boys from the local Catholic school. I didn't really know why we fought, it just seemed to be the thing you did when you ran into one of them. My dad was an Orange man and, although I didn't understand the politics, I knew from an early age that the Catholics were somehow different from us. Not that my father went to church – I don't think it was about religion for him, it's just that he wanted everyone to be like him. He supported Rangers and that said it all: there was a great divide between the Protestant Rangers supporters and the Catholic Celtic fans. Although I'd taken after my dad in looks, as a teenager I started to form my own opinions and I began to realise that I didn't want to grow up to be like him.

My father was an incredibly proud man; proud to be working class, proud to be a Labour supporter and proud to be a family man. He had fulfilled the dream he had, after surviving the POW camp, to live quietly, find a wife and raise a family. It seems a simple dream to us now, but in those days it must have been quite daring, and achieving it was by no means straightforward. To his credit, he had got what he wanted and he was contented with his life. He was a popular guy with a wide circle of friends from the veterans' club, the freemasons and the Orange order, so he had plenty of people around him who shared his attitudes. I have a lot of respect for my father and recognise what a huge achievement it was for him and my mother to raise and provide for a family in those years, but I just couldn't get excited about the same things he did. When the Orange parades happened each year he got very enthusiastic about them, but for me they were just a day to stay inside. Nevertheless, he was so keen for me to get involved that he arranged for me to learn the flute so that I could take part in the marching band! I only ever marched once, but I did play the flute in assembly at school once, and I seem to remember that the girls liked that. Not that I had a girlfriend in those days – I never even thought of girls like that then. I would occasionally walk a few girls home from school or carry their books; I liked girls' company, but it was still a few years before I had a girlfriend.

My father also tried taking me to football matches, to watch Clydebank and Rangers, but football wasn't a game that captured my imagination and I soon stopped going to matches. He was incredibly set in his ways: he always drank in the same pub, read the same paper and held the same views. I remember when I got bit older I tried to take him to different pubs, but he refused to go into 'a bar with a carpet in it just so I can pay an extra penny for my pint'!

That's not to say that we fought or didn't get on, we actually got on very well; he just seemed to be the only one who didn't realise that times and attitudes were changing. In the sixties I started to sense that there was a bigger world out there, as I'd seen things on TV that gave me glimpses of opportunities his generation had never known. The one thing my father and I did share, though, was a love of boxing, and when Cassius Clay won his first title in 1963 we were both transfixed. There had never been a boxer like him – his style was so beautiful – and we loved to watch him fight. To this day, seeing Muhammad Ali on TV makes me think of those evenings I spent with my father.

As I got a bit older, the differences between my family and I made me realise that I didn't want to spend my life working at the Singer factory, and that meant I had a problem: there was no obvious route out of Clydebank as I wasn't doing well enough at school to get any qualifications. The paper round had often made me late for school and I found it hard to catch up. I fell behind and began to get a bad reputation with the teachers. I got the strap so often that I achieved the class record for it and I think the other kids started to admire the way I took whatever punishment the teachers threw at me. Of course, that only egged me on to get into more trouble, as at this point there seemed little reason to pay attention in subjects like history and geography, although I was just about keeping up in English and maths. The only subjects I was actually good at were PE and woodwork, so it seemed my only career option would be joinery.

I had another reason for not trying hard at school: there was no way my parents could support me through college. Although my father had once dreamed that I might become a doctor, even if I had done well at school, I could never have gone on to further education without financial support, as there were no grants in those days.

School became pretty pointless and I left at the earliest opportunity without a qualification to my name. My teachers had often asked me what I was going to do if I didn't pass my exams, so I told them that I was going to join the Royal Navy. It wasn't just to shut them up; I really did want to join up. As someone who wasn't particularly well educated, academic or articulate, I just wanted to be more than one of the hundreds of people working at Singer's on a slave wage. I don't know where that desire came from and why I wasn't willing to accept my lot, but I didn't have my father's attitude that we are working class and we should be proud of that and that we shouldn't have ideas above our station. All I wanted was adventure.

I knew I didn't have too many options and that the armed services offered good prospects for a boy like me. I would have a career, a decent wage and some status – all things a job in a local cabinet-maker's couldn't give me – and, crucially, life at sea would get me out of Clydebank and help me see the world. I didn't have many ambitions at that age, but I was determined to travel.

My parents, especially my mother, weren't keen for me to sign up. Not only did my mum not want her little boy leaving home, but at the back of her mind she must have thought about my dad's ship going down. The fact that we were in the middle of the Cold War can't have helped: it seemed likely that a military career would see me take part in one conflict or another. After all, this was 1964, and it was only a couple of years since we'd all held our breath as Kennedy and Khrushchev had gone head to head over the Cuban Missile Crisis. But I was young and didn't think anything would happen to me – you don't at that age – and I was as determined to join the armed services as I had been to get a bike.

However, because I was under sixteen, I needed my parents' permission to join and my mother refused to sign the forms. It wasn't often that my mum refused to let me do something as she wasn't the kind of woman who put her foot down. For most of my childhood she had been a benign presence, going along with whatever my father wanted and offering unconditional support to her family. So when she said she didn't want me to join the Navy, I knew she *really* didn't want me to join. But, like my father, I was determined, and so I threatened to run away to London and become a tramp and a junkie if she didn't let me sign up. She eventually gave her consent.

At first, I'd thought about joining the Army, probably because my dad had been a soldier, but it was his experience of Army life that convinced me to join the Navy. The whole point of signing up was to see the world and my father told me that if I joined the Army I'd spend the whole time square bashing. If I wanted to travel, then the Navy was the place to serve.

I think there was about a six-week gap between leaving school and joining the Navy and I spent that time working at a local cabinet-makers. I can't remember who organised it, perhaps it was my parents hoping I'd change my mind, or maybe it was my woodwork teacher. If it had been my mum's plan to get me to stay, it failed: having a regular job only made the Royal Navy seem even more exciting. I couldn't wait to leave.

THREE

In the Navy

1964–68

*I always preferred to talk
my way out of trouble.*

Given my attitude to authority, I guess it was inevitable that I'd run into some problems when I joined the Royal Navy. But when I said goodbye to my family at Glasgow Central Station, I had no idea that within a few short years I'd be dishonourably discharged.

There were about fifteen lads from Scotland meeting at the station to travel down to the training base in England together. My parents, sisters and a couple of my brothers got the train from Clydebank to Glasgow to see me off. Although this was my first time away from home and family, I think I was too excited to be scared. I was leaving Clydebank to see the world and I felt great. I think I also felt proud and that I was an adult going off to do a man's job, but my Navy records show that I wasn't even fully grown when I joined – I was only 5 feet 3 inches.

I was fifteen years old and too young to join the Navy officially, so I was being sent to the boys' training base near Ipswich, known to everyone in the service as HMS Ganges. It had a reputation for harsh training methods that turned out self-reliant, professional sailors and was famous for its 143-foot-high training mast which all recruits were made to climb.

We arrived just as it was getting dark and a truck from the base came to pick us up from the station. After our registration, we were taken into the base, and as soon as we passed through the gate, the officers started shouting 'Left, right, left, right!' That was it, we were in the Navy, and from that moment on I entered a world of rules and regulations.

Bloody hell, I thought, I've entered Stalag 17.

Life at HMS Ganges was hard but fun as the officers put us through our paces to get us fit enough for life at sea. Mostly I remember running around the parade ground and going up and down that bloody mast. After having shared with my brothers for so long, I was used to a lack of privacy and found the transition to accommodation in the old Nissen huts pretty easy. Although I'd had a bit of a talent for answering back at school, in the Navy I knew I had to keep my mouth shut. As I was so young and so keen, and because everything was so new to me, I didn't feel the need to question things too much. Mostly I really enjoyed myself; I'd made friends with some of the other recruits and we would often go into town on our nights off to drink and meet girls. It didn't take me long to realise that girls really do like a sailor, and of course this meant that the local boys were jealous, so there were quite a few fights.

I acquired a bit of a reputation as a tough guy – I think it's the accent – but I never went looking for a fight and always preferred to talk my way out of trouble. My instinct was to back down and my attitude was non-confrontational. I'd always mutter, 'I'll show you' under my breath and use that anger to prove people wrong. I was what you'd call determined rather than hot-headed.

One morning after a fight, we lined up on parade for inspection by the divisional officer and one of my mates had a black eye.

'Did you get that fighting the local lads?'

'Yes, sir.'

'Well done, lad.'

There was a huge sense of camaraderie, even with the officers, and it created a tremendous sense of belonging, which meant I felt no qualms about signing up for twelve years' service. I would have been twenty-seven when I got out if things had gone to plan, and at the time I believed it would be my career, my life, and I was happy with my choice. Knowing how things turned out, and understanding myself a bit better, it seems almost funny to me now.

There are loads of different career paths in the Navy and you have to choose what you're going to specialise in before you join. I don't think we got a lot of guidance, which is probably why I ended up selecting to spend the next twelve years in the engine room as a stoker. Although ships had long since stopped using coal, the word stoker was still used for those sailors who worked with the engines. My choice was based purely on the fact that I'd been good at woodwork at school and thought I might be good with mechanical stuff, too. The good thing about being a stoker was that there was always something to do, adjusting pipes and monitoring valves. The bad thing about it was that the engine room was in the bowels of the ship, and if the vessel got into trouble you'd be last men to make it to the lifeboats.

My first commission was on HMS *Eagle* and I spent my first few months at sea going round the British Isles, which wasn't exactly the glamorous life on the open seas I'd imagined. But we were a small team and a tight unit in the engine room and I enjoyed the company of the other stokers. The only problems I had were with my commanding officers. The NCOs – the non-commissioned officers – were all right because they were working-class lads who'd earned their promotions, but the commissioned officers – who'd come straight in with their stripes from university – were prigs and bullies. Unsurprisingly, we took the piss out of them when their backs were turned. We were young and mischievous and constantly found little ways to break the rules without getting caught.

My favourite trick was a way of getting to spend more time on shore when I'd either used up my shore leave or had it suspended for some petty infringement of the rules. If you couldn't leave the boat, it meant twiddling your thumbs onboard when the bars and good times were only a few hundred feet away. So I used to put my clothes inside a big dustbin, cover them with paper, then cover that with rubbish and take the bin out to the bin stores. Once I'd dumped the rubbish I'd change into my civvies and spend the night on the town. The officers never checked you on the way back, so I'd just pick up my uniform and the empty bin and climb the ladders back on to the ship.

Eventually we got to leave British waters and by the age of seventeen I was incredibly well travelled. If life in Clydebank had been small – small dreams, close horizons and spending months at a time without even leaving the neighbourhood – those years in the Navy opened up my eyes and taught me things about the world that had never been discussed around the table when the Bannatynes sat down for tea.

When I was seventeen, we docked in South Africa for twelve days, and there were several families who were keen to have British sailors stay with them while we were on leave. My knowledge of international politics wasn't great, but the effects of apartheid were immediately apparent even to me. I was driven round by a white family, whose daughter I'd started seeing, when we witnessed the aftermath of a car crash that had injured several black people, all of whom were covered in bandages. The girl turned round to me and said: 'That's bloody typical, they always travel round in big groups and they're always having accidents. And do you know what? Even if they're not hurt they insist in being covered in bandages.'

I'm not sure what I was supposed to make of that – was she trying to tell me that black people were accident prone, or hypochondriacs? Or that they had such poor access to healthcare that they deliberately faked injuries so they could get some free bandages? I was too young and too unsure of my position to question her, and if I'm honest it was only later in life that I started to feel uncomfortable about what I'd seen: at that age I just didn't know where to put myself and didn't have the social skills to respond. She told me another story about a bus running over a black man and not stopping as if nothing had happened. She seemed to consider this a perfectly acceptable thing to do and I was just too shocked to argue with her.

I spent my time in South Africa with my eyes out on stalks, taking in every new experience with a sense of wonderment: this was exactly why I'd wanted to join the Navy and get out of Clydebank. The family I stayed with took me to a safari park and within a couple of days I had seen lions, elephants, rhinos, hippos and buffalos. It was an amazing experience, and again it wouldn't be until I was older that I realised how lucky I had been – many people can spend weeks on safari and never get to see lions or rhinos. I wrote letters home regularly, and I can't imagine what my parents thought of my stories: they probably thought I was making them up.

The one experience you couldn't make up, though, was a snowball fight we had on the top of Table Mountain. It hadn't snowed there for a couple of generations and most of the people in the city had never seen snow. We climbed to the top just to watch people looking at the snow! Of course, growing up in Scotland, snow was nothing new to me, but for South Africans it was a once-in-a-lifetime experience.

On another occasion, we docked in Split in what was then Yugoslavia, and it was the first communist country I'd ever been to. I changed my money at the onboard post office and went ashore like I'd done countless times before, though I wasn't at all sure what to expect. Although my knowledge of world affairs was limited, I knew that the communists were 'the enemy'. There were so many people on the streets carrying guns that we were a bit jumpy at first, but when we got into the bars we found that everyone wanted to buy us a drink. They were so friendly and so keen to speak English and show us their city. It was a real eye-opener and the kind of current affairs lesson you don't get from watching the news.

I changed ships many times but never saw active service. I took part in several training exercises and fake wars, but mostly when we were at sea we were just testing equipment and seeing how fast the ship would go. After a couple of years of that, and a couple of years of sucking up to my commanding officers, I realised that the Navy wasn't really for me, even though I still had ten years left on my contract. Unsurprisingly, I became pretty demoralised and didn't even bother putting myself forward for promotion.

There are only three ways of getting out of a contract with the armed services: you can either die, get so badly injured that you can't perform your duties, or misbehave so badly that they throw you out. Guess which one I preferred?

Even as early as my posting on HMS *Eagle*, I was seriously considering how I could get myself into so much trouble that they'd kick me off the boat. But when I entered the stokers' mess on my first day on board, I met some guys who instantly became friends, and I began to think that maybe I could stick it out to the end of my contract. My only problem would be taking orders from my commanding officer, a lieutenant called Stuart Hall. We didn't see eye to eye from the start and I took an instant dislike to him: he wore far too much aftershave and thought his stripes meant he was a better man than any of the sailors who answered to him. We both thought the other was a waste of space.

My best mate on board was a guy called Brian Smith, who was a great source of fun and trouble. We all called him 'Bwian' because his girlfriend at the time had a lisp, and to kill time on board Brian and I joined the boxing team. As we sparred most days, I guess it was inevitable that I'd end up with an injury: one day I was training with a much bigger guy who I'd cornered and who decided to get out of trouble by windmilling his arms around to create some space. As his arm circled, he landed an awkward punch that bent my nose flat against my face. It hurt like hell and poured with blood, but I told Brian that I didn't want to go to the doctor. Thankfully he insisted. The doctor took one look at me, held my nose between his finger and thumb and pushed it back into position – well, almost! Words cannot describe how much that hurt. Of course my nose is still bent to this day, and I get through loads of pairs of glasses because they always get twisted on my crooked nose.

I only ever had one competitive boxing match, when I fought for the stokers in an interdivisional tournament held on the deck of our aircraft carrier. Brian had trained me well and on the day he got me completely hyped up so there was no way I was going to let the stokers down. My opponent was a good fighter, but as I'm left-handed I box southpaw, I found I could dance around him and land a couple of blows on his undefended left ear. It was enough to win the match on points and the respect of the lads in the crowd.

Brian was a much better fighter than me – I had a great left hook but I lacked the killer instinct – and he would punch you pretty hard if he thought you weren't training seriously. With so much spare time, I was getting incredibly fit and filling out from a scrawny kid to a pretty fit-looking guy, despite my broken nose. And I wasn't the only one who noticed – the girls did, too.

Although I'd always enjoyed girls' company and been good at chatting them up, I'd never actually gone out with a girl and I'd certainly never slept with one. Many of the guys on the ship bragged that they'd slept with loads of women, but I'm not sure I believed them. Although this was the sixties, it was before the Pill had made an impact and sexual liberation hadn't really happened yet, so I was just waiting for the right girl.

One night when we were docked in Portsmouth, some of the guys from the ship and I decided to go to a dance on shore. I was heavily into the Beatles and had a bit of a mop top, and I reckoned I looked pretty good. Even though we weren't in uniform, all the girls knew we were sailors and we got quite a bit of attention when we walked in. We'd go to the bar, get a few drinks in and check out the girls. On this occasion, I saw the most beautiful girl I'd ever seen, with the prettiest smile, and so of course I asked her to dance.

Her name was Sallyanne Green and, in the coming weeks, I would fall head over heels in love with her. But after the first dance, I didn't realise that and told her I'd better go and join my mates without making her promise to save the last dance for me – something that sounds unbelievably old-fashioned now. At the end of the night, the last song came on, so I went to find her and was disappointed to see she was already dancing with somebody else.

'I thought you said you'd save your last dance for me,' I said while staring out the other guy.

'I thought you were joking.'

'I wasn't joking,' I told her seriously.

And so she ditched the other guy and danced with me and that was it: we were together. Like most eighteen-year-olds who fall in love for the first time, I thought that Sallyanne and I would stay together, get married and do the happily-ever-after thing. Suddenly shore leave became more and more important to me and I would take every chance I could to stay at her flat. It felt very grown-up – other guys were losing their virginity in the bins round the back of nightclubs, but I had a girl with her own flat. We would get up in the morning, have breakfast in bed and then spend the day together until I had to get back to HMS *Eagle*.

My schedule obviously meant I was away a lot, so in the whole time we were together we probably only spent about fifteen nights with each other, and in between visits I had to content myself with being her penpal.

Knowing that Sallyanne was waiting for me made taking the flak from Lt Stuart Hall even harder. I knew I had a better life waiting for me outside the Navy and he couldn't handle the fact that my career wasn't the be all and end all of my life. He started reporting me for every minor offence and all I was allowed to say was 'Yes, sir'.

Smithy also got on the wrong side of Hall and this made us even better friends. If we were on the ship we were boxing, and if we were on shore we were out having adventures together. There was one particular night I remember when we'd docked in Hong Kong and landed ourselves in some seriously hot water.

As ever, we made our way to a bar to try out the local liquor and see what the town had to offer. Whenever you go ashore, the Navy recommends that you stick in groups of three of four, as that way you're less likely to be attacked or provoke an assault. But Brian and

I were the best boxers on the ship and we were confident we could handle ourselves.

We walked up to this particular bar, and as we opened the door a group of six men spilled out who were about as drunk as it's possible to be while remaining upright. They'd been drinking for hours and were in the mood for a little excitement and when they saw us they decided they'd found their fun.

The first blow found the back of my head and I stumbled before several more rained down on me. The eight of us were trapped between the outside door and the inner fire door of this bar. I looked at Brian and he looked at me, and with a tiny nod of our heads we decided to respond in kind, two against six; then all hell broke loose.

I tore into one guy, punching and kicking him, and it took me a while to realise that Brian was taking on the other five by himself. I remember keeping my guy at bay with a few punches just so I could watch Brian. He was like something out of a Bruce Lee movie, bashing heads together and kicking one in the nuts while he smacked another in the face. He was incredible.

I finished my guy off just in time to see one of the other guys grab a crate and bring it down on Brian's head. Smithy put his arms up for protection, and as the crate came down on him it tore the skin off the backs of his hands. I jumped on the guy with the crate and finished him off, and we carried fighting on until we'd broken all six of them. They had black eyes and fat lips and when they couldn't take any more they sloped off, looking like they'd been in a fight against ten, not two.

After that, we walked into the bar to a hero's welcome. The lads we'd seen off had been causing trouble all evening and the manager had been trying to kick them out for hours. This sweet little girl pulled out a first-aid kit and started dressing Brian's wounds. I desperately wished I had a more dramatic cut than the bite I'd sustained on my thumb! Eventually she gave me a plaster, but she was clearly more interested in Brian.

The next day, we were back onboard when we happened to see the guys we'd been fighting with. Because HMS *Eagle* was the biggest aircraft carrier in the fleet at that time, with over 2,500 sailors on board, we'd never seen them before. For a moment I thought they were going to get their revenge, but they came up to us and acknowledged that they'd been beaten, showed us respect and shook our hands. I think they even apologised.

Word got round about our brawl, which helped my reputation as a boxer, and I was soon put forward for an interdivisional tournament. I'd represented my ship once before, but this time I was going to be fighting for the Navy against the Army. However, before I could really get down to training, I got myself into a major spot of bother.

FOUR

Dishonourably discharged

1968

*When I have a mission, it gives
me something to focus on.*

As I've already said, I didn't much care for my commanding officer, Lt Stuart Hall. The months of taking orders from him had started to take their toll, and what had begun as a petty annoyance had brewed into a major source of friction. He had been singling me out for punishment and kept reporting me for minor infringements that other stokers got away with, so I was starting to hate him and realised I didn't want to work for him any more. As there was no easy way of getting out of the Navy, though, I was going to have to do it the hard way: I was going to have get myself dishonourably discharged.

One night, when we were anchored off Lossiemouth in Morayshire, the officers were having a party onboard with guests from the mainland. Lt Hall was quite drunk and was intent on impressing his girlfriend, who was a guest at the party. The two of them got off the ferry boat that had brought them over from shore, and as Lt Hall climbed on deck, he caught my eye and saw an opportunity to show his girlfriend what a big man he was. He walked over to where Brian and I were standing and poked me in the stomach with his torch.

'Move back,' he said

'Please don't poke me with the torch, sir,' I told him.

'Move back,' he ordered and poked me again.

'Please don't do that again, sir.'

'Move back,' he repeated angrily.

So I took a step back and he walked into the party, leaving me fuming. I turned round to Brian and said something like, 'If he tries that again I'll . . .'

'You'll do what?'

'I'll bloody throw him overboard.'

'I bet you bloody won't.'

'I bloody will.'

'I bet you five pounds you won't.'

That very second I knew that he was going over the rail. In those days, when someone dared me, I found it very hard not to rise to the bait. So when Lt Hall came out of the party about half an hour later, I didn't think twice. I ran over to him, picked him up by the knees, lifted him into the air and hoisted him over the rail before anyone could stop me. There was a 20ft drop down to the cold North Sea – if the fall didn't hurt him, the cold water soon would.

Luckily there were a couple of people onboard who realised what was going on and they pulled me back and grabbed hold of him while he was still holding on to the rail. As he was hauled back on deck, he looked at me in a fury. That expression on his face was worth all the punishment I had coming to me: I felt fantastic, even though it was clear I was going to pay.

I was taken straight down to the cells, which were next to the paint store on a lower deck, and was left there to await my fate. The windowless cell was 8ft by 6ft, and all it had in it was a single metal bunk, a thin mattress and a couple of blankets. I guess I should have been scared, or at least sorry, but I was actually quite excited as I was pretty sure I'd found a way of swapping a twelve-year sentence for a much shorter one.

After a couple of days the captain summoned me for a hearing, where I pleaded not guilty to using violence. I was able to do this as no witnesses had come forward to say it was me. However, the captain decided that he couldn't decide the matter by himself and ordered a court martial, the military equivalent of a criminal trial. It would take about six weeks to prepare that case, and I was to spend the time in solitary confinement onboard the *Eagle*.

When there's only one prisoner in solitary confinement, the officer charged with guarding the prisoner can get pretty bored. So one day my guard asked if I'd like a game of draughts: as long as the chain remained on the door and I remained in my cell, he thought it would be all right. We spent several hours with the board table propping open the door, with me on the inside and him in the corridor. By the end of six weeks we'd got to know each other pretty well, and as friends brought me plenty of reading material, I rarely felt lonely. In fact, one of the things I remember reading was a newspaper article about a businessman who had started from scratch and was now worth millions. It got me thinking that maybe I could do something similar when I got out, and dreams of future success kept my spirits up. I also continued to write to my parents, and friends brought their letters down to me, which also helped keep my mood upbeat. As I didn't want to worry my mum and dad, I didn't tell them about the court martial, as there was always a chance I wouldn't be found guilty and they'd never need to know.

One of my senior officers was tasked with representing me, and he was determined that I wouldn't let the stokers down. He told me I was representing the whole team and made sure my uniform was spotless, and when he marched me into the court room, he commanded me to hold my chin up, look straight ahead and keep my arms straight.

I couldn't pretend I wasn't guilty any longer – and if I did there was a chance a 'not guilty' verdict would let me serve out the rest of my contract with the Navy – so I admitted the charge. Although the verdict wasn't in doubt, the sentence was, as my crime of 'showing violence to a senior officer' was considered serious enough to warrant a two-year stay in a civilian prison. I was lucky: I got nine months in Colchester barracks, an Army detention centre, followed by a dishonourable discharge.

When I left the court martial, I experienced a mixture of fear and relief that the trial was over and my sentence was relatively light. I was only nineteen and I didn't have a clue what I would do next, or how my parents would react. But whenever you change your life there's always that little bit of excitement about the future, and that's what kept me going. The thought of Sallyanne Green also helped: in just nine months I'd be able to spend as much time with her as I liked.

What I hadn't realised was that court martials are pretty big news, and Scottish sailors who get court martialled are particularly big news to the Scottish press. My mother tells me that she was quietly watching the local evening news with her supper on her lap and a cup of coffee in her hand when the newsreader announced that 'Nineteen-year-old sailor Duncan Bannatyne was today dishonourably discharged from the Royal Navy . . .' I'm not sure if the coffee stain ever came out of the carpet.

She was completely shocked as she'd only just received a letter from me saying how well things were going! She was sure there must have been some mistake, so she called up the naval base, made some enquiries, only to find out that the newsreader hadn't got it wrong. After several more calls from the local call box, she found out where they had taken me.

My mother was so worried about what the Navy had done to her little boy that she decided she'd have to visit me in Colchester. This was quite an undertaking for her – it would have meant a train to Edinburgh, then down to London, where she'd pick up the train to Colchester – and I'm not sure she'd ever been to England before. But that was what my mum was like when her kids were involved: nothing was too much trouble.

Having not told my parents about the court martial while I was on remand, I decided to continue writing to them as if nothing had happened throughout my sentence to spare them any unnecessary worry. When I was told I had a visitor, I told the officer he must have made a mistake – as far as I knew, nobody had a clue where I was. When I was finally led through to the visitors' area, I got the shock of my life when I saw my mother and Auntie Margaret staring back at me.

Of course my mother refused to believe that I'd done anything wrong and insisted that the Navy had to be at fault. Auntie Margaret was slightly more sceptical. When I explained that I had indeed tried to throw my commanding officer overboard, Mum soon began to see the funny side of it and relaxed. She was still a bit concerned about what I would do when I was discharged, but she said she was convinced I'd make something of myself. Hearing her say that was a huge boost to my morale.

It turned out that the Bannatynes had some distant relatives in Colchester and my mother arranged for them to bring me regular supplies of shampoo and toiletries, as all I got given at the barracks was a bar of coal tar soap. The small comforts they brought me made my nine-month sentence that little bit more bearable.

In actual fact, I didn't find the sentence all that hard, mostly because I was fit, and that meant there were always weaker, fatter guys who got picked on ahead of me. What I hadn't reckoned on, though, was that many of the other guys serving time had done some pretty horrific things to warrant their imprisonment. Two of the worst men I've ever met in my life were serving their fourth detention term for skinning cats alive, of all things. They weren't right in the head and were incredibly tough. They were also incredibly fit, and I made it my mission to beat them on the assault course. When I have a mission, it gives me something to focus on, and that small goal carried me through. It wasn't much, but it gave me enough of a reason to get up in the morning and do my chores.

There wasn't actually that much to do in the detention centre, and most of what we did involved training: many of the men would be going back into service after their sentence, and so the officers' job was to get us as fit as possible. We were on the assault course pretty much every day and I've never been fitter in my life. But no matter how hard I pushed myself, I couldn't beat the cat-skinners. Somehow this continued to spur me on – I was determined to beat them one day.

I had to wait until my last day in Colchester to get what I wanted. It was my final circuit and I had nothing to lose: I ran so fast, timed all the jumps perfectly and scrambled over the wall with just the right technique, and as I came to the last hundred yards I had both of them in my sights: I dug down and forced my legs to sprint. It was enough to catch one of them, but the really nasty guy still beat me. It was only after I crossed the line that I realised I had torn my trousers from crotch to knee and that I was in agony. Still, it didn't matter – I'd proved what I could do if I put my mind to it, and the next day I would see Sallyanne again.

We had arranged by letter to meet at London's Paddington Station under the clock. I hadn't seen her for months and I longed to take her in my arms and start our new life together: as far as I was concerned, we were going to get married and live happily ever after. I arrived at Paddington, my heart thumping with nervousness and excitement. I bought a bunch of flowers with some of the £21 – not to mention the eight shillings and a penny – I'd been owed in final salary at the end of my sentence, and went to wait for her under the clock.

The station was absolutely packed – I'm not sure I'd ever been to London before and I had no idea it could be so busy. I looked and looked and looked for her but I couldn't see her. I began to feel weak at the thought that she wasn't coming, as it had only been imagining this moment that had sustained me for so long. And then I saw her in the crowd and my heart practically exploded. I fought my way through the crowd, dropped my bags and wrapped my arms around her.

A few years later, when the song 'Tie a Yellow Ribbon…' came out, it made me think about that moment. Just like the lyrics, I'd come out of prison for a reunion with my sweetheart, and even though Sallyanne and I had split up by the time it was in the charts, hearing it took me straight back to Paddington Station. Other people of my generation have much cooler favourite songs by Hendrix, the Stones or the Beatles, but because of that long wait at Paddington Station I have the most uncool favourite song of anyone I know.

Sallyanne and I took the next train down to Devon, where she had arranged for us to stay in a B&B for a few nights. Only having had the company of men for nine straight months made those nights with Sallyanne all the sweeter, but just when I thought we would be together all the time, she told me she'd joined the RAF. I couldn't believe it. And what was worse she was due to start her training in four days' time! When we kissed goodbye at the end of that perfect week, we didn't know what the future would hold – she had her training and I needed to find a job, so we couldn't even plan to meet again.

It turned out to be the last time we ever saw each other, and so Sallyanne Green remains my first love, unsullied by rows, infidelity, boredom or all the other things that can turn love into complacency. I returned home to Clydebank, moved back in with my parents and signed on the dole. But I wasn't depressed – I knew it wouldn't be for ever and that I had a chance to do something more exciting with my life.

FIVE

Whatever it takes
1969–72

*Why wouldn't you want to buy
something that made you money?*

When I got back to Clydebank in 1969, things had changed. For starters, I had a new little brother, Sandy, who I hadn't seen before and who was already a toddler, and both my sisters were well on the way to getting married, both coincidentally to men named Smith. Helen's wedding had been planned for some time, but I seem to remember that Anne stole her thunder and got married first aged just nineteen. It wasn't a long-lived union.

Helen's marriage was more stable, and both her and her husband Leslie managed to get a bit of money behind them by buying tenement flats. There had been a scheme in those days where you could buy a room in a tenement, known as a 'single end', on a three-year loan, and as they were both working, they'd both bought one. Of all my siblings, Helen was the one who shared some of my get up and go: her plan was to sell the tenements and use the profits to emigrate to Canada, where her brother-in-law had already started a new life.

I was also starting a new life, although in very different circumstances. I had no qualifications, no money and no reference from my previous employer, of course. My prospects didn't look that good, so I signed on the dole while I looked around for work.

To get my dole money, the Labour Exchange insisted I enrol in a training course and get myself a trade, so they sent me to the job centre, where I was given a list of available courses and told to choose two. My first choice was to become a typewriter repairman, as I figured I'd spend all my time in nice offices talking to lots of secretaries. It seemed like a pretty good trade to me, so I didn't give too much thought to my second choice. Unfortunately the typewriter course was already full and the job centre automatically booked me onto my second choice: I was going to train as an agricultural vehicle fitter and welder.

The course took place in Balloch, up by Loch Lomond, so I spent quite a lot of money on train fares there and back, which meant I needed a job just to complete the course. As the training was over by four o'clock, it meant I could take on an evening job, and I ended up doing bar work at the Atlantis Bar next the Singer factory. I would get there just in time for six o'clock, when the workers would stumble out into the evening like zombies needing a few drinks to wash the factory out of their thoughts before they headed home. I also got a job at a hotel on Sundays – in those days only hotels could serve alcohol in Scotland on Sundays – so I was earning pretty decent money, which meant I could afford one of my childhood ambitions: a car.

Somehow I needed to fit in some driving lessons, so I arranged for the instructor to pick me up in Balloch and teach me as I drove back to Clydebank for my shifts at the Atlantis. Once I'd bought my car, a metallic green Hillman Minx with a matt black roof, I wasn't about to wait about for a train in the cold, so even though I hadn't passed my test, I drove myself to the training course each day. Inevitably I ended up with a few points on my provisional licence, but I didn't care because driving was the coolest thing I'd ever done. No one in my family had ever had a car before and it felt so good to be behind the wheel that I wasn't going to let a technicality stand between me and my car. I eventually passed my test at the second attempt.

Once the course had finished and I'd got my qualification, I was offered a job on a farm in Rugby repairing tractors. It was the start of a pretty scrappy chapter of my life where no job seemed to last for more than a few months, I spent a lot of time on the road and would often end up back at my parents when the work dried up. In the next few years I would live all over the country – Brighton, Leighton Buzzard, Leicester – repairing tractors, forklift trucks and buses. It was filthy work and no matter how hard you scrubbed your hands, you could never get all the dirt out. My hands were always grubby, and it was the sort of thing girls used to notice.

Having said that, I was also having a terrific time. After the confines of the Navy, where I was constantly being told what to do, I was now a free agent, walking into a new town every few months, finding a B&B and asking around for work. It was exactly what I needed. I made friends, I mended cars for favours instead of paying for digs or beer and just went with the flow. Occasionally I'd completely run out of money and have to hitchhike back to Glasgow, where I could always find work in a bar or driving a taxi. I didn't have a plan and I wasn't too bothered if I seemed to be going round in circles: it was enough just to be out of the Navy.

After muddling through for a couple of years, by the time I was twenty-three I'd begun to establish myself back in Clydebank and was earning enough money to get a flat on my own. It wasn't anything special – it didn't even have a phone – but after years of sharing either with my brothers or crew members, it was a chance to have a room of my own. I was able to afford the rent because, without planning to, or even realising it, I'd actually started my first business. I'd gone to an auction to buy a cheap car to repair using the skills I'd learned on my course. As taxis were unlicensed in Clydebank in those days, to make a bit of extra money I used to wait outside stations and pubs, picking up fares. I started making enough money to buy another car at auction, but as I couldn't drive two taxis at once, I got a mate to drive the other one and split the takings with him. And when that produced enough income, I used it to buy

a third car. I didn't see it as anything other than common sense –
why wouldn't you want to buy something that *made* you money? –
but looking back I realise it was my entrepreneurial drive looking
for an outlet.

Having spent so long away from my family on farms or at sea, I
actually enjoyed being back in Clydebank. I still didn't have any
plans, but I'd succeeded in not being poor, and for the time being
that was enough. It was also lovely to be able to pop round to my
parents for Sunday lunch and see my little brother Sandy grow up.
Occasionally Helen and her husband would be there, and they'd tell
me about their plans for selling up and going to Canada. I think my
mum had started to do a bit of cleaning work by then, so there was
a bit more money coming in, and all in all it seemed like a good time
for the Bannatynes.

But that all changed with a simple knock at the door in October
1972. I was at my flat watching TV and preparing for an evening in
the taxi when I answered the door to find one of the other taxi
drivers.

'Your family have been trying to get hold of you,' he said. 'They
called the office.'

His voice was faltering and I knew he had bad news.

'The controller radioed everyone and asked someone to come and
get you.'

'What is it?' I asked, not wanting to know the answer.

'Your sister's dead.'

'Which one?'

'I don't know.'

I drove thirty minutes from my flat to my parents' house not
knowing which sister I had lost.

SIX

Becoming the oldest
1972

---

*Life is too fragile and valuable to be
spent doing something you hate.*

Helen and Leslie had only left for Canada a week or so before. They had both been so excited about their new lives – they had even been excited about getting on an aeroplane – and we had been looking forward to her first letter telling us all the news of her glamorous new life on the other side of the world. It seemed impossible that she was now dead.

It was difficult getting information back from Canada, which made it even harder to believe what had happened. Bits and pieces filtered through to us and we learned that just a few short days after stepping off the plane, she had suddenly collapsed and died. She had been such a tall, fit young woman that this made her passing even more unbelievable: how could someone so full of life just drop dead? My parents were desperate for an answer – we all were – and the doctors eventually told us it was most likely to have been a brain tumour. At the time, people speculated that going on the Pill had caused the tumour, but I very much doubt that had anything to do with it. I now believe that it was likely to have been deep vein thrombosis, a condition no one seemed to know about or talk about some thirty-five years ago.

The family had a wretched week waiting for her ashes to come back from Canada so we could have a memorial service. We were all devastated and tried to do whatever we could for Mum and Dad. My mother seemed to cope by keeping busy, but in the days that followed we watched new lines appear on my father's face and circles darken under his eyes. Being forced to wait so long for information, and then for her ashes to be returned, delayed the grieving process and the whole family was on hold until we could lay her to rest.

I was now the eldest and I felt a huge responsibility to take charge. I had a car, I tried to do as much of the organising as I could and used to pick up relatives so they could come and sit with my parents. Auntie Margaret, who had offered so much support in the past, was yet again a source of strength to us all.

With three young kids at home – William, Campbell and Sandy – my mother had something to focus on just cooking and washing for them. My father, who didn't do any of the household chores, had been given time off work and he didn't know what to do with himself; nor did I know what to do with him except take him to the pub.

He had been drinking in the Mountblow Bar for over twenty years, and of course everyone in there knew about Helen and wanted to offer their condolences. It was impossible not to talk about her. We spent hours in there, talking and drinking, each pint making us more melancholy, and that's when he told me the horrific story of how he'd had to pile up the bodies of his comrades in the POW camp and set light to them. We got very drunk together that night and cried like babies. I'll never know what percentage of the tears were for Helen and what percentage were for his lost friends, but I do know that I will always love my father for his strength, honesty and pride. Obviously I had been told throughout my childhood that he had been a prisoner of war, but it was only then that I realised what that had meant – the suffering, trauma, rats and death. Seeing my father so emotional, and finally understanding the things he had overcome, gave me a new respect for him and brought us closer together. How unfair, I thought, that a man who had already suffered so much now had to grieve for his eldest child. It was heartbreaking.

Helen's death changed all of us for ever. The family dynamics shifted and my parents were never the same again. Many years later, at my fiftieth birthday party, in the middle of one of the best nights of my life, my mum – who was also having a pretty good time – was joined at her table by two friends of mine. All three of them had lost a child, a fact that only I was aware of. I stood there, the party going on at full pelt around me, quietly wondering if they could somehow tell they had something in common. Was that the magnet, I wondered?

While nothing can compare to losing a child – I cannot bear to contemplate something happening to one of my kids – it's also pretty hard to lose a sister. My brothers and other sister are the kind of people who remember the date Helen died and would never fail to go and lay flowers or commemorate the day in some way. I wasn't like that, and I don't know if over the years they thought that I didn't care. If they did, they were wrong: Helen's passing had a profound affect on me. I have no doubt that it changed my life and made me the man I became.

In the weeks immediately after her memorial, though, my priority was taking care of my parents. With no one to lean on myself, my behaviour became belligerent and I ended up in a few scrapes. I lost my licence for drink driving – a bloody stupid thing to do, not least because it meant I could no longer drive taxis, putting paid to my first business venture. That in turn meant I had to start travelling all over the country again, taking work as a fitter and welder wherever I could find it. I regularly visited my parents, though, and on one weekend back home I somehow ended up getting arrested for disturbing the peace. I'd been out drinking with some friends in a pretty rough part of Glasgow, and was walking home by myself. All I did was kick a bloody can, but as soon as I did a police car swung round the corner and an officer jumped out.

'What the fuck do you think you're doing?' he asked in that

smart-arse way all bent coppers seem to have.

'What the fuck's it got to do with you?' is how I probably answered, and within seconds he had me in an armlock and was calling for back-up.

Then, when the second car arrived, he started punching me in the stomach to make it look like I was resisting arrest – he just wanted to make the crime, and himself, look bigger. At the time the Clydebank force had a reputation among my friends for being corrupt, and a few years later I think the corruption came to light, but there was nothing I could do: I ended up with a conviction – and a fine – for disturbing the peace.

It was a pretty bleak time for me and I was arrested again in March 1973, only this time things worked out a little worse. It was on another weekend home, and after another night out drinking, that I was arrested for being drunk and disorderly. I was beginning to feel a little picked on, so I gave a false name, only in my drunkenness I gave a mate's name.

The investigation ran its course and it eventually came to trial. I got the day off work and travelled up to Glasgow for the hearing, as I knew I had to own up to my real identity, otherwise my friend would get into trouble. I stood up, confessed, and was immediately rearrested. I was charged there and then, pleaded guilty and was sentenced. The fine was £10, which might not sound a lot, but it might as well have been a million quid because I didn't have it. And as I couldn't pay, I was given an alternative sentence: ten days in Barlinnie gaol.

Barlinnie, in the East End of Glasgow, is one of those old Victorian prisons with a reputation for overcrowding and murderous behaviour. I couldn't believe I was being taken there for such a petty crime. The friend whose name I'd given had been at the trial and he promised to try and find the money. It took him three days.

Barlinnie was not a pleasant place, but it wasn't that long since I'd been in the Navy training every day, so I was still pretty fit. Although it was frightening, the real reason I was scared was because I thought I'd lose my job. My hunch was right, and when I got out I found myself out of work yet again, with an ever-lengthening criminal record to impress future employers with. There was a chance I could have gone off the rails at this point, but something stopped me: it was Helen. The tragic death of my sister had taught me that life is precious and can be short. Because of her, I knew I couldn't carry on wasting time and that I had to make some changes and get in touch with the dreams I'd had when I'd been in detention on HMS *Eagle*. I started to reaffirm that I was going to make life bigger and better for myself.

I've often wondered how my life would have turned out if Helen had lived. I've read many times that it's often the oldest child who becomes the most successful in any family, the one who breaks out and makes a different life for themselves. Perhaps it's only because I became the oldest child later in life that it took me so long to become a successful entrepreneur. In the aftermath of her death, grief sent me off course, but as the months passed, her memory only made me more determined to make something of myself.

I left Clydebank again and followed the money south through another string of welding and fitting jobs. Although I was still working for someone else, at least I had a trade that could potentially lead to something. At this point I had a renewed sense of self-belief, but when I found myself in yet another muddy field, shivering under the hood of another tractor, with oil under every fingernail and in every crease of my skin, I realised my future had to lay elsewhere. Helen's death had made me impatient because it had taught me that life is too fragile and valuable to be spent doing something you hate. I quit and decided I had to make some changes. I knew it was all down to me: *I* would be the catalyst, *I* was the only one who could make it happen. My instincts told me that I would know the right opportunity when I came across it, and until then, Helen's death would encourage me to make the most of my life, and in the next few years I had a wild and wonderful ride.

SEVEN

Jersey

1974–78

Why don't we just leave here and go and start a business and become millionaires?

Fed up with the cold, I headed as far south as I could get in the hope of picking up some bar work over the summer. When I'd worked on a farm outside Brighton, I'd spent a lot of time with holidaymakers – well, girls on holiday to be more specific – and I thought I could handle the easy money and easy sex of life in a resort. So I got on a ferry to Jersey, where someone had told me my driving licence would still be valid. If there was no bar work on offer, then at least I could pick up shifts as a taxi driver. I didn't know a soul on the island, but as soon as I got off the ferry – with just my rucksack and a few quid in my pocket – I liked Jersey, and I got the feeling Jersey liked me, too.

I followed my nose from the port into the centre of St Helier, looked for a cheap B&B, checked in and asked if the landlady knew any pubs that might need bar staff. After dumping my rucksack, I found the pub she'd mentioned and landed myself a job. Finding friends was just as easy – you just had to pick up a pool cue in the right pub and start a conversation. Within a few weeks of being on the island it felt like I'd been there for years.

It was 1974 and, like my idols Lennon and McCartney, my mop top had been replaced by shoulder-length hair and a moustache, while the girls all had long hair and talked about peace and love. I don't think any of us would have called ourselves hippies, we were just incredibly laid back and unconcerned about the future.

Working in a bar meant that I had the mornings free, so I'd often start the day at the beach. A friend had a camper van and we'd drive out of St Helier to Five Mile Beach to catch a few waves. Surfing is an incredibly intense experience – it takes all your thoughts and all your muscles and rewards you with one of the best natural highs in the world. I loved it and started to regain some of the fitness I'd lost since my Navy days.

I also discovered that girls find the rough, surfer look very appealing. I had a good body, smiled a lot and was growing in confidence. Having spent several years in very male environments – the Navy, farming and cabbying – on Jersey I had a more mixed circle of male and female friends. It wasn't just about the sex, or the promise of it, I found that I'd often have more interesting conversations with women, or perhaps it was just that when women are around, the conversation doesn't get too blokish.

Everyone had a different reason for coming to Jersey – usually they were either running away or searching for something – and that meant there was a huge mix of backgrounds in our gang. I wasn't just mixing with the stokers of the island, I was getting to know the officers and people from all walks of life, including university graduates and other 'middle-class devils' my father had warned me about, and I formed friendships there – most notably with a guy called Mick Doherty – which have stayed with me for the rest of my life.

I hadn't planned to hang around, but soon realised I'd been on Jersey for a year, and then in the blink of an eye it was two years. Life was easy and I was having so much fun that I didn't notice or mind that my dreams of making something of my life, perhaps even starting a business, had been put on hold.

These days, people talk about the swinging sixties as the era of the sexual revolution. That might have been the case in San Francisco, but in Jersey it was the seventies that swung. Girls on holiday were much more willing to experiment than they were at home, where their reputations might have been tarnished. This was long before anyone had heard of HIV, of course, and if we'd given any thought to catching anything – which we didn't – we'd have assumed a shot of penicillin from the doctor would have sorted it out.

Mick and I took a series of jobs; one week we'd be deck-chair attendants, the next hospital porters, lorry drivers or ice-cream vendors. There were plenty of wealthy people on the island, with million-pound mansions and boats moored in the harbour, and every so often there'd be a bit of work tending bar at a private party. That was the first time I caught a glimpse of the millionaires' lifestyle, and I guess I must have thought a few times, 'I wonder if this will be me one day'. However, we'd often find ourselves between jobs, and with nothing to do we'd head to the beaches or bars and find ways to entertain ourselves. We thought we'd got life sorted and although we'd occasionally get into a bit of trouble – I once got arrested and fined too, for selling ice cream on a Bank Holiday, which is illegal in Jersey – for a couple of years life was one long holiday. Even working was fun, as there was no better way to meet girls than to serve them drinks or sell them ice creams.

I survived on a tiny amount of money, but I never felt poor. My digs were cheap because, as a non-resident, I was only eligible for temporary housing. The accommodation was mostly appalling, but on the one occasion I found a half-decent room going cheap because no one else wanted to sleep in the same bed as the recently jailed 'Jersey rapist'. Once the rent was paid, everything else was pretty cheap: you never took a girl out for dinner, only ever for a drink – and perhaps a burger if you really fancied her – and there was nothing else to spend money on. Every job I did was cash-in-hand so I never needed a bank account, and as this was Jersey there wasn't any tax to pay. I probably earned about £200 a month, and spent every penny of it. If I did have something left over, it would have been stored in my spare shoes until the ferry brought the next lot of girls over. I didn't even need to spend money on clothes – my rough-and-ready surfer look would have been ruined if I'd worn decent threads. I couldn't have been any happier if I'd had a million pounds in the bank.

As it's virtually impossible for non-residents to start a business in Jersey unless they're incredibly wealthy, there was never an incentive to do anything other than part-time jobs. Over the years I worked out a few ways of making a bit of extra money, and one of the easiest was renting an ice-cream van for the day and buying some stock. I found out that you could pay extra to get an exclusive pitch, and if you were the only ice-cream van in sight you'd do better than if you were one of several around the main beaches. Without realising it, I was learning quite a lot about running a small business. I didn't realise I was learning at the time, or that the skills I was picking up would change my life, I just knew that if it was a festival day – Jersey has a huge flower festival – or if the weather was good, I could make enough to take the rest of the month off.

We partied hard. I was probably fit enough and young enough to have put away eight pints a night – no wonder so much of Jersey is a blur to me now! Vague memories of good times are occasionally peppered with moments of clarity, like the night the DJ stopped the music to tell us all that Elvis was dead. He played a couple of Presley songs, then went back to his playlist as if nothing had happened. I think I remember that so clearly because it was one of the few news stories that punctured our Jersey bubble. I could tell you precious little about anything else going on in the world in those days – I was too busy having a good time.

To make sure our fun wasn't spoiled by too much work, Mick and I often joined the Monday Club, which only had one rule: you didn't work on a Monday. We'd start the week with an all-day party and feel pretty smug that we weren't tied down by a nine to five, answering to a boss we couldn't stand. The problem with not working Mondays, was that it was harder to get a job on a Tuesday; so we also joined the Tuesday Club, which meant it was pretty easy to end up in the In Between Jobs Club, too.

As Mick decided to settle down – and marry – his girlfriend, I started to grow a little dissatisfied with the endless partying. I even got a bit tired of surfing and of always having wet clothes and sand everywhere. These days people often ask me if I regret spending so much time partying when I could have been doing something more productive, and I always tell them I wouldn't trade away a single day of my days in Jersey: it was fantastic – some of the best years of my life, in fact – and there's not a bum job or hangover I regret. I might have only had one pair of shoes and one pair of denims to my name most of the time, but I was very happy there, and I realise now that I actually learnt a lot about myself which helped me be more effective in business when I was older. Apart from picking up bits and pieces about the ice-cream trade, which would prove directly relevant to my future career, I got to know myself, learning my strengths and capabilities. I also got to like and believe in myself, and the idle notion that I might someday start a business began fermenting into quite a powerful brew. What was once a dream was becoming an intention.

And there's one other bloody good reason I don't regret partying for so long: Gail. I don't actually remember the first time I met Gail as she was just one of the gang. I probably knew two or three of her ex-boyfriends, and she probably knew a couple of my exes, too. Everyone's lives in our little gang were so entangled that there was always the possibility of friendship turning into something more. But even though Gail was blonde and petite – just my type, as it happened – I still didn't think of her as anything other than a mate for several months.

I think she started to see me in a new light when I shaved my beard off. It was very fashionable then, thanks to the Bee Gees, but it didn't suit me all that well, so I went back to just a moustache – I may also have had a Kevin Keegan perm around this time – and I noticed that she started to look at me differently and was suddenly a lot more attentive. She had a habit of coming up to me and saying, 'Laugh' because I had a loud laugh that she thought was hilarious. And she was so cute that I just had to oblige.

With Mick married, I began thinking it was about time I settled down too. Gail worked as a waitress at a golf course where she got a room with the job. Her digs were a huge improvement on the room I'd been staying in, so after a few weeks I moved in with her. And that was it: we were together and it immediately felt like something permanent.

Gail was the sort of girl you married, and I realised that if we were going to make a life together, then I was going to have to get myself a regular job so we could afford a place of our own. I applied to drive the Coca-Cola delivery lorry, as I'd got my HGV licence while I was on the island, and it would actually have been quite a prestigious job had I got it. But I didn't, and reluctantly I began to realise that I would have to leave Jersey behind me.

I wasn't far off thirty, and I was beginning to think it was time to start taking life more seriously. The looming threat of the big 3-0 finally helped me make the decision to start doing something about my long-held ambition to start a business.

The turning point came one Sunday morning after yet another Saturday night partying. I was sitting on the beach with Gail, looking out at the waves rolling in, when it dawned on me that I'd been the oldest person at the party the night before. There's no way I wanted to become the oldest swinger in town, and I realised the time had come for action.

Earlier that morning, we'd picked up the paper to read over breakfast and I'd read a story about a man who'd started a business on a shoe string and gone on to become a millionaire (I'm pretty sure it was an article about Alan Sugar). It was a real rags-to-riches story, and as I sat there looking out to sea I couldn't come up with a single good reason why I couldn't do exactly what he'd done.

Gail and I had been together for about six months at this stage, and I knew I wanted to marry her and start a family, but I also knew I didn't want to bring kids into the world without having something to offer them: I wanted them to have bikes and ice creams and toys – all the things I hadn't been given.

At the time I was in between jobs again, and the prospect of finding employment was looking pretty bleak. The only jobs on the island were the seasonal ones I'd been doing for four years, or banking or nursing positions, for which I was unqualified. And without a permanent job I would never qualify as a resident and never be able to rent a decent flat, let alone buy one. I'd thought about setting up in business on my own, but as a non-resident I wouldn't be allowed to raise finance or buy a lease on premises, assuming I'd had the money, of course.

I didn't see any opportunity for me to retrain or go to college and nor did I think there was any chance of me getting a proper job – who would want a twenty-nine-year-old beach bum in their company? After reading the Alan Sugar article, it seemed clear to me that the only way I could make a living was to create my own business.

'Gail,' I said, throwing pebbles into the sea, 'I think it might be time for us to leave Jersey.'

'Where would we go?'

'Somewhere warm, preferably, but I don't really mind.'

'And what would we do?'

'Oh, I don't know,' I said as I turned to her. 'Why don't we just leave here and go and start a business and become millionaires?'

I think she thought I was joking.

EIGHT

Duncan's Super Ices
1978–85

You should never let it get personal.

It didn't matter to me that I didn't know anyone who'd started a business, or that I didn't have any assets or capital, not to mention any contacts. Deep down I knew this Alan Sugar guy didn't have anything I didn't have, and if he could do it, so could I. My intention was to go to the south coast of England and try something in the tourist industry, so we got on a ferry and headed back to the mainland.

Before embarking on our new adventure, Gail announced that she wanted to visit her sister Irene in Stockton-on-Tees, as she hadn't seen her for two years, so we drove north in my little Mini for a quick stopover. I thought we'd only be there for a few nights – a few weeks tops – but we ended up staying for years, and they turned out to the most eventful years of my life.

I'd never been to Stockton before – to be honest, I don't think I even knew where it was. All I remember was that after Jersey it seemed cold and windy and I really wasn't very happy there at all. I'm sure it didn't help that the local paper had a front page story about a woman who'd stabbed her husband to death. Unsurprisingly, I thought it was a terrible place, I hated it and was itching to go south. However, while we were there it made sense to sign on the dole, as once you had registered in those days, you could move around to different places and still receive benefit. With a little bit of money coming in, things got a bit easier, and so a couple of nights turned into a couple of weeks, and then a couple of months. All the while I was thinking about leaving, but I started to see the benefits of staying put and owning our own home. Suddenly we weren't with party people any more, we were with people who had roots and purpose, and I guess it started to rub off.

Irene and her husband Peter lived on an estate called Bishopgarth, which was full of identical houses, ideal for first-time buyers. There wasn't much there apart from a pub, so that's where we spent most of our evenings. Then one night a friend of ours set me a challenge, or more accurately he dared me, and, of course, I just had to prove him wrong. He was a bit up himself – he had a three-bed semi, two cars, 2.4 children, everything I didn't have, and he was only twenty-four – and he was enjoying telling me I'd wasted my life. Like so many Brits, he insisted on telling me how much money he'd made on his house and what a fool I was for working in dead-end jobs. I told him he didn't have that much equity and that I could easily catch up with him. But then he pointed out that to get a mortgage I'd need to get a job first so I could provide the bank with proof of income. Then he went on to say that no one would give me a job because there were no jobs to be had.

'You'll never get a job round here,' he said.

'Yes I will.'

'No you won't.'

'Yes I will.'

'No you won't.'

'Want to bet?'

Of course, I didn't really have any interest in getting a job, but I was bloody determined to prove this sanctimonious git wrong! So the next day, Gail and I knocked on the door of every local business asking for work. All we got were rejections, but the following day the personnel manager of a local bakery phoned and said she'd been so impressed that we'd shown some initiative that she'd had a look round and found jobs for both of us. I had won the bet, but I soon realised it had a price: hard labour.

Gail and I worked at Sparks' bakery, a huge place where they made loaves for Mother's Pride and most of the supermarkets' own brands. It wasn't the most glamorous job in the world, but it was our plan was to save up for a deposit on a house, get a mortgage, then rent it out and move to the south coast. Not only would I be joining the property-owning classes, I would still get to be a beach bum – it would be the best of both worlds.

We worked nightshifts and started to stockpile the cash, and I also made a bit of money on the side, buying bread wholesale from the bakery and selling it door to door. It wasn't work I enjoyed – I can't understand why people would spend their lives working somewhere like that – and it went from bad to worse later in the year when we were two of only eighteen workers who agreed to work during the bread strike of 1978. People don't remember the bread strike now – it was followed by the miners' and printers' strikes a few years later – but, at the time, you had great difficulty buying bread anywhere in the country. All 600 staff had received letters reassuring them that their jobs would be safe if they went back to work, so I saw no problem with it, but most of the workers believed what the union had told them and thought they'd be fired when the strike ended.

During the strike we had people calling us scabs as we crossed the picket line, and there was a fair bit of intimidation out of work, too. The union had told its members not to speak to us, even if we bumped into each other in the supermarket. It was incredibly petty and completely ridiculous. Some members of the union were bullies who ruled by fear and we'd had people calling us at home saying they wanted to come back to work, but that they were being intimidated by the union. When the strike finally ended the atmosphere at work got even worse: people refused to sit next to me in the canteen, even moving tables if I sat down beside them, and that included some of the people who had phoned us at home to say they didn't support the strike.

It's partly because of this experience that I don't have unions in any of my businesses now. Having seen how a few people used the union to intimidate their colleagues, I realised how disruptive only a few union members can be and how unions often fail to represent their members' wishes to the management. Most of my colleagues had been happy with the pay rise we'd been offered, but those were the days of 'one out, all out' and the unnecessary strike went on for months. These days, however, it's fair to say that changes to employment law have made union membership less important, as employees now have many more rights than they did back then. Perhaps that's as a result of all those strikes, but I'd still be wary of letting the unions get a hold in any of my companies.

Despite the name calling and the threats, working at the bakery was worth it, as after a year we had bought our own three-bed semi, just like the one my friend in the pub had been bragging about. I think it cost £12,000 and we managed to put down a £2,000 deposit. I was still missing Jersey, but buying the house helped me to settle and I was starting to get used to the idea of staying in Stockton.

I'd always said that the only reason I wanted a job was to get a mortgage: I had no intention of carrying on as a wage slave once we owned a property. Consequently, it seemed like fate when just two weeks after we moved in I saw an opportunity to give up work and start my first business. All the time we'd been in Stockton, I'd made a bit of money on the side buying cars cheaply at auction, doing them up and selling them on at a profit. I was at yet another car auction when I saw an ice-cream van drive up, and I knew instantly that this was the business for me.

First steps

It was a little Vauxhall Viva ice-cream van with big green eyes, and it was called Catweasel and cost me £450. It was pretty ancient and it broke down quite a few times, but I thought it was just perfect for what I wanted to do at that time. Selling ice cream was a business I could start without much capital, I didn't need any staff and it was something I had a little bit of experience at, thanks to my days on the beach in Jersey. There was just one problem: I was too tall to stand up in it properly. The only way I could stand upright was if I didn't wear any shoes, so I drove round in my socks!

Of course, I didn't have any contacts in Stockton to get my business off the ground, but I did have a *Yellow Pages*, and that turned out to be all I needed. I simply looked under the heading ICE CREAM SUPPLIERS and phoned around until I found the company that offered the best deal – simple, huh? It was pretty obvious that you couldn't make much money selling Walls ice cream, or any of the big brands, because they spent so much money on marketing and subsidising fridges in newsagents that they couldn't offer me a decent price, which meant I'd be left with a tiny profit margin. I eventually found a company called Treats that only did wholesale, and at their prices I reckoned I could make an 80 per cent profit on some of their products. At first I just bought enough stock for a weekend to see how it went, but I soon worked out what sold and what didn't and got the van properly stocked. I also started selling cigarettes, pop, confectionery and milk.

At that time, every ice-cream seller in the country had started serving soft ice cream, or Mr Whippy, because it was faster to serve. But Catweasel didn't do soft ice cream, so I served scoops of hard ice cream, something that was meant to be a slow process. But that was only if you used a mashed potato scoop. My stroke of genius was importing a special scoop from America, like the ones I'd used in Jersey. These scoops meant I could serve hard ice cream as quickly as you could serve soft ice cream. (I also discovered I could hold eight cones in one hand – this was clearly going to be something I had a natural talent for!) As well as being fast, I found that my American scoop left a little mark in the ice cream like a smile. So I filled the smiles with strawberry sauce, and added some aniseed balls for eyes – suddenly I could charge ten pence instead of the usual eight for an ice cream with a face.

The face ice creams were, predictably, very popular with the kids, and Duncan's Super Ices got off to a good start. I then started giving all my ice creams names, calling them after the Muppets. Chocolate scoops became Muppet bears; raspberry ripple was a Muppet with acne and mint ice cream was a Kermit. From time to time I'd get some very confused parents coming up to the van saying, 'I've been told to ask for a frog smoking a cigar.' The cigar, of course, was a 99 flake.

I loved the ice-cream business. I loved the kids and I happen to think I was really good at it. I'd take pictures of the kids and put them up in the van, so when they saw me pull up they'd rush out to see the photos of themselves. And for some reason in the early eighties it was fashionable for kids to wear jumpers with their names on them, so when a kid came over, I'd give him the personal service.

'Hi, Johnny, how are you?'

He'd look confused, if a bit pleased. 'How do you know my name?'

For some reason they never worked out the answer.

It was a good business, and because I also sold ciggies and milk, trade was good 365 days of the year. It wasn't all easy, though, as I had rivals, some of whom took a dislike to me, and the feeling was often mutual. I had one competitor who was particularly good, but I managed to move him on because he was on the dole and wasn't declaring his income. I guess I made life hard for him, and in the end he got sick of me and he put his van up for sale. Naturally, I saw no reason not to buy it, but when I phoned him up, he refused to sell it to me and slammed the phone down. He was a fool: you should never let it get personal. He could have sold his van to me for 20 per cent more than it was worth to anyone else if he'd just negotiated instead of slamming the phone down.

Instead I sent a friend called Peter Bell round to buy his van at a lower price, and when he brought the van round to me, he realised

I'd need help, so offered to drive it for me. Suddenly I had staff, which was a little unplanned, although technically I seem to remember Peter was self-employed and got paid a commission. As the summer came to the end, lots of ice-cream vans came up for sale at auction, and as you can pick them up cheaply at that time of year, I soon had a fleet. Having four or five ice-cream vans parked in the driveway got up a few of our neighbours' noses and they found ridiculous reasons to complain. I wasn't doing anything illegal, though, so I carried on. I really didn't care if they thought it was an eyesore, it was my business and that was much more important to me than keeping the neighbours happy. In time, though, I did rent a depot as it made loading up the stock easier.

I also saw an ad in the local paper selling concessions in local parks, guaranteeing the highest bidder would be the only ice-cream vendor in the park. On a hot summer's day, they were pretty much a licence to print money. I had no idea where these parks were, as I was still pretty new to the area, so I bought a map and took a look at them. The concessions were auctioned off by the local council, so I phoned up for the application form, filled in the paperwork and calculated what I was prepared to offer. For a pitch in Stewart Park I thought £2,000 was about right, and a few weeks later I was told I'd got the contract. I made £18,000 in that park in one summer. It was some of the easiest money I've ever made, and to this day I can't understand why the other ice-cream vendors in the north-east didn't bid for it. I was new, both to the area and to the business, and if I could see what the concession was worth, why couldn't they? To me, that's the $64,000 question – why could I spot the opportunity and they couldn't? It didn't require any special skills, or even much intelligence, to realise that selling ice cream exclusively in a park would make money, so why didn't they go for it? People ask me what gives me my drive: I want to know why other people don't share it. The conclusion I've come to is that every other ice-cream seller in the north-east must have been happy with the status quo. I wasn't: I wanted more.

I remember having a phone conversation with my dad at this point, telling him about my expansion plans for the business. He wasn't as enthusiastic about my success as I'd thought he would be, so I asked him about it. I've never forgotten his reply: he told me that 'people like us' didn't start businesses. I got the feeling that he thought I was betraying my working-class roots in some way. He'd been proud to be a worker, and for some reason he seemed uncomfortable that my ambitions lay beyond earning a wage.

In the early eighties, we decided we had a good enough income to start a family, and I think it was less than a month after we'd made the decision to try for a baby that Gail told me she was pregnant. I was, of course, thrilled to know I was going to be a dad, but over the course of the next few days it occurred to me that my child wouldn't have my name unless we got married. It wasn't the most romantic of weddings – we just used the local register office and we didn't even have a honeymoon – but when I said my vows I really meant them. After the ceremony we had a meal in the Crathorne Hall Hotel a few miles out of town. It was pretty posh even then – it was later bought by Richard Branson's Virgin Hotel group – and it was certainly too posh for us: my brother had to ask me which fork to use and, of course, I didn't have a clue, and my dad was very confused by the little bowls of water they had on the tables. I had to tell him they were for washing your fingers in.

Life was definitely good in those days. Not only was family life everything I had hoped it would be, I also had a job where I could eat all the ice cream I could manage – a pretty good perk in any job. But the ice-cream business had another distinct advantage over working in the bakery: during the week it didn't really start until three o'clock, when the schools finished, so as a new dad I got to spend plenty of time with my new daughter, Abigail. At the weekends, however, it was different: you started early and finished late. Saturdays were always worse than Sundays – both were long days, but as Sundays were much busier I preferred them. Of course, the fact that we took about 30 per cent of our weekly turnover on a

Sunday might have had something to do with it. Although having staff meant responsibility and paperwork, the upside was that I no longer had to do the Saturday shift, as I made that Peter's responsibility.

A problem at home

Not long after Abigail was born our happy home received some frightening news. Gail had suffered from cataracts since she was a child, which is very unusual in children. Her treatment over the years had involved making pinholes in her lenses, which had eventually become opaque over the course of more than a dozen operations. After Abigail's arrival, we found out that the operations had also weakened her retinas, when the strain of giving birth made one of them start to detach. In effect, this meant the inside of Gail's eye had started to separate from itself, and if it wasn't repaired quickly her eyesight would be lost for ever. With a new baby, not to mention a business, to run this meant tough times on the home front. Gail decided to drive back to her home town of Prestwick to see the surgeon who'd treated her as a child, while I stayed in Stockton to look after the business. Her surgeon took one look at her eye and immediately admitted her to hospital for surgery – the problem was so bad that he wanted to operate within hours and said it was amazing she'd been able to see well enough to drive. As soon as Gail phoned me with the news I left the business in the capable hands of my most honest driver – or so I thought – and rushed to Gail's side in Prestwick. I arrived after Gail had been in theatre, and the surgeon had some bad news for us: he had looked closely at the problem on the operating table and decided he couldn't repair the eye as the muscles were too badly torn. However, he said he knew of a specialist in Edinburgh who'd been doing some research into new treatments that had been devised in America. As soon as Gail was able, I got her in the car and drove to Edinburgh to see the specialist.

At first the Edinburgh surgeon wasn't sure he could help either and told us he needed some time to think about it. I remember spending an agonising day walking round Edinburgh waiting for him to make a decision. He finally phoned us at our hotel and told us what we wanted to hear: he was willing to give it a go and would operate the next day. We were delighted and scared at the same time, but we had no choice – we put Gail's future in his hands and just hoped that he was worthy of his reputation.

The operation involved removing the eye from the socket and putting a tiny piece of rubber behind it which he could stitch the retina to. He then glued everything together and deliberately left a tiny air bubble that would create enough pressure to keep her retina in place. Once she came round, Gail had to spend forty-eight hours lying on her front so the air bubble would hold the retina in the right position. I spent two nights sleeping on the floor of the Royal Infirmary taking care of her and hoping everything would be all right. Gail was in a lot of pain and very frightened, and at one point she said she'd rather go blind than go through an operation like that again.

But it was worth it: the surgeon saved her eyesight and a couple of weeks later she was able to have the other eye operated on, too. She was a guinea pig for pioneering surgery that a few years later would help two of our children who had inherited her condition. The success of Gail's surgery was an enormous relief, but by the time we were back home, the ice-cream business was in a terrible state and I realised the supposedly honest driver I'd left in charge had been ripping us off. It was the height of the summer when we should have been taking over £10,000 a week in cash. I'd thought I could trust him when he offered to bank the takings for me, but as soon as I looked at the books it was obvious that something was wrong – I could tell from the stock orders that we'd been selling the ice cream, so there was no reason for the profits to be so low unless he'd been putting the cash in his own pocket.

I was with him in one of the vans one evening, going over where the money might have gone, when he cottoned on to my meaning and changed his attitude.

He said, 'I've got rights, I'm an employee, you can't just accuse me without proof.'

Something rose up inside of me and then, the next thing I remember is him going backwards through the window of the ice-cream van. My hand hurt, so I knew I'd hit him really hard, but to this day I don't remember throwing the punch.

Hitting people isn't something I've done since my youthful brawls – and I've certainly never hit anyone since – but I couldn't believe that someone would try and rip me off when I was doing everything to stop my wife from going blind. By ripping off the business he was putting my wife and child's future at risk, and all I was doing was responding like a protective father looking out for his family.

I eventually got the business back on track by working fourteen-hour days, and it continued to provide me with a good income. I remember being pleased when I read somewhere that an airline pilot earned less than me – and I remember feeling particularly smug the day I got a car with electric windows! It was long hours, though, and full-time responsibility: in the morning I'd be driving the vans out to the parks, where I paid someone else to do the selling, and throughout the day I'd be sorting out paperwork or going to the wholesalers. In the evening I'd have to collect the vans and do a stock take, and I often wouldn't finish until 10 p.m.

I carried on building up the business, and towards the end it had a turnover of around £300,000 a year, of which I reckon about £60,000 was profit that I took as a salary – the equivalent of about £120,000 today – not bad for an ice-cream seller! We'd moved out of our first house and into a bigger five bedroom, three reception house when my second daughter, Hollie, arrived in 1985. The house was in a bit of a state when we bought it, but I did it up room by room and made it look fantastic. By the end, I don't think there was a single surface in that house that I hadn't personally painted. I even fitted the kitchen myself. Thinking about that time now, I can't believe I wasn't constantly knackered. I had a physical job, I worked long hours, I had two kids *and* I was doing the house up. I'd stayed fit since I was in the Navy, but I think the real reason I could cope with all the activity was because I was enjoying myself.

NINE

Ice-cream wars

To be successful you must recognise your weaknesses and employ people with complementary skills.

By now I was starting to think I was doing quite well for myself. I had two beautiful little girls, a nice big house and the kind of income that let us take a couple of holidays each year, so when rivals tried to take my business away from me, I had several good reasons for protecting my turf – by any means necessary.

However, it wasn't always straightforward. At times rivals would try to take a piece of my business away from me, and as they were almost always on the dole and just doing it for a bit of extra income, I got annoyed. I was paying my tax, was VAT registered and was doing things right, and they were breaking the law. I got into quite a few fights with people that usually went like this:

'Look, I've got two kids to look after, I'm responsible for employees *and* I'm paying my VAT. Why should I let a little twat like you take my business away?'

'Piss off!'

'Thought you might say that. Perhaps you should know that it's against the law to sell ice cream without your name and address on the side of your van for the public health inspectors.'

'Piss off!'

'If I call the public health officer, he'll come tomorrow . . .'

'Just piss off or I'll do you!'

'And if your name's not on your van, he'll put you off the road.'

At this point they usually started to pay attention.

'And if your name *is* on it, then I'll phone the dole and check to see if you're registered. So you can do what you like, you can stay here and fight me or you can piss off yourself.'

Because the ice-cream trade was – and still is – a cash business, it inevitably attracted a criminal element, and over the years I've heard stories that the trade's been used for money laundering, been involved in protection rackets by organised crime and all sorts. I can't say if any of that's true, but I certainly met my fair share of less than reputable dealers. One of them tried to scare me by making threatening phone calls. Gail's sister Irene was babysitting for us when the phone rang.

'Is Duncan there?'

'No, he's out at the moment. Can I take a message?'

There was a pause.

'Tell him he's going to lose a leg!'

Irene was frightened by it at first, but Gail and I just laughed when she told us about it. It was the kind of thing that happened from time to time when someone thought I'd strayed onto their patch. I learned that people who threaten to do you harm over the phone are generally pretty spineless; it's the people who don't bother with a warning that you want to watch.

Although my Scottish accent helped me get a reputation for being hard, it wasn't enough to stop people trying to intimidate me. There was this one guy who sold ice cream in Middlesbrough, and to be fair I guess I'd moved onto his patch: I'd paid for a contract to sell ice cream in Stewart Park, but after the park closed in the evening it made sense to try and sell more stock locally. This guy – let's call him Paddy – didn't like this one bit, and he used to send his drivers to warn me to stay away. Even other independent sellers told me to steer clear.

'You don't want to mess with Paddy,' they told me.

'Why not?'

'You just wait till you meet him.'

'How will I know when I meet him?'

'Well, he's this huge black guy with two Dobermans and he drives around in a campervan.'

'And I'm supposed to be scared?'

Sure enough, one day while I was selling ice cream on a housing estate this campervan pulled up with an enormous black guy behind the wheel and two massive Dobermans fighting it out in the passenger seat. There was no mistaking who it was or why he'd come: he meant to see me off. What happened next probably changed my entire career.

I said to myself, 'If I run I'm finished, and if I look scared I'm finished.' If I'd have thought for two seconds longer I'd probably have been too scared to act, but I had a rush of blood to the head and acted impulsively. I jumped out of the ice-cream-van window, ran over to his van, jerked his side door open and just shouted at him.

'What do you want?' I demanded.

He just stared back at me while my heart pounded. I had no idea what would happen next, but I didn't falter, I just held his gaze. Then he spoke: 'Duncan, hi . . . um . . .'

And I knew I had him! It was a fantastic feeling because it was suddenly all over – he was just bluff and smoke.

'Duncan, let's work something out . . .'

Like most bullies, he was weak, and a few days later I heard he was walking round Middlesbrough telling people what a nice guy I was and that we'd come to an agreement.

I've been asked many times why I confronted him. The honest answer is I'm not entirely sure. I think it was because I was too scared not to stand up to him: I had too much to lose and the consequences of not seeing him off were far worse than the immediate danger. I've always been good at mental arithmetic, and I just calculated the risks quickly. The lesson I learned from that is that you have to stand up to intimidation. If you show any weakness it will be exploited. If I hadn't stood up to him that day, he would have started to erode my business, and who knows what would have happened after that.

Over the years, plenty of people tried to take a piece of my business, but I had four vans, plus another two working permanently on contract in Stewart Park and Albert Park, so we had the advantage of numbers when someone saw their chance. And if I needed an extra pair of hands, I could pull staff out of the café concession I ran in Preston Park.

We were very organised about seeing off our rivals: when any of us saw someone moving into our territory we just crowded them out. My wife and I both had CB radios in our Cortina estates – the ideal vehicle, it turned out, for humping ice cream from the wholesalers – and as soon as we saw a rival on our patch, we'd radio all the other drivers to come and park next to him. Suddenly he'd be surrounded and the kids would always buy from us instead of him, as we were out there every day and they got to know us. With no customers, they'd soon slope off. I guess we gave our rivals a hard time, but I figure that's all part of business.

Although I'd been in the north-east for a few years by this stage, I was still an outsider, and I realised that having a few more contacts would be good for business. I joined the local council pay-and-play golf club thinking that might be a smart way to meet some local officials or businessmen, but as I was usually only free to play during the day, I didn't meet too many useful contacts. However, one day I was playing a round with a guy who ran a local garden centre and he suggested I join the Freemasons and said he could make some introductions for me, so I rolled my trouser leg up, put on a pinny and joined the masons, hoping it would be good for business. It turned out to be a massive waste of time. All that happened was I met a couple of painters and decorators who overcharged me. I can see how some people benefit from networking, but for a single-minded entrepreneur like me, there was no point: my business success was forged from the strength of my personality, not my contacts.

Taking care of business

The admin side of running a business – VAT returns, accounts, stock taking and the like – turned out to be something I was very comfortable doing. While profit and loss came easily – thankfully the former more easily than the latter – I had to learn about VAT, pay roll and all my statutory obligations. I didn't know who to turn to for advice, but the one thing I did know was that accountants charged a lot of money, so I called the tax man direct for some information. I soon found out that the government produces a leaflet on absolutely everything, so I called up the VAT office and they told me about filling in the VAT returns. When I started employing people, I just asked the relevant government body what my responsibilities were and they told me, from making National Insurance contributions to health and safety responsibilities. I've never understood people who use an accountant for everything. Getting to grips with these issues isn't hard, and it means you really understand your business. That said, I do know a very successful businessman – I'll name no names – who can't add two and five and has had an accountant from day one. It wasn't a problem for him as he has skills I don't have – he's great with people and pays attention to detail, attributes I know aren't my strong point. What this teaches me is that you can run a business any way you want to, but to be successful you must recognise your weaknesses and employ people with complementary skills.

If only I'd taken as good care of myself as I did of my business. When I finished at 10 p.m., I would often go straight to the pub. It was only after closing time that I went home for something decent to eat, something I sorely needed after snacking on ice cream and sweets all day. I guess it wasn't all that surprising then that I started to get a bit fat. The intense boxing training I'd done in the Navy meant I'd been used to being fit and trim, so when my weight ballooned from 12 to 18 stone, I decided it was time for a change. My kids were growing up and I realised I needed a business that fitted in with school times, not one where the only down time was while they were in lessons.

TEN

Building the foundations of a fortune

1984–86

The government produces a leaflet for everything, so you never need to pay for an expensive consultant.

I had been making such good money with the ice-cream business that at times I actually had too much cash. I didn't see the point of keeping it in the bank where it only earns you what the bank will pay you, so I bought up little terraced houses to rent out. That way the money provided me with an income, and I'd made a sound capital investment in freehold property. It was a smart move that got even smarter when the government announced a new initiative.

They introduced a new policy that gave all unemployed people an entitlement to housing. And the best bit about this is that the government started paying £46 a week directly to landlords. Now a lot of people wouldn't want to rent to DSS tenants, but as far as I could see I was effectively renting to the government, so my rent was guaranteed. I started converting terraced houses into bedsits and renting them out. I picked up the houses for about £10,000 each and made a 30–50 per cent return on my capital each year in rent. There were, of course, a couple of downsides, the big one being that it took a few weeks for each resident to be processed for voucher payments, and while that was happening the Giros went straight to the claimant, which meant I had to be there at 7 a.m. to wait for the postman and intercept them. If I'd have stayed in bed I'd never have got paid, but it was worth it as it was such a good income, even if the odd tenant decided to sell their bed or smash a window when they were pissed.

From time to time I was asked if I would rent to elderly tenants who needed housing. I started looking into the market to see if it was a possibility, but there were so many responsibilities in terms of staff and support that I had to say no. But it got me thinking, and whenever care for the elderly was on the news, which was pretty much every night, as Maggie Thatcher had some radical proposals, I wondered if it was an area I should get into.

I've said all along that I've made it in business without contacts or a network, but I did have a telly and I did buy a newspaper, and they were pretty good substitutes for picking up leads. The story that really caught my eye was when the Thatcher government brought in the Registered Homes Act in 1984, which meant they would pay a flat rate – almost exactly £140 a week – for every elderly person who needed looking after. I did the sums in my head: if I had fifty residents that was £7,000 a week and a guaranteed turnover of £364,000 a year, the equivalent of almost £700,000 in today's money. I did another quick sum to estimate my costs and reckoned that if my home was 90 per cent full, I could make a 33 per cent profit on my investment every year. Who wouldn't choose to start a business with a guaranteed income like that? And who wouldn't choose to have the government as a client, as they were guaranteed to pay? It wasn't exactly a difficult decision, especially as I knew from owning the bedsits that people were looking for accommodation for their relatives.

Then, as if someone was trying to tell me something, three things happened in quick succession to convince me it was a business I should get into. First, someone bought a big house in the street where I owned some bedsits and announced they were turning it into a care home, and second, I read in the local paper about a couple from Scarborough who had made so much money from care homes that they had bought their own aeroplane. That very same week I was playing squash with a neighbour called Billy Morgan, who had also seen the news and wanted to know if I'd thought about going into the care home business.

'I've thought about it, Billy,' I told him. 'But I'm having such a great time with the ice-cream business, and the bedsits are such a goldmine I'm just not sure I need the hassle.'

I certainly wasn't against the idea of care homes, I just wasn't sure I wanted to be in business with anyone else. It wasn't that Billy couldn't run a business – he ran a local jeweller's, so I knew he was clued-up about making a profit – it's just that I'd never been much of a team player. I'm so single-minded that having a partner isn't my natural working style. But as we played our game, Billy continued trying to persuade me that we could work together. Afterwards he dropped me off at home where I put my feet up and read the local paper, the *Middlesbrough Evening Gazette*. I turned to the Businesses for Sale section, and there in black and white was a six-storey hotel for sale in Scarborough with planning permission to turn it into a residential home for the elderly.

Residential homes weren't as lucrative as nursing homes, as they only provided sheltered housing rather than medical care, but if I'd been a religious man, it would have seemed like someone up there was trying to tell me something. I called Billy.

'What are you doing tomorrow?'

'It's my day off. The shop's shut.'

'Fancy a trip to Scarborough?'

We agreed to buy it there and then, although it took us several months to arrange the finance, as even though we both ran our own businesses, it represented a big hike in our borrowings. During the delay, we drew up plans to convert it into twenty-two separate residences, and as soon as the keys were handed over, Billy hired an acquaintance of his to do the building work. Stupidly, he agreed to pay a day rate, and over the next few months I watched the costs rise while progress slowed. I kept a close eye on the work, and on one occasion I turned up to find absolutely nothing being done because the builder had taken on another job, while still charging us by the day. I was furious, but there was no point in blowing up at Billy or sacking the builder: neither of those things would get the job finished any sooner, so I decided to move in.

I still went to Stockton whenever the ice-cream business needed me and to see my family of course, but as I was on site I could greet the builders, every morning and each evening I was there to inspect their progress. Unsurprisingly, things started to get done, but we had already wasted so much money that Billy and I were going to have to finish the job ourselves if we were to avoid bankruptcy, and that included painting the outside of the building – all six storeys of it. We hired cherry pickers and long rollers and worked our balls off, and finally it was ready for inspection by Social Services.

During the renovations, we'd applied to the authorities for a licence to open as a residential home, and I got a shock when Billy told me all the paperwork would have to be in my name.

'I can't do it,' he told me, 'because I've got a criminal record.'

He tried to reassure me that he had been wrongly convicted and was innocent, but as far as the authorities were concerned, he had a black mark against his name. I was shocked, but I couldn't let that affect the business. We did everything in my name and got our licence, and it turned out to be a licence to print a fair bit of money. It was so successful that Billy wanted us to do it all over again; I told him I'd think about it.

Shortly after we opened, my parents came down to visit us, and as well as enjoying spending time with Abigail and Hollie, I think they got a kick out of seeing how well I was doing for myself. Although my dad had retired from the Singer factory at sixty-five, he carried on working as a porter at a hospital for war veterans until he was sixty-eight. Now nearly seventy, the trip to see us was one of the few holidays he'd had. During their stay, I took my dad to see the residential home in Scarborough and I don't think he could believe his son owned something so big.

'You're doing well for yourself,' he said as I showed him round.

As he spoke, I thought about how he'd told me 'people like us' shouldn't start businesses.

'I'm proud of you,' he said, 'really proud.'

It was one of the greatest moments of my life, and knowing I had made my father proud spurred me on. I felt I had to continue to be worthy of his pride. So when Billy Morgan next asked me if I wanted to open another residential home with him, I told him I had plans of my own. If my dad believed in me, I didn't need a partner to move forward.

The profit from the home in Scarborough was substantial, and unlike the ice-cream business it was pretty much guaranteed. If I had been interested in care homes before, I was now determined to build a business in the sector. The first thing to do was research, as you can't start a business on gut instinct alone. I spent time going round other nursing homes, pretending to be looking for a place for my mother. Thank God she didn't need their care, because if she had I would have been heartbroken. Ladies were sharing six to a room, often being forced to use commodes because the bathroom facilities were so poor. I saw some horrible things, like patients with sores on their legs which no one had the time to dress, and many of the places absolutely stank of piss and shit. It was both an eye-opener and a stomach-turner.

But in among the squalor and sadness, I saw a way to do it better. In business, it doesn't matter if you come late to the market: if you can do it better than your competitors, you can still make money. I realised that if I built a nursing home of single rooms with ensuite facilities I would always be full. I knew from my early calculations that there was money to be made, but those fact-finding missions made me determined to do it with integrity and I decided there and then that I was going to build a brand-new style of nursing home.

I'd learned from the ice-cream business that the government produces a leaflet for everything, from registering for VAT to paying National Insurance to health and safety regulations. In other words, you never need to pay for an expensive consultant. I called up the local council and asked for all the leaflets they had on the rules for care homes, and within a few days I knew that you had to have so many square foot per bed and so many members of staff for every patient – precisely the kind of information I needed to work out the best way to plan my first nursing home. And as I now knew more about care-home regulations than any architect I could find in the *Yellow Pages*, I sat down on my own and sketched out a building that met the government's guidelines perfectly, making sure that most of the rooms had ensuite toilets.

ELEVEN

Going it alone
1986–87

An entrepreneur in debt is an entrepreneur in business.

Most people have an idea for a business at some point in their lives, but they don't do anything about it – that's really the only difference between entrepreneurs and everyone else. And most people who run a business learn more about business on the job than any university could teach them. Simply by being in business, I gained the insights, confidence and experience to become a better entrepreneur. I had proved with Duncan's Super Ices that I could be the best ice-cream seller in the north-east, so why the hell couldn't I be the best nursing home provider, too? I became obsessed with the idea of opening a care home. 'It's a guaranteed income,' I kept telling myself. 'With a thirty-three per cent return on your capital.' I'd have been crazy if I hadn't followed it through.

I finally found what I was looking for when I took my ice-cream van into Stockton town centre and went to get a coffee before I opened up. It was a glorious day, so I knew I'd make a lot of money and was in a terrific mood. But it was about to get even better, because on my way to the coffee shop I passed an estate agent, and in the window was a plot of land for sale.

If it had been a movie, that card in the window would have started glowing, the music would have started up and my eyes would have bulged: it was exactly what I'd been looking for, *and* it was substantially cheaper than I had expected to pay. I walked in, got the details and when I read them I couldn't believe my luck: it already had planning permission for sheltered housing to be built on it. One phone call to the planning office told me that 'sheltered housing' included nursing homes: I wasn't going to walk away from this. I put in an offer of £30,000 and it was accepted.

The plot, in nearby Darlington, was three quarters of an acre of derelict land. It was a really horrible place, just a rusty old car park filled with old skips and burnt-out sofas. The reason it was so cheap was because it was next to vacant land that ran alongside the railway. At the time the government wanted to redevelop any land visible from a train to make it more appealing to the travelling public, and they were making grants available to pull down existing buildings and erect new homes. Consequently the railway land was being snapped up by developers, and my plot was undesirable because, as a car park with no buildings on it, it wasn't subsidised.

When people talk about 'location, location, location' in property, they don't mean buying in Chelsea or the Riviera. At least they don't if they're smart: I knew my grubby plot was a fantastic location because the efforts of Barratt and Wimpey and the big house builders nearby would push all the prices up. Even if I hadn't built on that plot it would have doubled in value just because the area was improving. Nevertheless, it was such a tip that the only way I could persuade the bank to lend me £25,000 to buy it was if I put my house up as security. No wonder then that Gail hit the proverbial roof when she saw it.

'You spent £30,000 of *our* money on *that*? Are you out of your mind?'

She had no idea how close I'd come to missing out on it and just how pleased I was to have pulled it off. When I'd been in the bank manager's office signing for the loan, the phone had rung and it had been for me, which was a bit unusual. It was my solicitor telling me that someone had put in a higher offer on the plot. I was furious: I had agreed a deal with the vendor and thought he was trying it on. Perhaps I'd sounded too eager and he thought he could chance his luck, or maybe he really did have a counter offer, I had no way of knowing for sure.

I didn't want to be conned and I didn't want to lose the land, so I negotiated a compromise: I told my solicitor I would exchange that afternoon, but only at £30,000, not a penny more. My bank manager pulled quite a face but agreed it could be done. The vendor, sensing the money was better off in his pocket than mine, accepted and we did the deal.

In my naivety, I'd thought that banks knew about numbers. I'd stupidly thought that a guaranteed income of £364,000 a year would be enough for them to feel confident enough to lend me the price of the land as well as build costs. I soon learned one of the great lessons of my life: people who choose to work in a bank like safety. They are by nature risk averse and if they could see the big picture they'd be writing this book instead of me. On one occasion I went to see a major high street bank and the business manager actually said to me, 'If it was that easy, everybody would be doing it.'

I told him that was a ridiculous excuse and demanded to see his boss.

'That won't be necessary,' he told me in a particularly patronising way.

'I've got a sound proposition here and I don't think it's unreasonable for me to want to know why you're turning me down.'

'To be honest, Mr Bannatyne, I think you've miscalculated your figures.'

'I haven't,' I insisted, 'but even if I only make a thirty per cent return and you're still charging me ten per cent interest, it's still a great business.'

He relented and asked his manager to join us. A few minutes later, a short, bald bloke walked in smoking a cigarette. He was the kind of middle-class snob I'd never had any respect for, and I knew he'd be a waste of space. He was a stroppy little berk who clearly didn't rate an uneducated ice-cream vendor very highly. He told me that I didn't have any 'sector expertise' and without it he couldn't see how I was going to make any money. With attitudes like that it's easy to see why the bank always offers the lowest possible rate of return.

Undaunted, I went to NatWest, but they also turned me down. It would take a relatively small bank, the Yorkshire Bank, which didn't have such a corporate culture, to take a calculated risk on me. The manager there, Peter Rouse, was ambitious and he already knew me as he'd remortgaged my house: he was ready to make the loan, but he had to get all the right boxes ticked on the form for his bosses to approve the loan. He helped me write a business plan and together we made adjustments to comply with the bank's lending criteria. Needless to say I'd never written a business plan before, but I didn't find it all that hard. It was easy to calculate the income, and the costs were fairly straightforward, too: if I had x residents, I'd need y staff and they'd get paid the going rate, a figure I found out by looking at the situations vacant in the paper. I estimated things like the electricity and gas by multiplying my bills at home. It was hardly rocket science, but it was all the bean counters at the bank's head office needed to see. I never looked at it again after we'd put it in the post, and as a business tool it proved entirely pointless. I have no idea what figure I'd calculated the business would be worth, but I can tell you it was a lot less than the £30 million I finally made from it.

For a couple of weeks I thought I was going to get all the money I needed and began to look around for an architect. I was stunned when I got a call saying that they would give me a 70 per cent mortgage, but only once there was a building on the site, *and* it would have to be fully occupied! I was going to have to find the money myself.

I'm often reminded of this time in my life when I'm in the chair on *Dragons' Den*. We see so many would-be entrepreneurs who are asking for backing because they're not prepared to back themselves. They don't believe in their idea enough to borrow the £50,000 they're asking for, or they're not prepared to offer their house as security, or even give up their jobs. They say they 'don't want to take the risk'. And that's when I tell them 'I'm out' because I know an entrepreneur with nothing to lose is just a daydreamer. An entrepreneur in debt is an entrepreneur in business.

I had already borrowed £30,000 and was meeting the repayments as well as the increased repayments on my remortgaged house. I was committed and had to make it work, and if the only way I could get the loan was to construct the nursing home, then I was bloody well going to have to get one built. And to do that I needed an architect.

Of course I didn't know the first thing about hiring an architect, but as I had already sketched out what I wanted, I wasn't looking for someone to produce a really marvellous design. When I found out that the standard industry fee for an architect is 6 per cent of the total cost of construction, I wasn't prepared to pay it. That meant the architect would have an incentive for the project to go over budget, and it seemed crazy that a professional should be rewarded for failing to do their job. In the end I negotiated a fixed price with a local architect who was more used to doing extensions on private houses. He saw it as a rare chance for him to work on a big project and was almost as motivated as me because he saw it as an opportunity to turn his career around. I learned early on that you do better deals when both parties get something out of it, and it helps when both partners are motivated by more than money.

He did a good job of taking my sketches and turning them into proper plans, as he knew about the required number of fire escapes and the right kind of disabled access. I also instructed him to handle the site meetings, as they were pretty technical. That said, I made bloody sure I attended every site meeting, too, so I could see exactly what was going on.

Originally I had planned to build a fifty-room nursing home, specifically because at night you needed one qualified member of staff for every twenty-five residents. Obviously it was most cost efficient to build either twenty-five or fifty rooms, but I could afford only thirty rooms, so I went ahead anyway, as I intended to build the extra twenty rooms as soon as I had a mortgage on the property.

The architect sent the designs out to tender, and we got some ridiculous quotes back from builders. I knew what the right price should be as there is a standard cost-per-square-foot in construction that any half-decent architect should be able to calculate reasonably accurately. I was determined not to be taken for a ride by builders who saw a chance to exploit my lack of experience. After nearly getting screwed on the price of the land, I was learning to play hard to get. Mostly it was those old feelings of injustice that kept me from doing a deal with anyone who I thought was taking the piss, and eventually one of the builders who had tendered caved in. He told me he'd been let down on another contract, so could start right away and at the right price. Was it a coincidence? Or was it what he'd been prepared to do all along? I never found out.

And what he didn't find out – at least not immediately – was that I had a small problem: I didn't have the money to pay him. The architect had explained to me that builders' fees are paid every six weeks in arrears. As the project manager, the architect visited the site at regular intervals to assess how much work had been done and then issued me with an invoice to pay the builder. So when the builder, John Scott, brought the first JCB on site, I knew I had six weeks to find the first instalment of his £210,000 fee.

Thankfully I was having a good time with the ice-cream business and was able to find the first £20,000 or so from there, and by the time the second payment became due I had sold some of the bedsits, so I could buy myself another six weeks. This carried on for the best part of a year: every six to eight weeks I had to come up with another twenty or thirty grand. In the summer the ice-cream business covered the cost, but in the winter it couldn't pick up the tab and I realised I would have terrible cash-flow problems that called for desperate measures.

I sold my car – a beautiful Mercedes 190E – and went back to driving round in an ice-cream van. I sold anything that had any value – my colour TV, the stereo – and somehow kept managing to scrape together the payments. My next option was to stall on the bills I owed Cadbury's and Walls for our ice-cream stock. The sales reps would call and tell me I was behind with my payment and I'd just say, 'I'm expanding at the moment,' neglecting to mention that I was expanding in a completely different area.

'That's all very well, but we still need to be paid.'

'Well if you could just help me out for a short while we'll all benefit – the bigger my company, the bigger my next order.'

This routine kept them at bay for a little while, but Lyons Maid soon announced they were taking court action against me to recover the debt. This might sound perverse, but I was actually thrilled when I got their letter, as I knew the court proceedings would take longer than it would for me to get the nursing home finished. At the very least it meant there was one less company hassling me every other day.

Inevitably, the time came when I had nothing left to sell, so I went and got myself three new credit cards and borrowed £10,000 on each of them. I think I was even able to defer the payment for the first few months. If everything went to plan I'd have the mortgage in place before I needed to start making repayments on the cards. I guess I should have been worried, but I had such faith in the figures that I wasn't: I knew the nursing home was going to make me rich.

The next asset I exploited was the residential home in Scarborough. When I talked to Billy Morgan about releasing some equity he was fine about it: he wanted to get his hands on his share of the equity, too. He was also planning to open a nursing home and could use the cash. This wasn't a complete surprise to me, but I thought it would be best if we came to gentleman's agreement not to hinder each other's progress. To that end, we agreed never to open care homes that would be in direct competition with each other, and never to poach each other's clients or staff. We needed to keep things amicable because for the next couple of years we would continue to co-own the Scarborough property.

But even the money from that wasn't enough. I was going to have to use the equity in our house. Although I'd added plenty of value to it with my DIY, I had already remortgaged it in order to buy the land. If I wanted to get any more money out of it, I was going to have to sell it, so that's exactly what I did. And to her credit, Gail didn't scream at me. She was completely supportive of what I was trying to do, and was prepared for short-term hardship for long-term gain.

Pretty soon I realised that the nursing home was going to make me fives times more money than the ice-cream business, yet Duncan's Super Ices continued to take up 80 per cent of my time. It was obvious I had to sell, and if I could sell it quickly it would help me make another instalment, so I sold it for £28,000 to one of my drivers and my milkman, even though the healthy turnover meant I could have got more for it if I'd been prepared to wait. But the truth was that it wasn't worth nearly as much without me in control, and a quick sale suited me just fine.

It was also around this time that the government changed the voucher system for the bedsits and started paying cash. It was no surprise that most of my tenants would rather give their money to the barman than me, so I sold the rest of my bedsits at a capital loss, although I can't say I cared as they had provided me with a good income when I'd needed it. However, this wasn't enough, and towards the end of the build I completely ran out of options. I could see the builder working hard to finish the development, and I knew I didn't have any money left to pay him. I'd wrung every penny out of every asset I could shift, and had no choice but to level with him.

'John,' I said. 'I have a little bit of a problem, I have a temporary cash-flow issue, can you wait until the job is finished for the money I owe you,' I asked.

'I knew you had a problem, Duncan – you've sold everything you own to finance this project, so I'll wait, but on one condition.'

'Name it.'

'I want interest at ten per cent on the outstanding balance.'

'OK,' I said.

'I'll get my lawyer to draw up some paperwork and you must get it signed by the end of the week.'

When the paperwork arrived, I got a bit of a shock. I had naturally assumed he meant 10 per cent per annum, but he was asking for 10 per cent a month! I was stunned, but I didn't have any choice: I had to agree. The truth is that I really didn't mind – I even got a kick out of it because I knew I was going to make a phenomenal amount of money. I never – not for one minute – thought it would go wrong, and it's that kind of absolute conviction I now look for in any entrepreneur who comes to me for backing.

It was obvious that I was going to have to establish a limited company in order to get the licences I'd need to operate, so I called Companies House, got them to send me the inevitable leaflet and began to fill in the forms. When it came to registering a company name I couldn't believe that my first choice wasn't already in use: Quality Care Homes.

I also knew I was going to need qualified people to run the nursing home, and perhaps even more obviously, I was going to need residents if I was to get the government's money. So long before the building was complete, I advertised for a manager and ended up employing someone who had worked for a rival. Her name was Margaret Little. When I told her at the interview that every resident would have their own room *and* their own bathroom, she was determined to come and work for me. Margaret knew how much happier residents would be in my home than anywhere else available locally. 'All my residents will want to swap,' she said. If I hadn't been convinced before about what a good business I was building, I was now. This is another example of how deals work better when both parties benefit: I couldn't pay her any more than her last employer, but I could give her job satisfaction. I quickly learned that it's a bloody cheap way of incentivising staff. I've also found that it's never hard to find people to work on new projects: whenever I've opened a new nursing home, or later on a new health club, enthusiastic people queue up to be in at the beginning of something.

Margaret was a very experienced and very caring nurse, and she brought with her from her previous employer all the information we needed about the rules and regulations we'd have to adhere to. She took care of all the red tape, dealt with the hiring of all the other staff and advertised for customers to fill the home we had called Springfield House – I should point out that this wasn't me nostalgically naming it after the house I was born in; it happened to be on Springfield Road. By the time it was finished, we were ready to hit the ground running.

Twenty patients moved in straight away, which was fabulous, but I knew I wouldn't get my mortgage unless I was *fully* occupied. The bank manager had made it quite clear I had to be at full capacity to get the 70 per cent loan. So I did what anyone else with an elderly mother would do: I got her to bring her friends round for a day out to make the place look full! When the bank manager came round, he saw thirty rooms and thirty old people, and agreed to give me my mortgage. He valued the business at £600,000. As it had only cost me £360,000 – for the land, the build costs, professional fees and everything from bed linen to kitchen equipment – I now had nearly a quarter of a million in equity in my new company and it was only my first week of trading. Not bad for a guy with no 'sector expertise'.

However, my excitement and happiness at getting the new business off the ground was tempered by the fact that my father didn't live to see my success. Given his experiences in the war and career in the foundry at Singer's, not to mention his forty-a-day addiction to Players, it wasn't a great surprise that he started to have problems with his lungs.

He'd started to get short of breath, even on fairly short walks, and needed to stop constantly. He was diagnosed with emphysema and was taken into hospital for tests. This happened just a couple of days before I was due to take Gail and the girls for a much-needed holiday in Spain, so I called his doctor and made sure it was nothing serious.

'He'll be fine,' I was told. 'Have your holiday. Enjoy yourself.'

Five days into the holiday I phoned home from a call box to check how he was doing. My brother George answered the phone.

'Has no one phoned you?' he asked.

'No. Why?'

'Dad died yesterday.'

My first thoughts were for my mum and I knew I had to get back to Glasgow to be with her. In those days, children didn't have their own passports, which meant Abigail and Hollie had travelled on mine. This was long before the days of EasyJet, and getting flights for the whole family to Scotland was almost as impossible as it was expensive. Gail agreed that she should stay in Spain with the girls and I should go to Scotland alone. When the funeral was over, I would fly back to Spain so we could all return to Britain together.

When I got home, my father's body was in an open coffin at the funeral home and I was able to say goodbye in private before the service. As I was the oldest, I felt a huge responsibility to sort things out, from taking my mum to the dole office to get her pension changed to getting the tenancy on the flat put into her name. With such a small window before I needed to get back to Spain, those days back in Clydebank are a tearstained blur.

There had been so much to sort out that it was only a few weeks after I had lost my father that his death finally sank in. He had only been seventy and had lived a life of service, first to his parents, then to the Army and his country, and then to his own family. He hadn't stopped work until he was sixty-eight. Two years of retirement seemed an insult to a man who had given so much.

My father and I had always had our differences, and at the time of his death I found it difficult to understand the decisions he'd made in life. Now, twenty years on, I realise what a success he was, raising a large family and holding down a job in difficult circumstances. Writing this book has helped me put his choices into perspective and has given me more respect for the decisions he took and the life he chose.

TWELVE

The first million
1986–90

You can run a business any way you like, but you'll run it better if you build it around your strengths.

As soon as the money from the mortgage on the first nursing home came through, I paid the builder, paid the credit cards off and started to build a twenty-room extension. I'd calculated that a fifty-room nursing home makes more than twice the profit of a thirty-bed one, as you don't up the staff, only the income. Not only did I have money in the bank, but thanks to Maggie Thatcher's policies, I also had a guaranteed income for years to come. It's no wonder I immediately started looking around for another plot. Some people would have been happy with just one nursing home, but all I could say was 'onwards and upwards'. If anyone asked me about the risk, I'd say, 'What risk?'

I can honestly say that it wasn't just the money that drove me forward. I knew what a difference my care home made to the residents: one lady came in who had previously been living six to a room, and she was so grateful and happy. The residents loved it, and that felt pretty good – you could see how well they responded to a better environment. It was another powerful reason to continue to expand and to make sure that with each new home we improved the facilities and learned from our mistakes. This meant making sure every home had single rooms with ensuite toilets (in Springfield House it had only been about 80 per cent to keep costs down) and designing more intimate dining rooms. In the first home, we'd built something that felt like a canteen and it was clear from what the residents told us that they would like to eat somewhere that felt more like their own home.

To this day I am incredibly proud of being at the forefront of the way caring for the elderly changed in Britain. I wasn't the only one, a couple of other companies such as Takare and Westminster Healthcare were also offering single rooms, some of them with ensuite facilities, and together we made a big difference to the lives of a huge number of people. Others might be happy to make money selling timeshares and robbing old people of their pensions, but I couldn't do that: I need to be proud of everything I do.

If I'm totally honest, the fact that Billy Morgan was talking about opening up other homes in the area also gave me a greater appetite for success. Having a rival is often a big motivator to me, spurring me on to greater success.

I found my next plot of land when I was driving home one day. I saw the For Sale sign, pulled over, got out of the car and peered through the chainlink fence at another grubby patch of ground. It was covered in weeds, was right next to a factory and was in a pretty shitty part of town – it was perfect. I stood there thinking, 'If I buy this plot there's room to build three nursing homes. I could build a little village. And with three homes in the same place, my overheads will drop and I'll make even more money.' I think it was there, gripping onto that fence, that I started to think I might end up with tens of millions of pounds. The rush was amazing.

When I got home, I did the maths and wrote myself a little business plan to take to the bank manager. The plan showed me buying the land for £130,000 and then building the first nursing home. It showed how the profit from it would fund the loan for both the land and the build costs. When the first home was full I'd start building the second, and when that was full I'd build the third. Each home had a build cost of £12,000 per bed, and at fifty beds each that came in at £600,000 per home, on top of the cost of the land. When I went in to see the bank manager and said I wanted to borrow £2 million he nearly fell off his seat.

'How much are you putting up?' he asked when he'd recovered his composure. This made me feel pretty confident: I could tell that with one full nursing home to my credit he was at least prepared to hear me out. I certainly beat the reception I'd had just over a year before.

'Not a lot,' I confessed, 'but I'm digging around and I reckon I could find about fifty thousand.' This was money I had left in the bank after the first mortgage had paid off my debts.

'Duncan,' he said, leaning over his desk, 'that's not very much against a two million loan.' I could tell he was trying not to be patronising; he just couldn't help himself.

'Perhaps I'm not explaining it right . . .'

I said that initially I only wanted him to lend me the money for the land, and a £50,000 deposit on a £130,000 plot wasn't a bad percentage. He said he could do that. Then I wanted him to lend me the £600,000 to build the first home on the basis that when it was built it would be valued at £1.5 million, based on the standard industry valuation of £30,000 per bed. As I'd already done it once, he agreed in principle and I went ahead and bought the land. Only when the first home was full would I go back to him for the money to build the next one. Within a couple of years he'd have loaned me £2 million and I'd be offering him security of assets worth nearly £5 million. If I defaulted, the bank was covered, so he agreed as long as he could get it past his bosses, which he did. To get their approval he asked me for a more detailed business plan, so I said, 'Here's your business plan: I build a nursing home for twelve thousand a bed and it produces a profit of four thousand per bed. That's a thirty-three per cent return on capital.' In other words, if I borrowed £1 million at 10 per cent interest, I'd make £333,000 and pay the bank £100,000 in interest, so I'd be left with £233,000. It was simple enough to me.

As a child, my family didn't have
a camera, so there are very few
pictures of me in those days.
(Right) Me, Helen and George near
our home in Canberra Avenue,
Dalmuir; (below) I'm on the right,
having already shown
my entrepreneurial streak by
getting a paper round.

In the Navy now. I joined the Navy at the age of fifteen when I was just 5 feet 3 inches tall, but I soon filled out and toughened up as I took the opportunity to see the world.

Some satisfied customers for Duncan's Super Ices, my first real business venture. After I'd invested £450 in an ice-cream van to start it up, I sold the business a few years later for £28,000.

Quality Care Homes was the business that transformed me from a small-time businessman to a multi-millionaire. As with so many of my businesses, it involved providing people with good quality facilities and having a clear idea of the market. These three shots were all taken at Roseworth Lodge.

Just Learning was the perfect business and, thanks to the quality and safety of the facilities, we were able to expand quickly. In five years I invested £2 million into the company, and then sold it for £22 million.

Bannatyne Fitness is now my most important business. The reception areas for Coulby Newham (above) and Darlington health clubs: it is important to keep evolving the look of each club and to pay attention to what the customers are saying.

Promoting the relaunch of alpha FM, a radio station that had been sinking until I came in and helped turn it round.

On site at the building of the second Hotel Bannatyne, in Durham, which is due to open at the end of 2006.

Outside Bar Bannatyne in The Gate, Newcastle.

Anyone can do it!

I immediately set about getting planning permission for the development we would call Norton Glades, and yet again I struck lucky in an area of construction that so often proves many projects' downfall: it turned out that the factory next door was in financial trouble and was closing down, which wasn't that unusual in 1988. The council wanted to announce that they were creating as many new jobs as possible and my homes offered them the chance to make that announcement. My planning permission was fast-tracked and I employed the same builder and architect as before. They'd done a good job on the first home, so I saw no reason not to use them again: I believe in rewarding loyalty and good work and it also meant that things would happen quickly.

Building on such a scale is never without its problems, but far and away the biggest hitch I've ever had with any of my projects has come from officialdom. I know the world is full of arseholes and you can come across them anywhere, but I swear the highest concentration in the world can be found in the departments of District Health Authorities that license nursing homes.

You can't operate until you've got a licence, and you can't get a licence until your nursing home has been passed fit for residents, which obviously means you need to build your home before it can be inspected. As the licensing department is so utterly dynamic and efficient, it takes a ridiculous three months between phoning up and asking them to inspect and the inspection actually taking place. Three months! That means you've got a fully operational nursing home lying empty for three months.

My solution was to make the necessary call three months before completion, but of course on the day before the inspection we still had a few walls unpainted and a few light fittings still unconnected. There was a mad panic to get it finished in time and I got all hands on deck to help with the decorating. By the time the convoy of inspectors turned up – and it was a convoy, I reckon they each used their own car so they could all claim the mileage and keep rate payers' bills higher than they needed to be – there were still a couple of chippies on site tending to a few last-minute jobs. But we were 99 per cent there, and the nursing home was obviously ready for residents to start moving in.

However, the guy in charge of the inspectors was a complete dickhead, even more than I'd come to expect from council inspectors. He saw the two guys in overalls and a screwdriver lying on the floor and announced, 'This isn't ready for inspection. Call me when you're ready.' They all turned round and headed for their cars to drive back separately to the same office.

'Are you telling me,' I asked, 'that even though I've got residents booked in, because there's one lousy screwdriver on the floor you're not going to carry out the inspection?' I was simmering with rage.

'This isn't ready for inspection,' he repeated.

'Well come and see the rest of the building, and by the time we get back here it will be finished.'

'It's not ready,' he said, 'and we're leaving.'

'It is *thirty* minutes away from being finished,' I told him, 'and you're really not going to let me open for another three months?'

I couldn't believe it. It was November 1988 and we had bookings from local hospitals to take patients in over Christmas, Social Services were planning to send people to us who needed care, but because of the dickhead from the council I was going to have to wait three months for my licence. For three months, my perfect nursing home was going to lie empty and I would have to make the mortgage repayments and pay the staff's wages out of my own pocket. I was furious.

Sometimes you can use fury to get you ahead, but sometimes you just have to know when you're beaten. There's no reasoning with people like that. They know the power they have and they get a perverse kick out of exercising it. I tell myself they must have little, mean lives, and that's why they take every opportunity to make themselves feel important.

Growing the business

Obviously with the new mortgage I was getting myself into a large amount of debt, something I was completely confident about, as I was absolutely sure that I was building a massive business. But this was the late eighties and interest rates were starting to climb, so I did the smart thing and bought into a 'cap and collar' deal when interest rates were at around 8 per cent. This meant that if rates went up, I wouldn't pay more than 10 per cent, but if they went down, I wouldn't pay less than 6 per cent. There was a chance that rates would start to go down again and that I would lose out, but the cap and collar deal allowed me to plan with a greater degree of confidence.

Most deals I do are still with fixed-rate loans: I see them as an insurance plan. I think over the years I'm probably slightly worse off because I could have paid less at certain times, but I've also paid out on a lot of insurance premiums that I've never claimed against. It's a small price to pay for certainty and peace of mind.

The next few years were good ones. I had plenty of time to spend with my kids, and the nursing homes were properly managed and needed little day-to-day input from me. When I wasn't with the kids, I was driving round the country looking for new sites, buying up bigger and bigger plots of land. It became something of an addiction as I started to dream of creating the biggest care-home business in the north-east. I loved every aspect of the business, from knowing we were making a difference to knowing I was building myself a fortune, there wasn't a day I wasn't happy to get out of bed and get to work.

I made a point of visiting our homes as often as possible, and whenever I could I always visited at lunch time, so I could eat with the residents and check the meals were of a high enough standard. If the portions were too small, I told the staff to be more generous, or if the menu was the same as the last time I'd been there, I told the cook to be a bit more creative.

Most of our residents were thrilled with their accommodation and had genuine affection for the staff, who went to enormous lengths to make sure they were entertained, stimulated and cared for, so the atmosphere was usually one of high spirits. Spending so much time with people at the end of their lives definitely had an affect on me and my future career. I sat down and chatted with several of our residents and was reminded how fragile and precious life is. Many of them would say to me, 'Make the most of every minute, you're a young man and you have no idea how quickly time passes.' When enough people tell you that, it sinks in, and I'm sure it was a motivating factor to do more with my life.

Of course running care homes wasn't without problems. It's the nature of the business that we had many residents who died, and that was always hard, and sometimes the families would blame us. These were usually the same families that hadn't visited their mums or dads for months at a time. And then there were the families whose first response on seeing the body was 'Where's her gold ring? I'm going to sue you.' Although our homes were developed to very high standards, they were mainly built in deprived areas to provide a service to the elderly in poorer communities. That meant we faced the full range of social-deprivation issues, and we got quite used to relatives trying it on.

I was more surprised to find that some of the trained nurses we employed would also try to rip me off. I made the mistake of thinking that all nurses were angels and that people attracted to the caring profession would be trustworthy. However, as our staff came from the same deprived communities as our residents, its more surprising that we didn't get more trouble, especially as, in the early days, plenty of residents were paying cash from their pensions.

I'm very good at taking action when I need to, so as soon as I noticed that the takings were down at one particular home, I started to perform spot checks on the safe to work out when the money was going. It quickly became clear which member of staff was the thief and so I confronted her. She confessed immediately, but told me that her husband had left her and she couldn't afford to keep her kids with her. When you hear a story like that it's quite hard not to give someone a second chance, so I did. She repaid the money and carried on with her work, so I never saw any reason to call the police in and let it affect the rest of her career.

Two months later, though, money was missing again and the same nurse was involved. This time she was sacked straight away. I still didn't see the point of getting the police involved, though: she hadn't been lying about having three kids and if I punished her any more then they'd have suffered, too. And to be honest, having the police on the premises is not something relatives, or residents, want to see.

Incidents like that made me very aware of security and I became frustrated with the matron at one of our homes in Norton Glades who didn't take simple precautions like locking her office door when she went on her rounds. I created a real scare one day when I visited the home and popped into her office without anyone seeing me and helped myself to the petty cash. A few hours later my phone rang.

'Duncan, look, I'm very sorry. I don't know how it happened, but it seems the petty cash has been stolen.'

'I can tell you exactly how it happened: you don't lock your bloody door!'

'Oh. Well, of course, I'll always lock it in future . . .'

She was so relieved that it had been me who'd taken the money that she never forgot to lock her door again. Incidents like that were rare, and most of my problems finding nursing staff weren't to do with their character or their qualifications, it was to do with money. Success creates its own problems, and for us the consequence of building so many nursing homes in the same area was that nursing agencies spied a chance to make some money of their own. They would rent an office in town and advertise their arrival in the nursing and local press by offering £15 an hour for qualified nursing staff when at the time we were paying £10 an hour.

In the course of just a few months several of our nurses resigned and went to work for the agency. And when we found ourselves short-staffed, what did we do? We had to call the agency, of course. But they didn't charge us £15; they charged us £20 an hour, taking the difference as their commission. In the space of a few months our staffing costs looked like doubling if we didn't do something about it. Of course, this wasn't just a problem for us, it affected NHS hospitals, too. My solution was set up our own agency to try and put the others out of business. However, it proved a slight conflict of interest: it only encouraged more of our staff to join an agency. In addition, it wasn't very successful.

Although the business was profitable enough to cover the rising costs, it made me angry, not so much for us but for the public sector. I knew from conferences I attended how hard elderly care was for our counterparts in the NHS, and I knew that they were also making sacrifices elsewhere to pay the agencies' rates. Ultimately, the people who really suffered were the patients and residents. It's still a problem for the NHS, and I'm starting to see the same pattern emerging in teaching and wonder how these vulture agencies will affect the quality of education.

When you're in the care industry, there are other kinds of problems that can come out of nowhere and plunge your business into the mire, like the time one of our male carers was accused of sexually assaulting a female resident. When something like that happens, the authorities descend and launch an investigation. Even if, as in that case, he was subsequently cleared, they probe their way into every bit of the business, asking questions in a way that's designed to make you feel guilty and taking up the time of the staff who had plenty of other things to do. On another occasion, one of our residents assaulted another resident, who fell awkwardly, hit her head and died.

By this stage of the business, I had learned that my strength as an entrepreneur was both my willingness and ability to delegate. I had employed a PR company on a retainer to handle the adverse press attention we got when incidents arose, and I had employed regional managers whose job it was to handle the fallout from those kinds of situations.

My ability to delegate is a major reason why I made it where others didn't. I know other entrepreneurs with completely different skills to mine and completely different outlooks. I know one very successful businessman who spends millions of pounds developing products he isn't sure he can sell. That's just not the way I like to do business: I like to own freeholds and assets I know the value of – whether that's an ice-cream van or kitchen equipment, I'd much rather own than lease. And I know of other entrepreneurs who are great at closing deals or motivating their staff. What we have in common is that we've worked out what works best for us. You can run a business any way you like, but you'll run it better if you build it around your strengths and delegation is one of mine.

I remember once bumping into Billy Morgan's wife when we both had a handful of homes to our names. She asked me how I was always able to leave work at three o'clock and get home to my kids when they were often working till ten at night. I knew it was because of the way I ran my businesses, whereas they bought fire extinguishers and kitchen equipment at auction – and there's nothing wrong with that, so long as you get everything serviced properly – or leased equipment cheaply, I bought everything brand new. So when they were racing around buying replacement equipment or being let down by their contractors, I had time free for my family. Of course that's not what I told her, I said it was because I employed good people and empowered them to make their own decisions.

'Yeah,' she said, 'but our homes are more profitable than yours.'

'Maybe,' I answered, 'but you were asking me how come I left work at three o'clock.'

I think what this illustrates is that there's more than one way to run a business. The art of delegation is about setting targets and boundaries for your managers, and as long as they meet their targets and operate within their boundaries then you trust them to get on with the job. It's the trust part of the arrangement that less successful entrepreneurs find difficult, but for me it was straightforward. When people don't meet their targets, you have to assess if that's because they're not getting the support they need, or if their job is too much for one person, if they're just not up to the job.

It may have been that some of my managers weren't great at the job straight away, but by letting them manage their department as they chose, they got the chance to learn a bit about themselves and develop their own style. And once they found that out they could mould their department around their strengths, just I have built a business around mine. This gave them a chance to become great managers, and that in turn gave me the chance to do what I did best: drive the business forward.

Of course it helped that I was delegating to the right people, and if there was one thing I was able to do instinctively it was to hire the right person for the job. As someone without any qualifications and a pretty unconventional CV, I was never going to be impressed by candidates with degrees. Years ago, when I was first looking for someone to make sure all the residential fees were paid, I didn't care about qualifications, or a specific age or even previous work experience. I knew the quality I most needed was loyalty, so when a CV came my way from a woman who had stayed in her previous job for twelve years before she was made redundant, I had a good feeling about her. Her name is Irene Readman and my hunch was right: she worked for me for twenty years until she retired in 2006. Irene ran a department monitoring fees paid by my nursing-home residents from an office we created from one of the bedrooms at Norton Glades. The staff outgrew that bedroom fairly quickly and some of them moved into a Portakabin in the grounds. In 1992 we finally had a purpose-built office in our third home on the Norton Glades site, which would eventually become a residents' lounge. I never did believe in spending money on unnecessary overheads!

One of the most enjoyable aspects of Quality Care Homes at that time was the team I was building around me. As well as Irene, I had a great financial director called Chris Rutter who could work out pretty complicated projections on the back of a fag packet. At one point I'd employed an FD who'd come from one of the big accountancy firms with a tremendous track record. But as soon as he joined Quality Care Homes it was obvious that he was institutionalised. He was used to having a department to call for everything from stationery to petty cash and was incapable of doing anything for himself. He was like a conductor waiting for his orchestra to turn up and he never realised he was the one who was supposed to make the music himself. He didn't last long. Chris, on the other hand, was an extremely hard worker with no airs or graces who just got on with the job. And he was accurate, too: if he prepared accounts for me, I knew they'd always be right, even down to the pennies.

Although I had a very formidable woman as my director of nursing, Susan Watson – who insisted on being called 'Mrs Watson', even by members of the board – the rest of my nursing staff were good fun and great at their jobs. One of the younger sisters, Joanne McCue, was clearly bright enough to go further, and after a few years with us she took over from Mrs Watson.

Everyone who worked for me was eligible for a bonus, which was paid if their care home achieved 98 per cent occupancy. This meant that it was more cost effective for me to be 95 per cent full, but it motivated the staff, which in turn meant the homes were happier places to work in and, more importantly, to live in. I felt it was important to include the cleaners and kitchen staff in that bonus scheme, as well as the nurses, as their jobs also had a big impact on the well-being of our residents. And if the rooms were clean and the meals were tasty, we were more likely to achieve 98 per cent occupancy.

While the bonus scheme was fairly generous, I got a bit of a reputation with my staff for being tight. I think this boiled down to paperclips. I couldn't see – and still can't – why any organisation ever needs to buy paperclips. Every morning when you open your post you get a letter with something clipped to it. All you have to do is take the paperclip and put it in a drawer and you'll never need to buy paperclips again. I also couldn't work out how one of our nursing homes got through 200 pens a month, yet whenever I monitored the stationery budget, that's how many pens they were buying. I came to the conclusion that the nurses had to be taking them home with them, so I put it into new contracts that staff had to provide their own pens.

I realise this must make me sound like an archetypal penny-pinching Scot, but it's actually part of my business philosophy: don't spend money unnecessarily. For every pound you overspend, you have to work harder to turn a pound profit. However, I'll admit that my need to account for every penny might have gone a bit too far with the 'Case of The Missing Eggs'. Joanne McCue teases me about it to this very day.

I had been visiting one of our homes where Joanne was working and at some point after lunch, I went into the kitchen and happened to notice that there were three boiled eggs in a bowl. After chatting to some of the residents and checking in with the staff, I went back to the kitchen and saw that there was only one egg left. I think I must have been at the end of my tether with petty thieving and things going missing, but anyway, I insisted on finding out who had eaten the eggs. It was company policy that if staff ate meals at work they had to pay for them, so I felt justified in asking who had eaten them. I told them I was determined to get to the bottom of it, and Joanne launched an investigation that went on for weeks until I finally forgot about it. I realise now that I should have probably just eaten the third egg myself and got on with the rest of my day. While I still don't like staff helping themselves to company property, it's not a good reason to get wound up. I now employ people to get wound up on my behalf.

THIRTEEN

Taking care of business

*It's impossible to think big
without thinking complex.*

As I'd worked out how to delegate, and because I'd appointed a great team, I found the transition to running a large business reasonably straightforward. I found out that it's pretty easy to find employees to look after things like payroll, and most of the admin side of things seemed obvious. Many of the people who come to hear me do public speaking are afraid of the legal responsibilities of managing anything other than a cottage industry. I tell them that they shouldn't let something like that put them off: if you get so successful that it becomes complicated, the chances are you'll be able to employ someone to take care of that side of things.

Being free to look to the future and work out how to grow is key to building a business: it's what a chief executive is there to do. If I had been consumed with how each manager was running their department, or had got personally involved in details like which bed linen we bought, I would never have been able to look for new sites, analyse the competition, negotiate new contracts or any of the other things that made us better and kept us competitive. If my thoughts were uncluttered by the minutiae of the business, then I was better able to see the bigger picture, to lead and problem solve. It also happened that I needed to have time available to deal with the banks.

Although the Yorkshire bank had financed my first two projects, I got the impression they were a bit worried about lending to me again. At the time I didn't really understand why, but I soon realised that a bank manager at a local branch only has the authority to lend a certain amount of money. As I was personally liable to them for over £2 million, they probably wanted to spread their risk a little more thinly. Once I had reached the local lending threshold, the manager had to get new loans approved by his boss, and when my lending extended further, then the boss's boss needed to get involved. This made the process of getting loans approved very slow.

So for subsequent deals I shopped around and ended up dealing with three other banks as well as Yorkshire: Barclays, the Co-Op and the Banque Nationale de Paris. I got a particularly good deal from BNP as a broker I'd used had told me they were desperate to get into the UK commercial market. I might have preferred not to pay a broker's fee, but it worked out cheaper to pay for his knowledge, and I've often found that specialist expertise can be worth the relatively small investment it requires.

Most people like their lives to be neat. They like to know how much they owe, and to whom, and in what size instalments they will make their repayments. I can live with complex, so borrowing from four different banks at different rates with different terms was easy for me. And of course, as soon as a bank knows it's got a rival, it makes you better offers. For a guy who had only recently been turned down for a loan, I got a huge amount of pleasure seeing banks fight for my business.

I don't think I'm unique among entrepreneurs for being at ease with complexity. I've read, and loved, most of Donald Trump's books and I've been amazed at how he's managed to broker such complex land and financing deals. Richard Branson is the same; his autobiography shows how much he relishes new ventures and adapts to ever greater complexity. It's impossible to think big without thinking complex. And by now I was thinking really big: I had an expanding chain of nursing homes, all of which were profitable at launch, and I could see that my net worth – the value of my nursing homes minus the value of financing – was several millions. If I could keep going, I was going to be extremely wealthy. The banks had other ideas, though. They could see that I was building homes they hadn't financed and they started to ask questions: they wanted reassurance that I wasn't over-committed, and unfortunately, it turned out that I was.

As the mortgage on each property was for more than it cost me to build them, each time I completed a nursing home I could inject some cash into the business. With positive cashflow, it became possible to start building new homes as soon as I'd found the land – I didn't have to wait for the banks' approval. However, what I thought made perfect business sense backfired when, several months into the building of two new homes, I set about seeking finance for completion. One bank manager explained his concern to me: 'Duncan, how do we know that you're not building homes all over the country?'

They couldn't verify my total debt, or my total assets, and I think they thought I was expanding too rapidly. When one bank catches cold feet, they all do, and I found it impossible to get finance. Reluctantly I had to tell the builders to stop work, and for months I had two homes left unfinished. It cost me a lot of money to leave them half-built, but I didn't have a lot of choice: all I could do was wait until I could finance the construction myself out of the profits from my other homes.

By the early nineties, most of my days were spent either with my growing family, taking the kids to school, playing squash or looking out for new sites on which to build. I'd have a few construction meetings a month and a few management meetings, but I certainly wasn't working a sixty-hour week. It just seemed so easy and I kept saying to Gail, 'Why doesn't everyone do this?'

I was feeling terrific about myself. I'd kept my promise to Gail and was getting to spend loads of time with my daughters, and as if that wasn't enough, I was sticking two fingers up to everyone who'd ever told me I wouldn't amount to anything. From my old school master to my commanding officers in the Navy to that stroppy manager at Barclays, I was proving them all wrong. There aren't many feelings to top that.

However, although it all seemed straightforward in my head, my body had other ideas and it started to protest. I might be with the kids or in the car, and I would feel myself falling asleep. I remember once waking up with a cup of coffee in my hand and thinking how bizarre it was that I hadn't spilt it. I dipped my finger in it and it was stone cold – I had nodded off sitting upright for twenty minutes or more. Something was clearly wrong.

I went to see my doctor and he immediately diagnosed narcolepsy and recommended that I see a specialist. By coincidence the specialist who came to see me, Dr Carr, was the same doctor who'd only recently given me the all-clear for a life-insurance examination. He knew there was nothing wrong with me – he'd tested me for everything under the sun – and after asking me loads of questions he announced that I didn't have narcolepsy at all: I was suffering from stress.

'But I'm not stressed,' I told him. 'I've got it easy.'

So he asked me if I lay awake at night thinking about opportunities or solving problems. I had to admit that I did, and he persuaded me that maybe I wasn't quite as laid back as thought I was. I spent so much nervous energy planning my next move or finding solutions that I wasn't sleeping properly. My body desperately needed to catch up on sleep, and he explained that drifting off was a release valve for the stress – the only way my body could cope was if it switched off the mind from time to time.

It turned out that there was a pretty easy solution: cutting down on tea and coffee, always going to bed at the same time and setting the alarm for the same time every morning, that sort of thing. And after a few months the problem drifted away. It also became clear that taking time off was important, as it was often only on holiday that I was away from a telephone – I didn't get a mobile until the mid-nineties and email didn't exist back then – and truly switched off. However, our summer holiday in 1987 nearly proved to be my last when a trip to the beach almost went disastrously wrong. We had gone down to the south coast to visit Gail's sister Irene, who had moved to Sussex. While Gail played with the girls on the beach, I went for a swim in the Channel. I put my head down and powered out from the shore, trying to cram as much exercise as I could into the holiday. It was a few minutes before I realised that I was making better progress than I'd thought, and after a few more minutes I realised it was because the tide was carrying me away from the coast.

At first, I wasn't scared: my dad had made sure I was a strong swimmer and I was still pretty fit, so I was confident I would make it back. All I had to do was put my head down and use all my strength to swim against the tide. I picked a point on the shore and headed for it. When I stopped for a breather after a couple of minutes, though, I realised I was even further away from the beach. I could see Gail and the girls on the shore, and I could tell they didn't have a clue I was in trouble, which meant no one would come and help me. For the first time in my life I thought I was going to die. If someone didn't spot me, I reckoned I only had a few minutes left before I'd go under. Somehow I was going to have to get myself back to dry land.

As going against the tide wasn't getting me anywhere except closer to the Isle of Wight, I calculated that my best chance to avoid ending up in the shipping lane was to let the tide carry me further down the coast, where I could see some timber groynes reaching out into the sea. If I could get hold of one of those, I reasoned, I could pull myself into the beach.

After ten minutes of some of the hardest physical exertion of my life, the tide slammed me into the old timbers, tearing my flesh against the barnacles and letting salt water into the wounds. The pain was so bad I nearly lost my grip. But I held on long enough to regain some strength and then began to pull myself slowly along the groyne towards the beach. When I was closer to the shore, the effect of the tide lessened and I was able to swim to safety. I emerged from the sea covered in blood but thankful to be alive.

It wasn't enough to put me off going back in the sea. I have a very strong bond with water – I can't put my finger on why – and am as happy on water, or in it, as I am on land. On one of our next holidays, we went to the Lake District, where we had such a good time on the water that I bought a yacht. I hadn't planned to, but when I saw the 'for sale' sign on a 30-footer, I thought it would be a nice idea, so I spoke to the vendor and told him that if he taught me to sail, I'd buy his boat off him. After a few hours, I reckoned I knew enough to take the boat out by myself – after all, it was Lake Windermere where you can see the shore at all times. How much trouble could I get into?

I soon found out when I took the staff on an away day to the lake to say thank you for all their hard work. We were towing a dinghy with an outboard motor in case the wind dropped, which doesn't often happen in Cumbria, but of course it happened to us – just as we sat in the way of the ferry. When I saw the ferry coming straight for us, I had no choice but to leap into the water and start the engine on the dinghy, but as I hit the water, a wave caught my life jacket and lifted it off over my head. At the same time it pulled me under and I was caught under the boat.

One of the other men on board realised what was happening, jumped into the dinghy and tried to pull me out. As he was hauling me on to the boat, the ferry was getting very close. It's a rule of boating in the Lake District that no pleasure craft can interfere with the timetable or route of the commercial ferries, so it wasn't going to change it's course.

Suddenly, booming across the water came a Tannoy announcement: 'KEEP CLEAR OF THE FERRY AT ALL TIMES! KEEP CLEAR OF THE FERRY AT ALL TIMES!'

We managed to get the motor started and pulled the yacht free just in time. Of course I was drenched and absolutely frozen.

'I've got some dry clothes,' one of the staff offered. Unfortunately it was a *female* member of staff, so I spent the rest of the day dressed in baby pink having my photograph taken by everyone on the team.

FOURTEEN

The extortion attempt
1991

---

*If you really want to be in business
and your partner is holding you back,
you have to look at your priorities.*

The wealthier I got, the better known I became, and when you're rich, there's always someone who's jealous and wants a piece of your money for themselves. It started without me noticing.

The first thing that happened was a parcel arrived at the Portakabin we were still using as an office. It was marked 'private and confidential'. Irene Readman asked if she should open it and I said 'of course' as I didn't have anything to hide. Inside she found a pair of beautiful black leather gloves and a card which said, 'Because I love you. D xxx'. I didn't know what to make of it, but being a happily married man I took the gloves home and showed them to my wife. She asked me what I was going to do about it, and I said I was going to wear them because they were so nice. I also thought that if I wore them, 'D' might approach me.

I don't think Gail thought D really existed, but she certainly wasn't about to have me wearing someone else's gloves, so she took them and hid them away. Once they were out of sight, they were out of mind, and I didn't give it any more thought.

The following week, the second strange thing happened. Someone daubed the words BANNATYNE SELLS DRUGS TO KIDS

106

in big letters on the gable end of a shop adjacent to one of my existing nursing homes. I got a phone call from the manager of that home at four o'clock in the morning to tell me about it, she was ready to paint over it because she knew it wasn't true, but I told her I wanted to see it for myself, so I went down there and painted over it straight away.

It's only with hindsight that I've made a connection between these events, and looking back it's clear that someone was cooking something up. At the time, though, they just seemed random and unrelated.

The next piece of the jigsaw seemed totally innocuous: a few evenings later, I left work late and rushed home as I was going out for dinner. I got changed quickly and as I ran out again, I saw a pot plant on the doorstep, which I'd noticed on my way in but hadn't had time to pick up. Gail and Abigail, who was seven years old at the time, came to wave me goodbye and my daughter spotted the plant.

'Dad, what's that?' Abigail asked, pointing to it.

'I don't know, darling. Why don't you take it inside? I have to rush now. Bye bye.'

Abigail picked it up and took it into the house; I remember the look of excitement on her little face.

It was the following day when the pieces started to fit together. I was at home helping my kids with their homework as Gail was out, so there were just the three of us in the house when there was a knock at the door at about 3 p.m. I opened the door to find myself face to face with four rather large men.

'Hello?' I said.

'We're the drugs squad.'

I was too gobsmacked to say anything as they flashed their badges.

'We have reason to believe there are class A drugs in this house. Who are you?'

'I'm Duncan Bannatyne,' I told them. 'This is my house and there are no drugs in here. You're talking absolute rubbish.'

'Well, we have a warrant, so we'll see about that.'

I was shocked but not worried: I knew there was no chance they'd find anything, I just wanted to make sure my girls were OK. But they refused to let me make a phone call, either to my wife or to our babysitter who lived across the street. I didn't want to scare the girls, so I didn't shout out to them or make a scene, I just hoped they'd stay in their rooms and wouldn't see anything.

As the four officers entered the house they pinned me up against the wall.

I said to the officer who was holding me: 'This is crazy. And thinking about it, it's the fourth odd thing that's happened this month.'

'What do you mean?'

So I told them about the gloves, the graffiti, and the pot plant.

'A pot plant? He asked, 'Where is it?'

'My daughter put it on top of the TV.'

At this point, they put on the rubber gloves and took a look at it: I was amazed when they pulled the plant out of the pot, and removed a bag of white powder from beneath the soil, which I assumed was cocaine. Obviously, I'd had absolutely no idea that it was there.

'Do you think it's a plant?' one of the officers asked in an attempt to show that the police have a sense of humour.

I told them I knew it was, but as far as they were concerned they had found the evidence they were looking for and they arrested me. They were about to take me to the police station when my wife came home. As they put the handcuffs on, I said to Gail, 'You know who's been doing this, don't you?'

She nodded.

I was damn sure I knew who was behind it: there was a guy I knew about town who was clearly jealous of my success, and though I'd love to name him, my lawyers won't let me. As Gail and I talked, the officers became intrigued and started to believe I really might have been framed. They asked for the name of the person I thought was behind it, and as soon as I told them, their attitude changed and they believed me straight away: he had a record for other offences and didn't have the best of reputations. They still had to arrest me, of course, and they took my finger prints at the station and established my prints were not on the pot, the only prints on it were that of a child. Obviously our story added up and they released me without charge, only cautioning me to say that if they ever found any drugs in the future, then they would use the events of that day as evidence.

If they hadn't believed me, things could have turned out very differently: at the time I was processing the registration of three nursing homes, and if I'd been charged with a drug-related offence, the registrations would not have gone through and I would have had a major cash-flow problem. If someone was deliberately trying to ruin me, they were either very lucky or very canny with their timing. It wasn't long after this that the tape arrived.

The brown envelope it came in was a lot like the one the gloves had arrived in. Inside was a little tape recorder and a tape, so I stuck the tape in and pressed play.

'*Good morning, Mr Ballantyne,*' a man's voice said in a fake Irish accent. '*We know you and have been following you. We have been fighting a war for a hundred years...*' It was at this point that the tape clicked, and after that they started saying my name correctly. '*We want fifty thousand pounds in used notes. Don't try and call the police, Mr Bannatyne, because if you do that, we will ruin you morally, physically and financially. Do not contact the police, Mr Bannatyne, or you will regret it.*' I inferred from that that they had planted the gloves, the drugs and painted the graffiti. The tape also said that they had been fighting a war for a long time and they wanted money to continue their campaign, though I found it hard to believe that the IRA were targeting me.

So what did I do? Well I called the police, of course. My babysitter's father was a police officer, so I contacted him at home, which was just over the road.

'What do you want to do Duncan?' he asked. 'You could pay up or you could work with the police to try and catch them; it's your decision entirely.'

'I want to catch them – I'll never pay an extortionist,' I told him emphatically.

'If that's the case, then wait in your house – I'll make a few phone calls and then I'll come and pick you up.'

As there was a chance the extortionists had my house under surveillance, he drove over to my place on some pretence and started unloading stuff into my garage. At some point during this charade, I sneaked into the back of his car and he covered me with a blanket. He drove me to Special Branch HQ in Middlesbrough where I met twenty or thirty officers, including some of the guys who'd searched my place a few weeks earlier. They explained that they wanted to use me as bait to get to the extortionist. If it was the guy we all thought it was, then he was suspected of all sorts of things and they wanted to catch him red-handed. So we started to set a trap for him.

However, as the police couldn't rule out that it wasn't the IRA behind the threats, Special Branch officers coached me to look for signs that I was being targeted by terrorists. I looked under my car every morning in case something had been planted, and instead of just getting in the car and driving off, they told me to reach in, start the ignition and then walk away, leaving the engine running for several minutes. I never put the girls in the car until I was absolutely sure it was safe.

Special Branch put us under twenty-four-hour surveillance and arranged for four unmarked police cars to be parked on the approach roads to the house Gail and I had moved to in Long Newton, near Darlington. Two officers were assigned to the office, and just in case the blackmailer was one of my staff, we had to say they were VAT inspectors. They spent a week in a room poring over accounts that meant absolutely nothing to them! (It was the same week that Chris Rutter joined the company as our financial controller. He'd asked me who the men with the accounts were, and of course I had to tell him they were VAT men. It was only in 2006 that Chris told me he'd felt too new to ask difficult questions, and that he'd spent the intervening fifteen years wondering what I'd done to warrant a VAT investigation.

On the Friday, as the extortionist had told me to, I went to the bank, withdrew £50,000 and put the notes in a black bin liner inside a holdall and taped it up with Sellotape. It was like something out of a movie, and it felt surreal to be a part of it. Nevertheless, I took the money home and waited for a call. The police sat round the house, and between endless cups of tea they'd coach me what to say when the extortionist made contact. They told me to take my time answering any questions as they would hold up prompt cards to tell me what to say. The phone eventually rang in the evening.

'Mr Bannatyne?'

'Yes.'

'Have you got the money?'

'Yes.'

'Good. Now what's your mobile phone number?'

I was silent. This was 1991 and I didn't have a mobile phone. I looked at the police officers in the room, who couldn't think of anything to write on their prompt cards.

'I don't have a mobile phone.'

There was silence on the other end of the line. I waited.

'Then we have a problem. We'll call you back.'

If it wasn't clear already that we were dealing with amateurs rather than the IRA, it certainly was now. We waited, and waited, and waited, but the phone didn't ring again. The police hung around all night, but when their shift ended they drifted off and we were left alone. It wasn't until Monday afternoon that the phone rang again.

'Mr Bannatyne, do you still have the money?'

I didn't. I'd gone straight to the bank when it opened and

deposited the cash – it seemed crazy to have it lying around the house if the police weren't with me for protection.

'We'll call you back on Thursday. Make sure you have the money.'

So on Thursday I went through the same routine again. I got the cash out, the police staked out my house and we waited for the phone to ring. And we waited, and waited.

I can't remember how long it took them to call back, but it was days if not weeks. When they finally called, Gail was in on her own.

'Can I speak to Mr Bannatyne?'

She recognised the fake voice straight away and she was livid.

'No you fucking can't, you bastard. We've got the police on the case and we're going to fucking catch you!'

And do you know what, that was the last we ever heard from them!

Although I was impressed that Gail had stood up to them, I was mad because she'd blown our chance of catching them. I was so angry with them and I wanted to face them in court: I wanted to know who had put class A drugs in the hands of my seven-year-old daughter. If I'd ever got them alone I'd have gouged their eyes out.

Nevertheless, it was a relief to have the whole episode behind us. Looking back, I realise how lucky I was to have been married to Gail at that time in my life. She was incredibly supportive of me and my decisions. She never argued with me – even when I sold the house – and she never told me my plans wouldn't work out. I think it helped that both her father and brother had run businesses, so she understood that what I wanted to do would require short-term sacrifices. Her support and belief in me drove me forward, and I guess it helped that I was also adamant it was going to work.

Not so long ago, I received an email from someone who'd heard me speak at an event for business leaders and was after some advice. She wanted to know if I'd had support from my family because her partner wasn't understanding of what she wanted to do. I just wrote back to her and said, 'Dump him!' I was only half joking: if you really want to be in business and your partner is holding you back, you have to look at your priorities. It's tough getting a business off the ground, and everybody needs support. Gail gave me that, and in doing so she made the hard times that little bit easier.

FIFTEEN

Shark-infested waters
1992

*You can only really learn about
business by being in business.*

By the end of 1991, Quality Care Homes Ltd had built and was operating nine nursing homes with a total of 428 registered beds, and in doing so had racked up debts in the region of £6 million. I wanted to borrow more, but the banks refused to play ball. I really believed in the industry: I thought we were improving standards of accommodation immensely for the elderly population of Great Britain, in fact I believe we were at the forefront of revolutionising elderly care and I really wanted to expand faster. I had chosen to keep using profit to finance expansion, and this meant I had a relatively modest income and only took out of the business what I needed to live on. In 1991 my total salary was £35,704 which was relatively low when you consider the company's turnover was £3,317,980 in that year. Although I knew on paper I was a multimillionaire, I certainly wasn't living a multimillionaire's lifestyle. Unsurprisingly, though, I quite fancied the idea of getting my hands on some of the wealth I had created.

I had a few of options: I could sell a couple of the nursing homes and, after I'd repaid the mortgages on them the company would have had a few million in the bank with which to build more homes. Or I could have accepted an offer from a South African firm to sell the entire company which would have seen me walk away with about £6 million. It was tempting, but their valuation was only five times the projected profit, which seemed far too low. I wanted at least fifteen times profit, but no one was prepared to pay that much.

I wasn't being greedy: there was a very good reason why I wouldn't sell for less. I had discovered that you can get the accounts of any publicly listed company from Companies' House and had been doing some research into the fortunes of a number of similar companies listed on the London Stock Exchange. You could see what the directors took in salaries, their profits and their costs. It's still a very good way of seeing how your rivals operate, and my research enabled me to see that the share prices of similar companies, such as Takare plc and Westminster Health Care plc were nearly 35 times profit. As soon as I knew that, there was no way I was going to accept the South Africans' offer.

Despite following my rivals in the financial pages, it never occurred to me to join them on the Stock Exchange until one night I found myself in the local pub and a friend mentioned the word 'flotation'. I didn't have a clue what he meant, but I made it my business to find out.

At this stage, I didn't know the first thing about stocks and shares. I'd never bought a share in my life, and apart from that bit at the end of the news where they tell you about the Footsie and the Dow, I'd never even heard people talk about the 'City'. So I went to the library, picked up a few books and found out that when a company floats on the Stock Exchange, its value is divided into shares. Investors buy those shares if they think the business will do well and increase in value, thereby increasing the value of individual shares so they can make a profit. When a company is first floated, the income from what's called an Initial Public Offering of the shares passes back to the company. As I owned Quality Care Homes at the time, that meant City investors would pay me cash in exchange for a stake in my company. I could take their money *and* still run the company – it seemed like a good idea.

If only I'd known where to start. Without any contacts, I simply called the Stock Exchange in London and told the receptionist I wanted to float my company.

'Well you won't want us then,' she said matter-of-factly, 'you'll want a broker.'

'Oh,' I said. I didn't really know what a broker was. 'Where do I get one of those?'

'I'll send you a list.'

So a few days later, when the list of brokers arrived, I started calling them up. The next week of my life provides a brilliant illustration of what I've always said: you can only really learn about business by being in business. The first few calls I made were disastrous: brokers were asking me things like 'What's your PEM?' or 'What's your market cap?' and, of course, I didn't have a clue what they meant. I must have sounded incompetent and not like the kind of person who'd built a hugely successful business in the space of five years.

As these conversations went on, though, I began to pick up bits and pieces, and with each phone call I sounded more and more plausible. I discovered that some brokers only deal with companies worth more than £50 million, so I asked for recommendations of brokerages that would take me on. I could then say 'so-and-so at such-and-such a firm recommended you to me', and this made a better introduction than a simple hello.

A couple of times I thought I was making real progress when brokers showed genuine interest in Quality Care Homes, but just when I thought I was speaking their language, I'd realised they were taking the piss: they were the brokers for rival care home companies. They'd sounded interested only because they were pumping me for information to pass on to their client: I found out there was no way they could have taken me on, as that would have been a conflict of interest.

There were a few times that week when I felt completely patronised, as if these posh City types were treating me like a regional small timer. I considered telling the lot of them to piss off, but I also sensed I was beginning to get through to them. After a week on the phone, I finally spoke to a broker called Bob Lederman at a company called Beeson Gregory, who told me he was actively looking to add a nursing home company to his portfolio, and so he took me seriously and agreed to a meeting. By now, I was fluent in brokers' jargon and not only knew that PEM stood for Price Earnings Multiple, but what that meant in real terms. So I put my suit and tie on and got the train down to London with my finance controller Chris Rutter to meet with Bob, who seemed a nice guy and had a firm hand shake, which I like. Normally when I meet people I can tell pretty quickly if I want to do business with them, but the problem with City brokers is that we spoke different languages and I couldn't be entirely sure I was making myself understood. It *felt* like a positive meeting, and without any comparisons to draw on I just had to trust my hunch: which was to trust them to do a good job. A few weeks later, I got to meet them again when they travelled up to the north-east to see my properties. I think they were quite surprised to see that our head office was still in one of the rooms at Norton Glades, and I suggested that one of the things the flotation would help me fund would be a new head office. They started to get quite excited about the chance to float Quality Care Homes and told me I could end up with as much as £12 million – I began to think they really were the firm to handle the flotation. They liked what they'd seen, both on paper and on the ground, and we agreed to the flotation. I didn't really know what I'd let myself in for.

Almost immediately, Bob started to instigate changes that would prepare the company for the market, and at times I felt as if I had little say in those changes. Although he'd use phrases like 'I'd strongly recommend', 'the market likes to see', or 'we can't interfere in the running of your business, but there's someone you really should talk to', it was bloody clear that I had to do what he said. That's not a nice feeling when you've never had to answer to anyone before.

Although I was about to get a masterclass in how the market operates, I sensed that I wasn't quite on top of the situation. At the time I felt the people around me were trying to take advantage of the fact that I didn't know much about City financing. In the months leading up to the flotation, I would meet lawyers, brokers, bankers and all kinds of hangers-on, who were all out to make a profit from me. I was half-excited and half-worried, and the more of them I met the more I thought, When this is all over I'm going to write a book about this. The title of that book would have been *Shark Infested Waters*. There were several breeds of shark, of course: there were brokers, bankers, lawyers, PR people and non-executive directors, all of whom fancied taking a bite out of me.

The major change Bob suggested was the creation of a board of non-executive directors. Normally, non-execs represent the interests of the shareholders, and so investors like non-execs to be professionals with good track records. In effect, it's a case of jobs for the boys: friends of the broker who were already non-execs of other companies he'd floated were appointed to my board, just as they'd been appointed several times before to other companies' boards. Every board needs a chairman and mine was no different, so my broker put me in touch with a very well-respected man from Edinburgh called Hamish Grossart. When I met Hamish, I liked him immediately and respected the fact that he really knew what he was talking about. He was a good-natured character with a great deal of knowledge about the City and how it worked. I could understand why investors liked to see a man like him represent their interests, so I offered him the chairmanship. Hamish was already a non-executive director of Hicking Pentecost plc and British Thornton Holdings plc and a number of private companies. His salary was to be £20,000 per annum for two days per month, and he also required what I considered to be a very large share option. It felt like a big drain on the company, but I kept reminding myself that in a few months' time I would get my hands on millions of pounds worth of shares.

There were a lot of things I would be expected to pay for on top of the brokers' fee of £80,000 and the board members' salaries. For example, it was necessary to hire a PR firm to sell the company to potential investors. So we agreed a fixed monthly fee, plus an additional allowance. However, when their first bill came through, their expenses added 22 per cent to their total bill. I checked and double-checked, but there was no documentation telling me what the 22 per cent was for, so I called the PR firm up.

'What's this twenty-two per cent for?' I asked.

'Oh, don't worry about that. It's usual practice.'

'Usual practice!' 'Don't worry!' I couldn't believe it!

'But I didn't agree to pay this,' I said as calmly as I could manage.

After a few minutes of arguing, the PR guy finally said: 'Would you prefer us to withdraw from the arrangement, then?'

Well, of course, I didn't want that: without a PR firm I wouldn't be able to float and I wouldn't get my hands on millions of pounds worth of shares. I tried to put it in perspective and told myself it was a small price to pay for a bigger reward. Nevertheless, that phrase 'usual practice' got under my skin and whenever someone has used it to justify something that costs me money, I'm liable to hit the roof.

Perhaps the worst example of someone taking the piss was when an executive from the PR company came up to meet me. During his visit, I took him out for a three-course meal, but when I got his expenses claim at the end of the month, I found out that he had claimed for 'sustenance' on the train on the way back down to London, so of course I called him.

'You don't have a receipt for this meal, do you?' I asked.

'No,' he confessed.

'That's because you didn't eat on the train did you?'

'No, Duncan.'

'I know you bloody didn't because you were bloody stuffed when I dropped you off at the station. So why the hell are you claiming for "sustenance" then?'

'Well, it's usual practice, Duncan. Everyone does it.'

And, of course, it was also usual *fucking* practice to add 22 per cent to his bill, too. I was furious.

'So it's normal for you to claim for something you didn't pay for and then add twenty-two per cent to the total?'

'Yes, Duncan.'

'Well,' I fumed, 'I'm not fucking paying it!'

The fights were immense. I couldn't believe how differently they operated. There was I building a real company, with real value and offering a real service, and there were they, engaged in some kind of shadow play where it was all sleight of hand, smoke and mirrors. There were many days when I considered pulling out just to spite them.

It's important when you feel yourself getting isolated to try and see the situation from everyone else's point of view. I realised that as far as they were concerned, they were about to make me very rich, so what did it matter if they siphoned off a quarter of a per cent here or some commission there? I didn't think they were total rip-off merchants, but it riled me that they operated in such a sly manner. It was as if they were trying to pull the wool over my eyes and I was determined I wasn't going to let them do that without a fight.

One of the biggest conflicts I had with the broker, ideologically speaking, was that it was in their best interests to keep the share price down, whereas it was in mine to see it go up. Obviously, if they undervalued a share, then that attracted investment. For example, if a similar care-home company had a share price of thirty times its earnings and they offered my company to the market at twenty times its earnings, investors were likely to sell the other company and buy stock in mine. This technique creates demand which would make the share price of my company go up, and eventually the price of both care-home companies would probably settle out at about twenty-seven or twenty-eight times its earnings.

I could see the logic of that, but the lower the initial offer price, the more shares I would have to sell to realise the £500,000 in cash I would personally be allowed to make on the first day of trading.

Of course, the brokerage would make a percentage on every share traded, so they had an added incentive to make the starting price low. And as brokers underwrite Initial Public Offerings as part of their contract with the Stock Exchange, if any shares were left unsold, the broker would have to buy them. I asked if that wasn't a conflict of interest.

'Oh, no,' I was told, 'we have Chinese walls.'

This particular bit of jargon baffled me. What it meant was that the people who worked putting our deal together weren't allowed to talk to their colleagues who would actually trade the shares. They shared offices and ate in the same canteen, but they weren't allowed to *talk* about our IPO. You couldn't see the Chinese walls between them, but they assured me they were there.

We also clashed when we determined how much money we wanted to raise from the market. From their point of view, it made sense to release as many shares as possible so they could make as much commission as possible. They suggested raising as much as £20 million, but I didn't see the point. The more shares I sold, the more I reduced my stake in the company, and I didn't like the idea of going from owning 100 per cent to owning a minority stake. Aside from my own stake, it didn't make sense to raise £20 million as the company didn't need that much: I told them £20 million was ridiculous as the money would just sit in the bank earning a low interest rate. All I wanted to raise, I told them, was enough to pay off the £6 million in mortgages and put a few million in the bank to cover the next stage of expansion. In the end we settled on offering just over 27 per cent of the company to the market: my holding after the flotation would be 72.8 per cent, meaning I would still be firmly in charge.

In a sense, this was quite attractive to investors as one of the things they were investing in was me and my proven ability to oversee rapid expansion. Because the City likes to see continuity, I was told early on by the broker that I wouldn't be able to sell my shares for the first two years. This meant that I would have as much interest in the share price going up as the investors would. As we got closer to the IPO, we established a window for our launch price of between £1.30 and £1.50 per share, which would make my shares worth between £12.5–14.5 million and value the entire company at around £17–20 million. It certainly beat the South Africans' offer, *and* it left me with a controlling stake in the company I'd created. Despite the hellish confrontations I'd had with the brokers and their associates, I was beginning to realise that it had been worth it.

Amazingly, it only took about six to eight months from calling my brokers to Quality Care Homes being offered to the market. It was an incredibly stressful time, and as the IPO neared I became increasingly tense. In the final week, I left Gail and the girls at home to spend a week in a hotel in London as part of an intense few days of networking and schmoozing.

Every day I had to give a presentation, and to start with each one filled me with dread. I had never done any public speaking before, and I found the scrutiny the presentations put me under hard to handle. I stumbled over words, fumbled with paperwork, forgot figures and didn't want to shake anyone's hand afterwards as I knew my own was wet and clammy. But I soon learned that public speaking, like so much else in life, is just a matter of confidence and persistence. Each time I did it, I got a little better and my confidence grew, and the more confident I got, the better I performed and the more convincing I became. I even started to enjoy it.

Some people charge a lot of money to teach public speaking, but the truth is there's nothing that can substitute for getting up there and doing it. Ten years on, I now get paid £10,000 a night on the after-dinner circuit, so I guess I must have got pretty good at it. These days, whenever I find myself in a situation that makes me feel uncomfortable, I remember those £10,000 cheques and try and see everything as an opportunity to learn.

The week before the IPO was exhausting and I survived on precious little sleep. It didn't help my mood that I would be the one picking up the tab for all the dinners, canapés, drinks and taxis everyone else was ordering in the flurry of activity before the launch, either. I was having three-course meals for breakfast, lunch and dinner, just to fit in all the investors I had to meet, and eating so much rich food was making me feel sick and gain weight. All I wanted was to get it all over with and get back home with half a million quid in my pocket.

On the day before the flotation, it was time for lunch with the new board of directors. For the first time all week, someone asked me where I wanted to eat. Instead of suggesting one of the many pricey restaurants I'd been eating in for the past few days, I told them that I wanted to eat at McDonalds. Hamish, the chairman, thought I was joking, but I told him I wasn't. After all, this was just the board; there were no investors to impress so why did we need to spend loads of money?

'But I've never been to McDonald's,' said one of our directors, Magnus Mowat. He was fifty-two years old and he'd never been to McDonald's! As we sat there with our burgers and fries, I realised this was the perfect example of how different I was from the rest of them, and it underlined why we'd clashed so badly. They clearly weren't used to dealing with someone like me; in fact, I can't think of another CEO of a plc in those days who was like me – they were all university graduates with corporate CVs. Stories like the trip to McDonald's helped me get a reputation as a bit of a maverick, a reputation that was enhanced by what happened on the night of the flotation.

SIXTEEN

The night of the flotation
July 1992

*When you do something others
don't have the balls to do, respect
starts to roll your way.*

There had been a fairly lavish dinner for everyone involved in the deal, ostensibly to thank the investors who had already been allocated shares. The fact that shares had already been guaranteed made a mockery of the thousands of pounds that had been spent putting together a glossy brochure that Royal Mail was preparing to deliver while we ate. The brochure was designed to entice new investors, and would land on their desks the following morning in time for the market to open. However, there would be no shares available for them to buy. Just as I had given jobs on my board to people recommended by the broker, now shares in my company were being guaranteed to his best investors. This had upset me as no shares were being made available to my friends and colleagues in the north-east, and as a local company it seemed only right to me that local investors should have an opportunity to share in it. Although the broker promised to release some of the stock through a northern broker, to my knowledge that never happened.

Everyone else at the dinner seemed to be having a good time, drinking champagne on my tab, but I was reaching the end of my tether. By the time we got back to the broker's office to sign the paperwork and release the shares, it was 2 a.m. and I was tired and fed up with all the pointless excess. As I sat in the boardroom with solicitors, bankers, brokers, Hamish, Magnus and a few hangers-on I'd never seen but was pretty sure I was paying for, I wondered if maybe I should have sold to the South Africans after all.

Eventually the paperwork was produced and a copy was passed to me to sign. I glanced at the contract and was just about to sign when I saw that the broker's agreed fee of £80,000 had somehow ballooned to £92,500. Anger seethed inside me. If one more idiot said the words 'usual' and 'practice', I was liable to lash out. I thought for a moment about just signing it and getting it over and done with, but I couldn't – the sense of being ripped off, of being taken advantage of, wouldn't allow me – so I opened my gob.

'I thought we'd agreed a flat fee of eighty thousand pounds,' I said to the broker, trying hard to keep my voice even.

'Yes, but there's just over twelve thousand in expenses to add to that,' Bob replied.

'We agreed a fee of eighty thousand pounds,' I said as calmly as I could. 'Not eighty thousand plus expenses.'

He insisted that it was standard for expenses to be added to the bill.

'Well I'd like to see a list of the expenses, then.'

They couldn't produce a list, but I imagined the kinds of things that would be on it: lavish lunches for clients and charging me twenty pence per page of a fax that would have cost them about a penny a page to send. I knew right then that I wasn't going to pay it. It wasn't to do with the money: it was the principle. He had agreed to a contract and I felt he ought to stick to the deal.

'Our contract doesn't say anything about expenses,' I reiterated. 'It just states the fixed fee and I think you should stand by our contract.'

No one around the table could believe what they were hearing. I think there were a few laughs as one or two people assumed I was joking. Bob, who was looking me in the eye, knew I was deadly serious, though, as he could see my rage.

'It's usual practice,' he said stupidly.

'Is that so?'

The room was completely silent and it felt as if we'd entered a different time zone where everything happened in slow motion.

'If you're not going to pay it,' he said with disgust in his voice, 'we'll pull the flotation.'

'*You'll* pull the flotation? *You'll* pull the fucking flotation? Then fuck you,' I shouted as I threw the contract across the room, just as I'd once thrown my commanding officer overboard. As I stormed out, somewhere deep inside me a little voice told me I was an idiot, but I told the little voice to fuck off as well.

So there I was, in a strange office block, in a strange city, at four o'clock in the morning looking for the lift so I could get the hell out! I wanted to run away from it all as fast as I could. The little voice told me I had just walked away from the chance to make a lot of money, but I didn't care: I told myself that in the morning I was going to call the South African and take his £6 million instead.

I was halfway down the corridor when the broker followed me out of the boardroom.

'You know what really pisses me off?' he stormed. 'It's that lots of people in this building worked really hard on this and now they're not going to get anything out of it because you're pulling the flotation.'

'*You're* the one pulling it,' I shouted back as I carried on walking.

When Bob had finished his tirade, Hamish ran after me before I could find the lifts. The building was otherwise empty, so he just bundled me into the nearest office.

'Come in here and talk to me.' He was a born peacemaker and was trying to hold the deal together. 'I completely understand why you're angry, but isn't it worth looking at the bigger picture?'

'I'm standing by my principles,' I told him. 'I'm not budging.'

'You're really prepared to blow the whole thing over twelve grand?' He couldn't believe it.

I assured him I wasn't bluffing.

Somehow he kept me talking for the best part of an hour and I slowly began to calm down. Every so often, there'd be a knock at the door from someone with a message from the broker telling me there was no room to negotiate. Of course, while Hamish was talking to me, someone else had the broker in another office, no doubt saying exactly the same thing to him: 'You're really prepared to chuck a multi-million-pound deal away over a poxy twelve thousand.' It seemed we both really were, and neither of us had any intention of budging. But Hamish, as well as pretty much everyone else who'd been in that boardroom, had been promised shares they could make a quick killing on, and so they – especially Hamish, who is a terrific negotiator – kept us talking.

What I failed to realise then was that I was actually in the stronger position. If I didn't sign it I still had the company, and I could still sell to the South African or float through another broker at a future date. I really didn't need them at all. If he didn't get the deal, however, he lost face with all the non-execs involved and all the potential investors he'd tempted. Not only that, but his firm would miss out on the 2.5 per cent commission they'd get on every share sold. By the time the sun started to redden the windows of the buildings, the broker had backed down and Hamish had persuaded me to return to the boardroom. I had won, but I was too bloody shattered to be happy about it.

On the table in front of us were several copies of the amended contract with the £80,000 figure on them. I thought about the empty building beyond that room and wondered which secretary had been summoned to type up the new document. I reckoned it would have taken at least thirty minutes to get the paperwork ready, so I knew he'd decided to back down pretty much straight away. The broker couldn't even bear to look at me, so I just signed and walked out. There was no champagne and no offers of congratulations.

When the market opened a few hours later, the shares were listed on the Stock Exchange, £500,000 was credited to my personal bank account and just over £4 million was paid into the company's bank account. I got the train home to Darlington exhausted but elated: I had swum with sharks and hadn't been eaten alive.

When word got out about my stand-off with the broker, I started to get a reputation as something of a hard operator, a tough negotiator and a man of principle. Unsurprisingly, I didn't mind at all, and when non-execs and investors came up to visit me, they often wanted to talk about that night. I realised that I had done what countless others had wanted to, and when you do something others don't have the balls to do, respect starts to roll your way.

The early nineties should have been good years for me: the company I loved was doing well, we were expanding into new areas – like the nursing agency – and I was amassing wealth beyond my boyhood dreams. My two girls, Abigail and Hollie, were a source of immense pride and joy, but something was wrong, and for reasons I couldn't understand I became incredibly depressed.

There were days when I'd find myself leaving the house in the morning, going down the motorway, pulling into a lay-by and crying my eyes out. This happened every day for a long time, and at first I didn't know what was causing the sadness. But over a period of months I began to realise what it was, although it would be few more months before I could bear to put those thoughts into words: my marriage was making me unhappy.

As Quality Care Homes had expanded, I had grown in confidence and discovered that not only did I have a talent for running a large company, it was something I enjoyed. But while I was getting a kick out of doing deals and meeting the lawyers and brokers who would transform my financial life, it became clear that this was a world in which Gail was not comfortable.

She had been a director of Quality Care Homes – she was a 50 per cent co-owner of the company when I started the business – but as we geared up for the IPO, Gail lacked the confidence, desire or ability to move up to the next level. I've often heard divorcees saying that they had 'grown apart', but I felt that we were growing differently.

Although divorce wasn't uncommon in the early nineties, it was still something I associated with soap stars or Hollywood. I wasn't close to anyone who had been divorced and I didn't consider it an option. I wondered if it was just the 'seven-year itch' that needed scratching, but a brief affair proved that my misgivings weren't to do with anyone else. I didn't actually want anyone else: I desperately wanted my marriage to work. I wanted it so badly, but no matter what I tried, Gail and I couldn't seem to communicate. It felt like we were in a trap and I couldn't see a way out, which made me immensely depressed; it seemed to me that the only way I could set us all free was by ending my life. Although I never went out and bought pills or planned exactly how I would do it, I was absolutely suicidal.

At work, no one suspected a thing. After I had cried my heart out, I'd sit and listen to the radio until the tear stains had left my face before starting the engine. I'd then walk into the office as if nothing had happened. I had no one to talk to about my problems: I didn't have that kind of relationship with my siblings, and my closest friend, Mick Doherty, was still living in Jersey. The best thing I could do was occupy my thoughts with the business and finding new ways to expand. The contrast between my work and home life couldn't have been greater.

When Abigail and Hollie had been little, Gail and I were so good together that I thought another child might remind us of when things had been better, and so I asked Gail how she felt about trying for a third baby. She thought it was a wonderful idea, and within a few weeks she told me she was pregnant again. We were both absolutely delighted, and it finally felt as if we were back on track. The relief was immense.

Jennifer was born two days after my birthday on 4 February 1992 and she was the best birthday present I've ever had. The age difference between Jennifer and her big sisters meant that she got plenty of attention and ours was a truly happy home again. As I looked at my beautiful girls, it seemed to me that part of the answer to making my marriage work might be to separate work and family. As it happened, the broker needed Gail to sign over her half of the company to me before the flotation anyway, and with a new baby to look after, she wouldn't have had the time to help out with the admin and board meetings she had previously taken care of. It seemed like good timing and after some negotiation Gail saw the sense in it too.

Over the next few months I was so busy that I didn't see much of my wife and daughters. As well as visits to the City, I was desperately trying to tie up land deals so we could spend the money we'd raised from the flotation. The less time I spent at home, the better Gail and I seemed to get on. Sensing this at some unspoken level, I began to work longer hours and spend more time at the gym: I found countless reasons to be home late. The routine seemed to work for both of us and I really felt as if I'd found a system that would keep my marriage alive.

SEVENTEEN

Making my money count for something
1992–95

The problems are so complex that before things can be changed an entire generation must first be educated.

When Quality Care Homes floated, my wealth became public knowledge. But not only did my children – 'Come on Dad, you've got twelve million pounds and you won't let me have a pony!' – and customers know how much money I had, so did thousands of people I'd never met. When you're a public company director, and especially when you're in the *Sunday Times* Rich List, you get a steady flow of begging letters asking you to donate to one good cause after another.

Fairly early on, I became involved with the Charter for Business, as it funds the Duke of Edinburgh awards scheme that promotes entrepreneurialism in schools, which is something close to my heart. Thanks to Charter for Business, I have been invited to garden parties at Buckingham Palace where I got to meet the Duke of Edinburgh and Prince Edward. This impressed my kids no end. Most of my charitable work, however, is pretty low key.

Over the years, I've helped out a number of people, sometimes anonymously, both as a private individual and as the director of a company. Wherever possible I've tried to help local people – I've never understood why a charity in Sussex would write to me when there must be more millionaires in the south-east than anywhere else in the country. That said, I take all the requests I receive seriously and have tried to help in a number of ways. I once paid for a little girl to have a growth removed from her face, and on another occasion QCH got involved with a refuge for women and children escaping domestic violence in Hartlepool. We found out that at Christmas the children usually got second-hand toys that had been left on the doorstep, so we found out the names and ages of the children staying there and bought them all brand-new presents. The staff then wrapped them up and addressed them individually. We then bought all the mothers perfume and said it was from Santa.

In 1993, I received a letter from a man called Bob Shields who had been so moved by the plight of orphans abandoned in Romanian orphanages that he'd started a charity to help them. Twice a year, Bob drove from Newcastle, where he was a police officer, across Europe to deliver medical supplies to a town called Brasov, about 100km north of Bucharest.

I had seen the same appalling pictures on the television after Romania's dictator Nicolae Ceausescu had been assassinated in 1989 after a popular uprising. Children – many with HIV and AIDS – were chained to their cots where they spent their entire childhoods, eating, shitting and sleeping on the same filthy mattress. Many of them had never been held, and those who had gone into the orphanage sane became deranged by the experience. Kids with mental and physical disabilities were treated identically, often by uneducated and poorly paid workers without a clue about cleanliness, let alone medicine. Unlike most of us, Bob decided to help by collecting supplies in the north-east and taking them straight to the children who needed them.

The reason I responded to Bob's letter wasn't so much that I wanted to help him, although I did, I got in touch with him because I thought it would be useful to know a local policeman – I thought it might get me off the odd parking ticket or speeding fine! I offered to raise funds for him by holding a charity dinner and ball, which was the kind of thing I'd been invited to many times as a guest. My secretary took care of all the organising and all I had to do was turn up and take the credit. I invited Bob to come as my guest, but he impressed me by insisting on buying enough tickets to fill a table with guests of his own. Although organising the ball meant extra work at the office, the team really responded to the challenge and enjoyed doing something different. It was very good for morale, and when we totted up the money received from ticket sales and an auction on the night, we'd raised about £20,000. Bob was thrilled, and so we promised to do the same for him the following year.

He suggested that I visit Romania with him so I could see how the money was being spent, but at the time I made my excuses. We carried on raising funds for Bob, and each year he suggested I go to Romania with him, but I kept on making my excuses. I was getting used to a life of luxury and I had commitments I couldn't easily relinquish, even for a short trip. In the end, though, I couldn't keep saying no. There's no way I could have known that when I finally agreed to go with him, it would change my life for ever. Over the course of the next few years, I would see things that would break my heart, but I would also meet some people who would make my life richer, truly remarkable people who have given my life a new dimension – Mona, Ioanna, Sister Marta, Magnus MacFarlane-Barrow, and someone I will call God, because I don't know what else to call him.

When we got off the plane at Bucharest on my first trip to Romania, the first thing I noticed was how small the airport was for a capital city. The queues to get through immigration control were immense and the arrivals hall was absolutely packed with people. When we stepped out into the car park, I saw that it was also packed because it was clearly too small for a capital city's airport. Cars were tooting to be let in and there was almost total gridlock.

I asked the Brasov chief of police, who had come to collect us, why the airport was so full.

'Ceausescu,' he said ominously.

'What do you mean?'

'The dictator thought the working man wouldn't need to fly, so he built the airport just for himself and his aides.'

I couldn't believe it, but that was just the start of my painful lesson in how a leader had neglected, and destroyed, his people. The car journey to Brasov only took about an hour and twenty minutes, but in that time I think I must have spotted fifty adverts for Coca-Cola, a drink I suspected few of the people I saw by the roadside could afford. People held their hands out to the passing cars, begging us to stop and buy what they had to sell, which was often just a handful of apples or nuts. Many of the people doing the selling were old ladies, and it made me think how differently we treated the elderly women in our care homes. It was heartbreaking, but that was just the beginning.

When we made it to Brasov, the police chief asked if we wanted to go to our hotel – a former Ceausescu summer residence that was now half derelict – or straight to the institute to deliver the supplies we'd brought. We went to the institute, which was in an old convent, so I could meet some of its ninety-six patients.

I was led through a labyrinth of corridors and eventually found myself standing in a dormitory. To my left was a little girl of about eleven or twelve, who was mentally disturbed and making the most painful noises. Next to her in another metal cot was a girl who was completely sane but was in the institute because she had a misshapen leg. Next to her was a ninety-year-old woman who didn't have any legs and who got around by dragging herself across the floor with her hands, and next to her was an old man. The room stank – the entire building made do with four toilets and one bath – and I had to remind myself that this was one of the better places, because Bob's donations had made a difference.

We hadn't brought much with us compared to Bob's overland trips, but I hoped that the supplies we'd delivered would help. The next day, however, I realised the problems Bob had getting his donations to make a difference: within twenty-four hours, many of the items we'd brought had disappeared. The drugs, clothes, mattresses and everything else people in the UK donated all went missing. The people working in the institute were paid so poorly, and had such a poor understanding of how the drugs or clean socks would make a difference to their patients, that they saw no reason not to sell the items. That way at least they could get enough carrots to feed their own children for a week. I had to constantly remind myself that this was Europe in the late twentieth century – it felt like something from the time of the Black Death, or from some war zone in the developing world.

On another occasion, I went to an orphanage and found that when I gave toys to the children, they took them and threw them against the wall until they smashed. I only later worked out that this was because, in the past, whenever they had been given something it had been taken away by their 'carers' the moment the donor had gone. I realised early on that there was no easy way to fix things. I remember saying to myself on my first morning in Romania: 'This is going to take fifty years. We need a fifty-year plan.' The problems are so complex that before things can be changed an entire generation must first be educated. I realised I was about to make a life-long commitment and would support Bob however I could.

Broken country, broken people

On that first trip Bob and I went to eat in a restaurant in Brasov, and when we walked in no one would look us in the eye. I remember thinking that it was like there was nothing behind their eyes: they had completely shut off and seemed unable to express emotions. I learned this was a hangover from the Ceausescu era when the tiniest of remarks could see you and your family rounded up and 'disappeared' by the authorities. We also went into a pub where there was just one other person in there, as no one else could afford beer. After a day of not making eye contact, I really wanted to talk to someone and see if they could explain why their country was the way it was.

'Hi,' I said to the huge man at the bar. 'Do you speak English?'

He nodded. I've since met children who live in the sewers but can speak four languages.

'We're here visiting your country,' I began.

'I am Valentine.'

'I'm Duncan. Listen, I'm trying to understand your country and how it works,' I said. 'For instance, what's the tax rate here?'

He looked at me with anger and started banging his chest. 'I am Valentine. I fought in war. I don't pay tax. I freed my country.'

We had to calm him down, and over the course of the evening we made a friend of Valentine by drinking huge amounts of his favourite Romanian vodka. He was one of the few people who would talk to us the whole trip. I've since spoken to charity workers who have worked with poor people all over the world – they say that in Africa the children will always laugh and ask you to play with them, in Thailand people will always try and sell you something, but in Romania, in those days, the people were so broken they couldn't even make eye contact.

The next morning, Bob – who's a big six footer and can normally take a drink or two – and I had the most appalling hangovers. We managed to get up for breakfast in the hotel to find that there was no milk – they only got milk two days a week – and only had two eggs. We were lucky to have coffee. On the way to the institute, we were walking through some woods when we were encircled by a pack of wild dogs – we thought we were going to get rabies.

'Don't run,' Bob advised. 'If we walk they'll be less likely to chase us.'

When we finally made it to the institute, our heads were throbbing, so we asked one of the staff if we could have a couple of painkillers. There weren't any: all the pills we'd delivered the night before had either been taken by the patients or pilfered by the staff.

From then on we always sent one of our nurses whenever we sent over medicine, to make sure it reached the people it was meant for.

That night we were invited to the institute manager's house for dinner. In Britain he'd have had the status, and salary, of a surgeon, but he still lived in a tiny house – perhaps 25ft by 12ft in total – which he shared with his wife, children and dog. At exactly ten o'clock, the lights went out: there just wasn't the money to generate the power. The country's entire infrastructure was on the verge of collapse. It turned out that the locals were used to the power switching off: during his dictatorship, Ceausescu had decided that the working man should go to bed at 10 p.m. so he could do a full day's work the next day, and to encourage an early night he would deliberately shut down the grid.

The manager lived in comparable luxury to some of the other homes I visited. A few years later, when I started an association with Unicef, I met a woman who shared a single room with her four children and a thousand cockroaches. In the corner was the kind of single-bar electric heater that people in Britain threw out a generation ago: she used hers to cook on. Her flat was in a towerblock on an estate of five towerblocks that shared a single standpipe between them. It was their sole source of water for drinking, washing and cooking. Needless to say the place, and the people, were absolutely filthy. One of the first projects I funded with Unicef was a scheme to reinstate the power and water supply to those towerblocks.

When I got back to Britain, I told my staff what I'd seen and together we made a commitment to see if we could make a difference. We sent out one of our nurses with each delivery of medicine, and she would stay there for two or three weeks at time, teaching the staff, sharing best practice, and caring for some of the patients. I also discovered that if we hired our own company pharmacist, we could exploit a law in the UK that said if a patient in one of our care homes died without taking all their prescribed medicine, then their pills had to be thrown away, unless they could be officially logged by a pharmacist. With our own pharmacist, we could take back unused medicines and send them on to Romania for next to nothing. It also produced cost savings across the company as it enabled us to pay trade prices for many of our everyday supplies. We also opened a chemist shop in Darlington called Simpsons in the mid-nineties and started sending significant quantities of medicines to people who really needed it. It was part of my life-long commitment to do everything in my power to help charitable projects overseas.

EIGHTEEN

Looking to the future
1993–95

As I pumped iron I started to pump my instructor for information... I realised it was a business with a healthy income.

After the flotation of Quality Care Homes had gone through, I decided the best way to celebrate having half a million pounds in the bank was to go on holiday, and in the winter of 1992/93, we went skiing three times as a family. The skiing holidays worked out well for us – we all enjoyed being on the slopes, and as we spent some of the day apart having separate lessons, when Gail and I got together in the evening, the conversation flowed naturally as we showed off our bruises and sprains. The money helped, too: we stayed in a fabulous hotel where the staff doted on our daughters, and in the evenings we'd treat ourselves to wonderful meals.

About four days before we were due to come home from our last skiing trip, my instructor thought my group was getting good enough to do a bit of off-piste skiing. It seemed like a great idea until the moment when, just as we were returning to the pistes after an awesome trip down the mountain, I hit a mogul and landed awkwardly. My skis were pushed apart and I could feel the muscles in my groin starting to tear. But just as I thought it was going to get really painful, suddenly the pain stopped and I fell over. I got up, and instantly fell over again. As I couldn't feel any pain, I didn't think it could be serious, so I kept on trying to get up and then falling over. My instructor skied over and instantly diagnosed me: I had snapped the ligaments around my knee.

The complete lack of pain meant I wasn't too worried – how bad could it be if it didn't hurt? A snowmobile was summoned and I was taken down to the resort, where a luxurious private ambulance was waiting to take me to hospital. I thought to myself: the Austrians really know how to run a ski resort, this is a fantastic service.

'How would you like to pay, sir,' the ambulance man asked in perfect English.

There was a good reason why the ambulance looked as plush as a limo. I handed over my credit card and was taken to the hospital where I was seen pretty much instantly. The doctor explained that I had actually snapped three ligaments in my right knee, which explained why the pain from the muscle strain had stopped as I'd fallen over: as the ligaments were no longer connected to my bones, they were no longer under any strain and my nerves couldn't feel a thing. No wonder I couldn't stand up!

'You couldn't have snapped them cleaner if you'd done it with a knife,' he informed me.

Reattaching the ligaments was a lengthy operation and would have to be booked in for a few days' time, so he put my leg in a full cast while I waited for surgery. I had the choice of having the procedure carried out in Austria, or I could go home where the medical insurance the broker had insisted I take out prior to the IPO would cover the cost. I'd also get an English-speaking doctor – and no matter how well the Austrian doctors spoke English, there was always a chance that something would get lost in translation. I told him I would get the operation done at home.

'Just make sure you have the operation within ten days,' he said. 'After that, the damage will start to become irreparable.'

With that warning, I got a taxi back to our hotel and started to see if I could get myself on a flight back to the UK. As soon as I got out my passport and tickets to try and re-book my flight, I realised

I had a bigger logistical problem than I'd thought: the girls were all on my passport; if I went back to England, we'd all have to go. Getting one seat on a plane was one thing, but last-minute travel for a family of five was another matter. I had no option but to wait for our booked flights in four days' time.

Once we were back home, I faced a further wait as I couldn't get an appointment with a surgeon – even a private one – without a referral from my GP. The British system of referrals still seems antiquated to me now, but as the ten-day window for getting the operation done narrowed, I became furious with the medical bureaucracy. However, as I was unable to work, I had time to sit on the phone and I eventually got myself an appointment.

On the tenth day, I finally saw a surgeon and had the operation to reattach my ligaments. It was a complete success, but I was told it would take months of training in the gym to help lengthen the muscles so I could walk properly again. I clearly wasn't going to be back in the office any time soon, but thanks to having mastered the art of delegation, I knew the company would be fine without me for a couple of weeks.

The real question was, how was I going to be without the company? As I lay at home recuperating, I had more time on my hands than I'd known since childhood. And without the distraction from work, there was nothing to hide the fact that our marriage still hadn't got back on track, despite Gail's announcement that she was expecting our fourth child.

I have a very precise memory of lying in bed one morning while I was still unable to move easily and realising that, yet again, Gail hadn't put any clothes out on my side of the bed as I'd asked her to, because getting dressed was so bloody difficult with my leg in plaster. It sounds really trivial now, but I remember lying there thinking, If she really loved me she'd have put some clothes where I could get to them. I lay there looking at my shirts on the other side of the room and started to cry: that was the moment when I finally recognised that it was over. But I didn't know how to tell Gail – how do you tell your pregnant wife that you want to leave her? – so when my leg was better I again buried myself in work in the dim hope that our problems would resolve themselves.

The physio I needed on my leg gave me the perfect excuse to spend even more time away from home. The fact that the nearest gym with a leg press – the essential bit of equipment needed to lengthen my muscles – was a twenty-minute drive away meant that there was no such thing as a quick trip to the gym. I had always enjoyed exercise, since my PE lessons at school, but once I got into the rhythm of training again, I found I had another reason to spend time at the gym: I had begun to think I might open one myself.

It seemed to me that there was an opportunity to start a gym in Darlington where there wouldn't be any competition, so while I pumped iron I started to pump my instructor for information. Obviously I knew what my membership cost, and when I found out how many members the gym had, I realised it was a business with a healthy income.

When a purpose-built gym opened on the A1 at Scotch Corner, I joined that, too, and as I lay on my back on the leg press, I looked up at the ceiling and started to count the ceiling tiles. They looked to be about a foot square, which meant I could calculate their income per square foot, and as I knew from the nursing homes roughly how much the build cost was per square foot, I did the sums in my head. I reckoned I could get a 35 per cent return on capital per year. However, Quality Care Homes was taking up too much of my time to do anything about it. For the time being, the plan to open a gym would have to remain a nice idea. But just having thoughts about a possible new venture was exciting: I was feeling confident about my skills as an entrepreneur, and thinking about my next move gave me cause to be hopeful when so much at home filled me with fear.

Although Quality Care Homes was a very well-run organisation, it still made a difference to the staff to see the chief executive turn up and ask them how they were getting on. I always made a point of taking a detour whenever I was near one of our homes to pop in and meet staff and residents. It was good to remind myself why we all put in so much effort, and I enjoyed those trips. There were also a couple of matrons and senior nurses who I got on well with. Some of them were so friendly they even asked the boss to join them for a drink, which was quite brave of them, and as the boss didn't want to go home, there were a couple of members of staff who became good friends during those months. One of the nurses, Joanne McCue, seemed to have a particular knack of lifting my spirits and I would often 'just happen' to drive past her nursing home on the off-chance that she'd be finishing her shift.

It was a busy time for the company. With cash in the bank after the IPO we entered a period of extremely rapid expansion. I'm aware that I like to do things faster than most people in business – I don't see the point of opening one nursing home at a time when I could have three, or five, under construction: the sooner they were built the sooner they'd be making money. Some members of the board expressed concern that we were expanding too quickly, but with the money in the bank their concerns weren't enough to slow me down.

I thoroughly enjoyed running a public company and thought it was a job I'd gladly do for life. I even enjoyed putting on a suit and tie once every six months and making presentations in the City. However, from time to time I felt that having to report to the board, and through them to the shareholders, was slowing me down, so occasionally I would get nostalgic for the days when Quality Care Homes had been a private company and I could run it without interference.

One area of friction between the board and I was gearing. We had agreed at a board meeting after the flotation that the gearing – that's the relationship of assets to debt – wouldn't go above 60 per cent. I hadn't really understood what it meant at first, but once it had been explained to me, I made sure that we got as close to that 60 per cent figure as possible as we continued to expand. I wanted to continue to borrow to build new homes, while they wanted me to raise the money from the stock market. It made no sense for me to do it their way: if I borrowed the money I could still grow the company while retaining my 72 per cent stake. Nevertheless, they continued to try and persuade me to return to the market.

'If you sell shares at two pounds fifty you'll get a lot of interest from investors,' they told me. Well of course I bloody would, they'd risen to three pounds each! I told them there was no way I was going to devalue my holding by releasing stock so cheaply.

'But you'll make the money back in the long run,' they said.

'I'll make more if I borrow it in the first place,' I countered.

However, when the price was right, I did return to the market in 1994 to raise a further £1.9 million from selling new shares at £3.10 each. From time to time the broker would call to give me the 'good news' that a potential investor wanted to visit the properties to assess their value. It dawned on me that such a trip – the investor was to be treated like visiting royalty – would come with a price tag, so I called the broker and asked him who would be picking up the expenses.

'It's usual practice for you to, Duncan,' I was told.

'Usual *fucking* practice? Are you joking?'

He wasn't, and our conflict of operating styles continued to rile me.

I also had a few run-ins with the various construction firms building the new homes. On one occasion a contractor estimated I owed him £50,000 when I thought the figure was more like £10,000, so when a CV was sent to me by a project manager who said he had some experience of conflict resolution, I asked him round for a chat. Tony Bell was, and is, an extremely experienced quantity surveyor who, like a lot of people in his field, was feeling the pinch in the early nineties, when construction was in recession. Although conflict resolution was only a sideline to his work as a surveyor, he was pretty keen to prove himself and get me a result. The trouble was, I wasn't willing to pay him.

'What's it worth to you to put this situation behind you?' he asked.

I thought about it for a moment. 'Twenty thousand.'

'Well,' he offered, 'how about I take twenty-five per cent of anything I save you under twenty thousand?'

'Done.'

I think he did a deal at £15,000 and took £1,250 as a fee from me for what amounted to no more than a few conversations with the contractor. I thought he was a pretty smart operator, but unfortunately I didn't have a job I could offer him. A couple of years later, however, when I was looking to recruit someone to oversee my construction projects, I was very pleased when Tony sent me his CV again. And when I eventually sold Quality Care Homes, he came with me to my new company, where he's director of projects and one of the lynchpins of my organisation.

Two years after the flotation, I felt I was ready to take over as chairman as well as being chief executive. It didn't help that Hamish had countless other commitments and it was getting increasingly difficult to schedule the company around his diary. I was paying him £20,000 a year for two days a month and I didn't think I was getting enough value for money. Much as I liked him, it was time to ask him to move on.

'I have to tell you Duncan, it's very unusual for the same person to be chairman and chief executive,' he said, when I suggested myself as his successor.

'What about Hanson?' I offered, citing one of the most profitable British companies of recent times.

Hamish had to admit there were some precedents, and although it wasn't against the law, he didn't think the shareholders would like it.

'The share price will go down,' he warned me.

'I don't really care,' I answered. I just wanted to get back in control of my own company. However, I couldn't persuade him to resign, so he remained as a director while I took over as chairman and chief executive director. Although the share price did stumble for a few weeks after we announced my chairmanship to the City, I used it as an opportunity to buy back shares with the spare cash I had left from the flotation, as I was convinced they were undervalued. Once I had asserted my authority, the share price began to climb again. I wasn't the only one watching our continued progress in the pages of the *Financial Times*, and in 1996 we were approached by an American company with a takeover bid. We arranged a board meeting to discuss the offer, however Hamish couldn't make it and instead sent a letter recommending that we accept the offer, and if we didn't accept, the letter said he would have no option but to tender his resignation. Although I would have accepted his offer there and then, it would have to be a decision for the entire board.

By this time I had appointed some of my own non-execs and got rid of a few that had originally been recommended by the broker. Among my appointments was my finance director Chris Rutter, who'd been working with me for a long time; Ronald Norman OBE, now Sir Ronald, the chair of a newly formed development corporation for the north-east; and the local Tory MP Michael Fallon. A fellow Scot, Michael had been an education minister under Maggie Thatcher and had got the nickname 'Two Brains Fallon' because he was so bright. We got on well and I found him very straightforward to deal with, and that's not something you can say of many politicians.

We sat down to discuss the American offer, which I thought significantly undervalued the company at £3.30 a share. I told the board I wasn't happy with the offer, but the first thing I wanted to discuss was Hamish's letter. I read it out to them and suggested that we should take a vote to see if we accepted his resignation. We all did: it turned out they were equally pissed off that Hamish often couldn't make our board meetings. Hamish left the company and, despite the fact that he had been given a substantial number of shares and had taken a generous salary for the past few years, he never made contact again. No thank you note, no Christmas Card, nada.

Rejecting the bid from the American company was a formality after that, primarily because I was having too much fun to sell at that point. However, I had been impressed by the man leading the bid. His name was John Moreton, and though I didn't know it then, he would become one of my closest friends.

NINETEEN

Moving on
1993–95

Over the years there have been a few key employees, without whom I wouldn't have had such an easy ride or had so much fun.

My success with Quality Care Homes was not enough to hide the immense pain Gail and I were putting each other through at home. Neither of us had ever spoken about splitting up, and if it had seemed unthinkable before she got pregnant, it was even more unlikely with a fourth baby on the way. Although I was thrilled about the baby, Gail's pregnancy made me feel even more trapped, and I became really miserable when I was at home. It wasn't going to be long before things came to a head.

I've since spoken to several people who have been through a divorce, so I know the story I'm about to tell isn't unique. Word for word, I know other people have had the exact same conversation we had. Gail came home after a night out while I'd been at home watching TV and keeping an eye on the kids, who were asleep upstairs. I have no idea what was on the TV as I wasn't really watching it, and Gail could tell from my face that I was somewhere else.

'What's wrong?' she asked.

I flicked off the TV with the remote and turned to look at her. I didn't know what I would say next, but then words just tumbled out.

'I can't go on living like this.'

She knew exactly what I meant, and while our children slept above our heads, we began to talk about ending our marriage. My timing was awful, and I've asked myself many times how I could have been such a bastard to leave my pregnant wife, but as soon as I admitted out loud that I wasn't happy, I began to feel more positive.

Gail was shocked but not shocked, in the way I now know so many other partners are when their husbands tell them they want to leave. She knew deep down that I had been unhappy, but we'd got ourselves into such a rut that neither of us had been able to make the necessary changes. She said she was still in love with me and she wanted to make me happy, even if that meant letting me go. She was adamant, though, that she didn't want to divorce. She knew of a few couples who had regretted ending their marriages quickly and so we agreed to a trial separation. I think she secretly hoped that we would get back together.

I rented a three-bed semi in Darlington, about four miles away from the family home in Long Newton, and started to move some of my stuff in. Before I could move in myself, though, I had to tell the girls. I sat Abigail and Hollie down and told them I had some sad news.

'It's not the baby, is it?' Abigail asked. 'It's dead, isn't it?'

'Oh God, no, it's not that bad!' In a flash her question made me realise that there were worse things a father can tell his children, and this gave me some comfort as I proceeded to tell her what was about to happen.

'The baby's fine, your mother's fine. That's not it at all. It's just . . . It's just that . . .' How the hell do you tell your kids you're leaving their mother? I had to fight for every word. 'It's just that . . . your mother and I, well, we've decided to . . . live apart for a while.'

As soon as they'd been told the baby was all right, they took the news pretty well and I reassured them that they'd have their own room at my house, too, and that I'd still see them every week. They seemed to accept it very calmly, although they were obviously upset. It's not unusual for kids today to come from broken homes, and many of their friends' parents had already separated, which I think helped them take the news in their stride.

One of the conditions of our trial separation was that neither of us would sleep with anybody else: if there was any chance of us getting back together, we didn't want third parties standing in our way. This suited me as I wasn't looking for anyone else and wanted time to adjust to being apart from my family, although the girls stayed with me every other weekend and every Wednesday night.

At first I didn't tell anyone at work about the separation: it was a private matter and I didn't want my private life to become office gossip. But about a week after I had moved into the new house, I was desperate to talk to someone about what had happened, so I drove round to a new home that was gearing up for opening and dropped in on Joanne McCue, one of the best employees the company had, who would soon become our Director of Nursing, becoming the second youngest female director of a publicly listed company.

Joanne was very supportive and listened while I babbled on, and over the next couple of months she proved great at casually asking if I'd like to join her and her sister at some function or saying she fancied going out for a beer. She never made it obvious that I was a charity case, and I never felt like a spare part who was making up the numbers. It was incredibly kind of her, and thanks to her efforts to include me in her social life, I avoided many lonely nights at home licking my wounds.

After a couple of months of seeing a lot of her, I finally asked Joanne if she might like to go out with me, just the two of us. She was initially reluctant: she didn't want to be anybody's mistress and she knew I had a lot to sort out with Gail, but she could sense there might be something going on, and so we started to go out for the odd meal. We got on so well that entire evenings passed in what seemed like minutes. We'd always be the last couple in the restaurant, and occasionally, if it was late, she would stay over at my place.

Joanne was adamant that I wasn't going to see her as some gold-digger. She knew I was rich, and if something was going to happen between us she was determined that I wouldn't doubt her reasons for being with me. And of course I had made a promise to Gail not to sleep with anyone else. So there were nights when Joanne would draw an imaginary line down the middle of the bed, and we would lie there talking and laughing our heads off, without anything happening between us.

It was wonderful to love being with someone as much as I loved being with Joanne without sex becoming an issue. I hadn't been in the position of waiting to have sex in a relationship since Sallyanne Green, and the anticipation was all part of falling in love with her. And that's what was happening: I was falling hook, line and sinker for Joanne, and in doing so I started to shed the layers of unhappiness and grief that had clouded the last few years with Gail. Not only was I falling in love, I was shunning depression and starting to look forward again. It was a magical time, and in the middle of this euphoria my fourth daughter, Eve, was born.

I loved the weekends that my children stayed with me. Eve would sleep in with me in a carrycot, Jennifer would have a room to herself and Abigail and Hollie would share. We had fantastic days out going to the park or the beach, and it was wonderful spending time with them without spending time with Gail: I was able to get to know them all over again. I took them swimming and made sure they all learned to swim, just as my father had made sure we could. It was great to re-establish our relationship, and I remember thinking how much easier divorce is when you have money. From time to time, I'd see dads in McDonald's spending their allotted Saturday afternoons over a Happy Meal. I was so grateful that I could afford more than a bedsit, and that I had somewhere my kids could come and visit me. I would have hated to have been a McDad: my weekends with the kids were messy, noisy and a whole lot of fun. Sometimes the four of them were more than I could handle, and I'd invite Joanne to come and join us. When I saw how the kids took to her, it made me want to be with her even more.

Finally I asked Joanne to come away with me for the weekend. We flew to Nice where a helicopter picked us up and took us to Monte Carlo, and there a limo was waiting at the helipad to take us to our hotel. Having spent so long as friends, I wanted to make a big romantic gesture that would make it clear how I felt about her. It turned out she felt the same way, and the next days, weeks and years would be the happiest of my life.

There is nothing better than being in love with someone who is in love with you. I had been in love before, but I'd never felt anything as intense with anyone else. Joanne and I became inseparable. We'd go to the gym together, go to work together, have lunch together and still have plenty to talk about when we got home. If I got an invite to a sportsmen's dinner or a gentlemen's club, I'd turn it down, even if it might have been good for business: I didn't want to go anywhere without her.

One of the invites we accepted was from John Moreton, the chairman of Southern Cross, the company that had tried to buy QCH. He wanted us to help him celebrate his fiftieth birthday, and when we arrived at the party I realised that John and I were wearing the exact same outfit: chinos, denim shirt and leather jacket. It was just one of many coincidences – not only did we both make our fortunes in the care industry, we both had girlfriends seventeen years our junior. The more I got to know John, the more I realised we had in common, and over the years coincidence has become an emblem of my friendship with him.

Gail seemed to take the news of my relationship with Joanne very well, and for the first few months it was very civilised, although I suspected that this was because Gail thought Joanne was something

I needed to get out of my system and that ultimately we would get back together.

Things changed, though, when she learned that I was taking Joanne to Barbados for a holiday. Gail had always wanted to go to Barbados, and it was the trigger that made her understand our marriage was over. When she learned that we'd be staying at the Sandy Lane Hotel and flying on Concorde, she hit the roof. By this stage, Joanne was working at our new HQ in Darlington, and Gail stormed into her office and tipped Joanne's desk upside down. What she didn't realise then was that the divorce settlement I was about to offer her would mean she could fly on Concorde as often as she liked and spend the whole year in Barbados if she wanted to.

Neither of us wanted a messy divorce or to end up in court fighting over the kids. We agreed that we wouldn't start divorce proceedings until we had been separated for two years, as this meant we didn't have to apportion blame on the divorce petition. We also promised each other to do everything in the best interests of our children: she had seen other couples compete with each other by buying the most expensive Christmas presents for the kids, so we agreed that we wouldn't buy any presents for the children without first discussing it with the other. Neither of us liked the idea of letting the court decide when we could see our children – the idea of formally sharing custody went against our desire to put our children's best interests first – so we sat down together with the divorce petition we'd got from the county court and decided how we would look after our children. When it came to filling in the 'custody' section of the form, I simply wrote: 'Both parents will act as adults at all times and act in the best interests of the children.'

Her solicitor pressurised her to fight for custody, but she said she didn't want to: we wanted to do it our way. My solicitor was quite sure our custody clause wouldn't be accepted by the court, but when the judge saw it, he was impressed. 'Wouldn't it be nice,' he said, 'if more parents could behave in this way.' Looking back, I think waiting two years to start divorce proceedings meant that we went through the process with clearer heads.

I agreed to give Gail a settlement that was worth just over £6 million, which included the house we had owned together, some shares and around £5 million in cash, money I raised by selling shares in the company, which reduced my stake to 50.8 per cent. It was a lot of money, and represented almost exactly half of my wealth at the time of our separation. Although it was – and still is – a massive amount of money, I was about to make a whole lot more.

As my life took an upward turn, however, fate dealt a cruel blow to one of my most valued employees. In December 1993, about a year after we moved into our new HQ, I became aware of a commotion outside my office. I could hear people saying 'You can't drive' and 'Don't be silly, I'll take you'. It was a small office – I had only about twelve staff there – so I was usually able to hear everything that went on. I went to see what was happening and realised that the receptionist had left, and so had Irene Readman.

'What's going on?' I asked one of the team.

'Irene's just had a phone call from her daughter saying her husband's collapsed.'

'Where is she now?'

'She's gone home.'

Irene was a hardworking woman, the kind of woman they coined the phrase 'salt of the earth' for. She had lived all her life in Billingham and had been happily married to Doug with two kids all the time I'd known her. Sadly, by the time she got home her husband had died from a massive heart attack. She arrived to find an ambulance outside and paramedics in her house. When she saw his body lying on the floor, she started punching him and screaming in typical Irene fashion, 'Don't leave me, you bastard! Don't you dare leave me!'

The next day I went round to see her and it was clear she had been sedated. She was in a state, so I sat with her on her bed for hours while we talked and cried. I told her not to worry about her job and to take as much time as she needed. Irene had been such a big part of Quality Care Homes that all the staff knew her and sent their condolences. Many of them knew Doug, too, and several of us went to his funeral, which even more cruelly was on Christmas Eve.

A few weeks into the new year, Irene handed in her notice.

'I can't accept this,' I told her. 'You're too important to the company.'

'But I can't work, Duncan. I can't even think straight at the moment.'

'That's OK. We'll wait for you.'

I put her resignation letter in the bin and kept her on full salary for eight months until she felt ready to come back to work. I know others on the team felt that I was being too generous and that my generosity was allowing Irene to wallow in her grief, but I didn't care: Irene had been loyal to me and now I was repaying her. Irene is one of the people who I have been able to rely on and build my company around. Over the years there have been a few key employees, without whom I wouldn't have had such easy ride or had so much fun, and Irene was one of them. I was very moved when she told me, after her retirement in 2006, that she couldn't have got through that time without my support.

TWENTY

Just Learning
1995–2001

Success depends on recognising
when your moment has come.

The mid-nineties was an incredibly exciting time for me: I was madly in love with Joanne, I was earning a phenomenal amount of money and I was enjoying spending it in style. I was also bursting with ideas and enthusiasm and felt there was nothing I couldn't do. With Quality Care Homes running itself for most of the week, I was freed up to look to the future and work out where the company should go next.

I was still interested in getting into the gym business, but when Gail and I had difficulty finding suitable day care for Jennifer and Eve, I started to wonder if perhaps Quality Care Homes should start a subsidiary in the nursery sector. I began looking into it and realised that there was a sizeable opportunity there. In much the same way as the government had paid for elderly care, they were now offering incentives to get mothers back to work. Yet again, I could start a business with an income effectively bankrolled by government money. I put my idea to the board and I couldn't believe it when they said they didn't think it was the right move for Quality Care Homes.

'But it's practically guaranteed money,' I told them. 'And we can build on land we already own.'

They weren't persuaded, but I was lit up by the thought of going into the day-care industry, especially as I had stockpiled hundreds of thousands of pounds from my share dividends and salary from QCH. Of course I could have out-voted them, but I believe in democracy and didn't think it would be right for me to steamroller them. However, there was no way I was going to miss out, so at the end of the meeting I asked the board, since I was technically an employee, for their permission to pursue the business outside of Quality Care Homes. They consented, and when the meeting broke up, Michael Fallon followed me out of the room.

'You know,' he said, 'I think you might really have something with this day-care business. Would you consider doing it with me?'

Of course I would! Who wouldn't want a former education minister who knew his way around red tape helping to start a new business that had the potential to be a bureaucratic nightmare? We agreed a partnership that would provide Michael with a salary, and as he couldn't match my level of investment, we negotiated that he would have a 10 per cent stake in the company, which we called Just Learning Ltd.

Aside from the money the government was making available, the big reason I saw such an opportunity in the day-care business was because demand would easily outstrip supply when the public wised up to the government's subsidies. The lack of a nationwide childcare brand also meant we would have little competition if we ran our business well. The timing was perfect, but I don't want to give the impression that I just got lucky by having the right idea at the right time. I believe we're all in the right place at the right time at some point in our lives: success depends on recognising when your moment has come.

Just as I had done with the care homes, I started visiting day-care centres to see how the competition ran their operations. On one occasion I heard that a child couldn't go to the toilet because there wasn't a member of staff available to accompany them. The rules were very strict about how many adults were needed to supervise a certain number of children at any one time and there was a very good reason for that rule: a child once famously took himself to the toilet, and then took himself off home! Ensuite facilities had been the difference for us at Quality Care Homes, and I saw no reason why a similar move couldn't produce an equivalent transformation in the day-care industry.

I had learned a lot from the nursing homes, and one of the reasons for the success of Quality Care Homes was our architecture. Don't get me wrong, we didn't build beautiful buildings, we built the buildings around the needs of our residents. I saw that we could do the exact same thing with nurseries. Most day care at that time was provided by individual operators in converted garages or spare rooms in their home, so the facilities operated around the carer's needs, not the children's. And as the law was so strict about the ratio of carers to children – it was 1:3 for babies under two – these individual operators couldn't easily grow their businesses. Their lack of flexibility was partly why Gail and I had had problems finding care for Jennifer and Eve, as no one had the capacity to take both of them on the same day. I knew it had to be possible to offer a better service to parents and their children.

Yet again, I got my hands on every bit of government literature available and genned up on staffing levels, educational responsibilities, payment vouchers, liabilities and anything else that would need to be factored into our projections. I had learned from the care-home sector that bureaucracy can strangle a business, but I had also shown with QCH that if you build your business around the legislation red tape can actually help you structure your company more effectively. Used the right way, red tape can give you processes that propel your business forward. Between us, I knew that Michael and I had the experience, the money and the aptitude to start a perfect business, and from the day we started to the day we sold, that's exactly what we did. Just Learning Ltd is the best case study I can offer of how to run the perfect business.

If research was the first thing we got right, the second was the location. I had found that you often come across the best opportunities in your own community because you have an insider's hunch on how the community will respond to a new facility. The best opportunity is one you understand, and I knew when I saw a large car showroom for sale that it was the perfect location for our first nursery. An outsider might have just seen the showroom, but I saw an industrial plot in the middle of a residential neighbourhood, and I knew the residents would rather have a facility that benefited them than a garage used for industry.

I negotiated to buy the premises subject to planning permission, which is a very smart way to buy land as you can tie up the deal without committing any money until you know you can do what you want with the plot. It proved to be a very sound move when, to my complete surprise, planning permission was recommended for refusal. Because I knew the community, I knew it couldn't be because of objections from local people, so I actually went knocking on the doors of nearby residents and told them about my problems with the planning department: I wanted to assemble as much ammunition as possible before taking my case back to the planners who had decided that a nursery would be too noisy.

However, my doorstep conversations revealed that the residents were already disturbed by the lorries delivering cars, often after hours so that trading wasn't interrupted. The residents would much rather hear the sound of children playing – which would stop anyway at 6 p.m. – than be disturbed throughout their weekends by the constant toing and froing of delivery vehicles. Several of the people I spoke to were willing to support my appeal against the planners' ruling, and not just because of the noise issue: they needed more flexible childcare themselves. Eventually we got our planning permission, and I bought the land using my own money.

Michael and I had worked out that because the staffing levels need to be so high, the best way to make a profit in childcare is to open a centre big enough to make savings at management level. Just as I had determined that a fifty-bed nursing home was more cost efficient than a forty- or sixty-bed home, I calculated that the ideal size for a nursery, financially speaking, was one that could take eighty to a hundred children.

We instructed an architect to design a nursery around the needs of the legislation. In addition to ensuring that each room had ensuite toilets, so we could keep staff levels to a minimum, we also made sure that each room had doors directly on to the playground. Not only was this nicer for the kids, it cut down on supervision and again helped keep our staffing costs down. As I said, we were building the perfect business, not just the perfect building. Other improvements we made on existing centres included integral kitchens and wash rooms, so if the kids had an accident, we could send them home in clean clothes. We also installed state-of-the-art CCTV to keep an eye on the kids and the staff, and an alarm system that alerted the police and emergency services if anything went wrong. We were determined to build the best, and safest, nursery possible.

One of the many similarities between the care-home and day-care sectors is that they're both serving the public *need*, so neither business has to spend very much on advertising and marketing as customers will come looking for us. In some businesses you need to spend the bulk of your money on client acquisition, and as marketing is imprecise and expensive, it's much better if you can find a direct route to your customers. With Just Learning we had exactly that. So as soon as word got out that we were building a day-care centre, parents started coming to us. It didn't happen overnight, though: day care was an option many parents hadn't considered until we started offering a reliable service, and so it took us a few months before we were full. But I never had any doubt that eventually we would have a waiting list of parents wanting to take advantage of the government's incentives and our excellent service.

I might be giving the impression that running a perfect business is easy: it's not, and any business that ultimately relies on government money for its income can expect to have to deal with plenty of policy hassle. Both care homes and day care are bureaucratic industries and you have to have the patience and diligence to attend to seemingly petty details. This really wasn't something that interested me, so part of making it a perfect business for me was working with someone like Michael. He'd probably tell you that Just Learning was a lot harder to get off the ground than I remember.

One of the government rules we had to abide by was that half our staff had to have nationally recognised childcare qualifications. Finding qualified staff, as I had discovered with Quality Care Homes, can be problematic, so we realised early on that the best way to get them was to train them ourselves. All our workers were encouraged to use their work with us towards NVQs and other formal qualifications, and this had the added advantage of motivating staff who might otherwise have seen the work as casual. Although our staffing levels were necessarily high, the recruitment and costs were modest as half our workers were unskilled and there was no shortage of young women wanting to work with little children.

We opened the first day-care centre towards the end of 1996 for a total cost of £1 million, all of which I funded myself. It was liberating to start a business without involving the banks, and it was also wonderful to be in sole charge again. I was finding running a large plc frustrating, and Just Learning made me realise how much more fun a business can be when you don't have men in suits running around making sure arcane Stock Exchange practices are being adhered to. I ran Just Learning from my front room, with just Joanne and I taking care of the paperwork and admin. With such low overheads, the profit was maximised, and as Michael was taking care of the day-to-day running of the company, he made it very easy for me to enjoy one of the most rewarding chapters in my career.

Of course, Michael's hard work is one of the major reasons why I look back on Just Learning with such fondness: it might have taken up a fair bit of my money, but it took up surprisingly little of my time, so I was free to take Joanne and the kids on holiday or get involved in other projects. I was also free to think strategically, and this enabled us to build up the business quickly: in the space of five short years Just Learning would be operating over twenty day-care centres, becoming a major player in the sector.

As I'd shown at QCH, one of the things I'm good at is orchestrating rapid change, so as soon as our first day-care centre was open, I was already planning to open several more. I knew that the secret to rapid expansion is to have good systems. For instance, there was a time at QCH when I was spending days driving round the country inspecting pieces of land that employees had already seen. To cut down on these unnecessary trips, Joanne came up with a reporting system that allowed any member of our team to assess a plot's value to our business. She established a set of objective criteria that needed to be met, so that anyone taking on an inspection could fill in a form which we could assess back at HQ. It was simple, but it worked brilliantly and I adopted an identical system for Just Learning.

The other key to rapid expansion is having the necessary funds available. Although I had funded the first centre with my own money, I didn't have sufficient cash to bankroll the entire venture. My total input was £2 million, with the rest of the investment coming from bank loans, all of which I had personally guaranteed. If we'd waited for each centre to become profitable enough to fund expansion from cash flow, Just Learning would have been very small scale. The rate of investment and expansion was such that Michael couldn't match my investment, but I knew how valuable he was to the business, so I offered him a share-option deal that enabled him to keep his stake at 10 per cent.

In addition to building our own day-care centres, we also acquired several, which gave the impression of even more rapid expansion. We were able to buy a chain of day-care centres in Kent quite cheaply as the company running them had fallen foul of the regulations and lost its licence, meaning they needed to sell quickly.

A motivated seller, like a motivated buyer, is an opportunity not to be missed in business.

Unsurprisingly, I was very happy with the way the business was working out. I had put into practice everything I'd learned from QCH and was proving that I was very good at business: I'd always known I wasn't a one-trick pony, but it's always nice to prove it to other people. Our good reputation meant that we were occasionally approached by third parties interested in doing business with us, as happened in 2000 when the investment company 3i asked if we'd be interested in taking over a chain of Scottish nurseries they'd help launch. 3i felt the time was right to cash in their investment and take their profits. Michael and I were interested in the deal, so we travelled to Scotland to meet the two women who had started the business. As soon as we met them, however, it became clear that they didn't want to sell: this was a business they had started from scratch and they were hugely emotionally attached to it. They told us they were still hungry to expand and obviously wanted different things from their investors.

Michael and I came to the conclusion that if these two women were serious, then *they* might want to buy *us*. One of the characteristics that singles individuals out for success is their ability to respond to chance and opportunity, and Michael and I instantly saw a way of realising some of the massive wealth we'd created with Just Learning. We put the proposition to them and they said they'd think about it. We eventually negotiated a sale price for Just Learning of £12 million – not bad for a five-year-old business that I'd invested only £2 million of my own money into and which I still owned 90 per cent of.

However, as the sale proceeded, the Scottish women tried to get us to lower our price. We refused and said that if they didn't come up with the agreed £12 million we would put Just Learning up for sale on the open market. This pissed them off and they instantly backed out the deal, which was always a risk. Nevertheless, Michael and I felt we'd been saved from dealing with them, and quickly advertised the business for sale. Within a few months, about ten interested buyers came forward, so the obvious thing was to go to sealed bids, a process where each bidder makes their highest offer in writing, unaware of what anyone else has bid. Assuming our reserve price was met, we were then honour-bound to take the highest offer. We gave each of the potential buyers the same deadline to get their bid in.

On the afternoon of the deadline, Michael and I went to see the solicitor handling the sale. The first envelope was opened with a certain amount of expectation, but we were quickly disappointed when we read the bid was for just £5 million. Perhaps we should have stuck with the Scottish deal after all. However, there were still another four envelopes to open and the range of bids went from £7 million to a massive and totally unexpected £22 million from the investment company Alchemy Partners. Michael and I couldn't believe it.

'Is it a mistake?' I asked the solicitor.

It wasn't, and I realised in a flash that, with Just Learning, I had made in five years what had taken me nearly ten years to make with the QCH. Didn't I say it was the perfect business? Michael became a millionaire with the deal and I would have even more money to plough into other projects.

However, it nearly came unstuck at the final hurdle. I went down to London with my finance director to sign off the final paperwork after months of diligent work. We were in a cab on our way to Alchemy's HQ when my phone rang. My solicitor had checked the figures and found that – guess what – they had deducted £300,000 for 'disbursements'. It was almost an exact rerun of the situation when I'd floated Quality Care Homes, and I had an almost identical reaction

'The deal's off,' I told my solicitor by way of ending the call.

My FD, who was sitting next to me in the cab, was shocked.

'Look, Duncan,' he tried to placate me, 'this represents a tiny percentage of a twenty-two million pound deal. Are you sure you want to do this?'

'Yes. Absolutely.'

I told the cab driver there had been a change of plan and to take us to the nearest place where we could get a drink. We were sitting in the bar of a hotel downing a pint when my phone rang again. It was my solicitor: they had agreed to waive the £300,000 and wanted us to go to the office to sign the deal.

'You knew they were going to cave in, didn't you?' my finance guy asked.

'I certainly thought they might.'

I knew how much firms like Alchemy spend on professional advisers and it was possible they would have a multi-million pound invoice to pay and no deal to show for it. I also knew how important, strategically, Just Learning was to them, so I'd been pretty sure they'd soon see things my way.

Of course there's not much point in running a business, even a perfect one, if you don't learn anything from it, and what makes Just Learning the perfect business for me is that right at the end I learned a very valuable lesson about selling companies. Just as a motivated seller is a great opportunity, so is a motivated buyer. There was no way Just Learning was worth £22 million at that stage, but it was so strategically valuable to Alchemy that they were prepared to pay over the odds for it. Yet again, it proved to be a change in government legislation that had benefited me.

When Gordon Brown became chancellor in 1997, he changed investment regulations for all venture capital trusts, of which Alchemy was one, forcing them to invest 70 per cent of their money in qualifying industries, which included day care. Alchemy had previously wanted to buy Rover, but when that deal fell through, I assumed they had a deadline for investing their funds. If they didn't, all their backers would no longer be eligible for the 60 per cent tax relief – 40 per cent capital gains and 20 per cent income tax – that had encouraged them to invest with Alchemy in the first place. Buying us at an inflated price kept their investors' tax bills to a minimum, and therefore their investors happy. And if they didn't keep their investors happy, they'd have lost a valuable reputation.

No matter what it is you have to sell, somewhere out there is a buyer who wants what you've got. I realised then that finding the right buyer can make an enormous difference to the price. And with my profits from Just Learning I decided to treat myself to something: I spent £3 million on a villa in Cannes.

Joanne and I had been on holiday there and decided we loved the weather, the food and the views and wanted to have a base there. We were walking along the Croisette in the height of summer when we passed an estate agent's that had a magnificent villa in the window. I went in to ask about it, but they didn't take me very seriously as I was in flip-flops and shorts. We went back a couple of days later in smarter clothes and got a different response.

Sadly – or so we thought – we missed out on the villa in the window, but several months later another place came up for sale, and we were very glad we'd had to wait. It's in a beautiful neighbourhood, with views out across the sea and along the coast to Antibes and it's one of my favourite places in the world. I've sat in the pouring rain looking at that view, watching a storm move across, and it's completely beautiful. Although I bought it as a holiday home, I actually spend several months of the year there.

I'm not one of those millionaires who's always buying the latest toys – I own only two cars and as I'm a complete technophobe the only gadget I have is a mobile phone – so my villa is one of my few luxuries. It gives me great pleasure to spend time there with my family, and it's also wonderful to be able to invite people to come and stay.

Some of my guests in Cannes include my brothers and sister and their kids. I don't see much of them these days, but if I didn't have the villa I'd see even less of them. I don't know if any of them think I should be using some of my wealth to help them out, but I do know that some of them are slow to offer to buy a round a drinks whenever I'm around.

It's different with my mum, of course: for her I would happily pay for anything. However, she has three pensions, including a war widow's pension, and always tells me she doesn't need anything. I still don't seem to have very much in common with my siblings: most of them are happy to live what I would call an ordinary life, taking their monthly pay cheque and paying the rent. Aside from our genes, it seems we don't share much else. Over the years I have occasionally given them all cheques at Christmas or birthdays – sometimes for as much as £5,000 to help them along a bit – but none of them have ever asked me to help them start up in business, which is something I find amazing.

TWENTY-ONE

Getting involved
with Unicef
1997

---

*I prefer to fund projects that
have a long-term benefit.*

The year after my first trip to Romania with Bob Shields in 1995, he was forced to take early retirement from the police force because of an injury. I tried to maintain contact with the institute he'd taken me to in Brasov, but for some reason I never discovered, Bob had fallen out with the management – and that meant they didn't want to hear from me either.

In 1997 I found myself at home watching a TV appeal on behalf of Unicef, the United Nations organisation that cares for children worldwide. As I watched it, I realised that it had been a couple of years since we'd done any fundraising for Bob, and I felt ashamed that we hadn't done anything to help, so I wrote a personal cheque out to Unicef for £50,000 to help with their appeal – in those days I was earning around £700,000 a year with dividends. I didn't know it at the time, but when a charity receives such a large cheque, they go out of their way to track down the person who sent it, and a few weeks later I got a call from a woman called Laura Boardman, who worked for Unicef in London. She wanted to know if I fancied meeting up to talk about other ways I could help. She invited me to a dinner where I heard Lord Deedes give a passionate speech about his involvement with Unicef, and his words made me realise I wanted a real connection to the projects I funded.

I told Laura that I was happy to donate more money, but only if I could see where it went; I didn't want it disappearing in a balance sheet at some HQ somewhere; I wanted to see it actually make a difference. She asked if there was anything in particular I wanted to get involved with, and I told her I wanted to help people in Romania.

A few months later she took me to Bucharest, where we looked at a couple of projects Unicef was funding. One was a day centre where street kids could get a decent meal and another was a wonderful theatre school run by a charity called Parada where children were taught juggling and acrobatics. Not only did this entertain them and bring them a bit of joy, it also enabled them to put on productions, which they toured the country with for profit. They were both simple and effective schemes and the kind of thing any donor to Unicef would be happy to see their money spent on. One of the acrobats there – a muscular sixteen-year-old called Thomas – could hold four people on his arms, and his was one of many stories that would break my heart over the next few years. I heard that he'd run away from his orphanage, choosing instead to live in the sewers for the past six years, and I wanted to know what had driven him to make that choice.

'Why did you run away from somewhere with food and beds to live in a sewer?' I asked him.

'I was bullied,' he told me. 'By the big boys.'

'Surely it couldn't have been so bad that you had to run away?'

'I was bullied and beaten up every night,' he confessed quietly.

People aren't generally beaten up without a reason, so I asked him why. He looked at me with piercing blue eyes that seemed to say, 'Don't you know anything?'

Again I asked him why.

'For sex,' he said simply. When he moved to the sewer, he did 200 press-ups a day and ran for miles up and down hills to build up his body and make himself strong.

'Now I take care of myself,' he said with pride.

My travels with Unicef took me to a town called Negru Voda on the Black Sea coast. I was taken to an institute that is possibly the worst place I've ever visited in my life. There was little more than one adult to care for a hundred children. They were completely deprived of any human contact; it's quite possible they had never been hugged in their lives. I arrived with a freelance photographer called Tom Craig, who was working for the *Telegraph*, and a new doctor who showed us around. As she spoke, I realised that she had already become something of a zombie and that the enormity of the challenge facing her was breaking her spirit. When she finished showing us round, Tom and I sneaked off to see what was happening elsewhere in the building and found entire floors that we hadn't known existed. Of course, away from the guided tours the conditions were disgusting. The matron found us walking around and was furious.

'Why do you always focus on the bad things?' she demanded. 'Why can't you stay where you're told. Can't you see that we're making progress?'

But she couldn't deny that while a few things were moving in the right direction, there was still a lot left to do. Seeing the degradation in those forbidden rooms made me determined to help fund projects that would help people in that institute. However, when I went back the following year with my friend John Gamble, the chief executive of Life Fitness Ltd, to see how my money had made a difference, I realised that the mattresses I'd paid for hadn't arrived. Even worse, the doctor I'd met the year before had given up: it had just been too much for her to cope with. The problems were so immense and complex that I accepted not all of my money would reach its intended destination.

A few months after my first trip to Negru Voda, Tom's photographs formed part of a Unicef photographic exhibition. At the launch party I got talking to the actor Roger Moore, who I'd previously met at a couple of Unicef benefit nights. Roger (now Sir Roger) is a Unicef ambassador and a neighbour of mine in the South of France, and he's since become a good friend. He was particularly intrigued by a very dramatic picture of a cot, but he couldn't quite work out why it made such an impact, especially as there weren't any children in it. I asked Tom to talk to us about the photo.

Tom explained that he'd taken it in Negru Voda, at the institute where the matron hadn't wanted us to see the rooms that hadn't been renovated. 'Remember how she insisted they no longer tied children up at night?' Tom asked.

'Of course I do,' I told him, remembering that awful place.

'What do you see when you look at the picture?'

'I'm not sure what you mean. It's a cot isn't it?'

'At first sight you think it's a just an empty cot,' Tom explained, 'but when you look again, you see that there's cord tied to each corner.'

Suddenly Roger and I realised we weren't looking at a cot, but at a cell.

'Why's that cord there if they're not still tying children up at night?' Tom asked.

For a moment I was completely overcome, thinking of children being tied up all night long in that horrible concrete room. It was an incredibly powerful image.

Unicef recognised that the best way to help the children being kept in such awful circumstances was to get them out of the big institutions, so they started funding smaller hospices. I have since been told stories about those hospices that are truly miraculous in the very real sense of the world.

One hospice was converted to take thirty severely physically disabled children from the institute in Negru Voda that we'd visited. None of them were mobile, yet within a few days of being in their new home, twenty-seven of them were walking. People I spoke to talked of seeing their faces light up when they were taken into the hospice, where it was warm, brightly painted and full of toys. These children had never been given a reason to cross to the other side of a room before, but now they had a toy box to play with, and carers to give them a hug, they had a reason to walk. As I looked around the room and saw everyone's faces, it seemed to me as though the whole of Romania needed a hug.

I prefer to fund projects that have a long-term benefit. Knowing that education is the best foundation on which to build a future, I have put money into several schools projects in Romania. Laura took me to a housing estate of several towerblocks, where I had been told my money had paid for several of the children to get an education. As we arrived, I could see it was a complete hovel. It was absolutely filthy and without power for most of the day. The only source of water was a standpipe and I could see no evidence that my money had made any difference at all. And then, all of a sudden, ten schoolchildren in immaculate school uniforms came running down the stairs. Seeing them so clean when everything around them was so filthy was like a camera trick.

'How come?' I asked Laura, slightly gobsmacked.

'You,' she said, 'And your money.'

The parents had been told that their child would only be allowed to go to school if they were clean, and as the school guaranteed the children a decent meal each day, the parents made sure the children lucky enough to get a uniform were always spotless for school. They were so proud that their children were getting an education. With more donations, more children would get the chance to learn and eat a decent meal. We were still at the towerblocks when the children came home, and they went straight to their apartments, got changed into their filthy rags and went out to play. Their uniforms were precious: they were a passport to a better future.

Over the years, on many different trips, I have met children living in the most awful places, enduring the most appalling suffering. Sometimes the only way you can understand such a big problem is by getting to know individual stories. Only then do you realise that you can make a difference and that a huge, seemingly impossible task, can be reduced to smaller, achievable challenges.

Unicef once took me to a place called Resita to visit an institution where I saw a little boy in a metal drum wearing a bright red suit. He was banging a tambourine and the radio in the room was blaring out loudly. As I got closer to him, I could tell that he was deaf. I knew this because he didn't have any ears. So I asked the interpreter to find out the little boy's story from the nurse.

'Oh that's not a little boy,' she said, 'that's Mona.'

The director of nursing told me that Mona was eight years old and still wearing nappies. She had been born with a cleft palate, a condition that in the UK is treated at birth with a simple operation. But in Romania it was assumed she was a freak of some sort, so she was put in an orphanage. Tragically, with her cleft palate untreated, and with the staff in the institute so badly educated about basic healthcare, bits of food stayed in her mouth – largely because they didn't even take the children out of the cots to feed them and simply spooned it in while they were lying on their backs. Over time the trapped food caused an infection that spread to her ears. The pain was so bad that she pulled away at her ears until she pulled them off. The infection also got into her eyes and made her blind.

On another trip, I visited an establishment that helped street children by feeding them on a daily basis. The deal was that they only got fed if they attended school, so food became a major incentive to get educated. The children at this place were the lucky ones, as there were only funds to support a small percentage of the local population. We joined the children for lunch and I observed one young girl taking a paper bag from her pocket. She diligently cut her food exactly in half and put one half in the paper bag. When dessert was served – a small but tasty cake – she took another paper bag from her pocket and did exactly the same again. I knew that my kids would have eaten the whole lot, so I asked her why she did it. She told me, 'Half is for my sister, who cannot come to school.' There just wasn't the money to send both of them.

In Bucharest, I met a twelve-year-old girl called Alexandra at a halfway house that had been established to offer food and shelter to homeless children during the day, but that didn't have the facilities to give them a bed at night. I asked Alexandra how she came to be homeless, and she told me that she had lived at home with her mum and dad until her dad developed cancer and was hospitalised. Her mother sold their house to pay for his hospital treatment, forcing her and her mother to live on the street. Then her father died in hospital, her mother died of cold and she was left on her own. When I met her she was living in a sewer.

Unsurprisingly, there have been times when I've come home from Romania and been unable to sleep. I often have to get up and write down the stories of the children I've met before I can sleep, but even then it's difficult. Some of the things I've seen are too painful to keep to myself, yet also too painful to share. I remember once being in a hotel in London and it was 2 a.m. and I couldn't get to sleep. I'd been crying so much my pillow was soaking wet. I had appointments in the morning and I was desperate to sleep, but the more desperate I got, the more wide awake I felt. Eventually I dropped off and was woken at 7 a.m. by my phone ringing. It was John Moreton.

'What's wrong?' he asked.

'How did you know something was wrong?'

'Well I couldn't sleep at two o'clock this morning for worrying about you, so I knew something was up.'

John is one of the few people I can talk to about the tragedies I've seen in Romania, and later that day he came round and took me out to lunch to a restaurant on the Strand called Loch Fyne. I sat there and told him about a little girl called Lorridana who I'd met on my last trip. This is what I wrote in my diary about Lorridana when I got back to my hotel:

We were at the halfway house at Resita when I saw a girl who was about eight years old, dishevelled and filthy, sitting on the gate. I went with an interpreter and asked her name. She said, 'My name is Lorridana.' I asked her her age. She said she didn't know. I asked her when was her birthday. She said, 'What is a birthday?' I asked her where she lived. She said she lived in the fields and she ate raw potatoes.

We took her to the halfway house and bathed her, changed her clothes and put her in a skirt. She protested and screamed: she didn't want to wear a skirt, she wanted to look like a boy.

I never saw Lorridana again, but I still keep her photograph in my kitchen.

TWENTY-TWO

Selling Quality
Care Homes
1997

I can't stress enough how important it is to agree fixed prices when agreeing deals with suppliers and contractors.

When it became clear that Just Learning was going to be a good business, I decided the time was right to sell my remaining shares in Quality Care Homes. It was an emotional wrench to leave the company I had started little more than a decade earlier, but I was having an increasingly fractious relationship with the City and a few run-ins with investors. In 1996, the share price started to perform weakly and I came in for a lot of criticism. When we got to the stage where we couldn't borrow any more money because of my agreement with the board not to let gearing rise above 60 per cent, I suggested to the directors that we shouldn't increase the dividend that year, but should reinvest the profit to expand. As I was the major shareholder, I was the recipient of the largest dividend and, of course, I was paying 40 per cent tax on that income. It seemed daft to me when we needed the money to grow the company, and I persuaded the board to approve an announcement that we wouldn't increase our dividends for one year. Of course it was a move that didn't go down well with the other investors and, consequently, our share price stumbled.

This is still something that frustrates me about the City: doing what's best for a company isn't best for the share price. If I had announced an increased dividend that year, my share price would have gone up but my company would have been in worse shape. It's a crazy situation that rewards bad choices and shows how directors and investors can have a conflict of interest.

When we'd floated in 1992, I had thought I was going to be a public company director for the rest of my life. I enjoyed a huge salary, respect and ran a company I loved – I never imagined that I would sell it – but the experience with Just Learning had reminded me how much more fun it is to run a private company, and it had made QCH seem dutiful by comparison. I realised I could pay somebody else to go into the office every day and do what I did: the company didn't actually need me any more if there weren't the funds to expand. I had long ago become disillusioned with the City's rules and regulations, and the cost of the annual listing, not to mention the fees for professional services, had started to grate.

However, selling up meant I would have to do one of two things with my profits: I would either have to pay 40 per cent tax on them, which totalled around £10 million, or I could go and live in Monte Carlo for five years. I'd looked into the Monte Carlo option, but had only been able to stay there for two nights before it drove me crazy. Then, in 1996, when Kenneth Clarke was still chancellor, the government introduced a new rule that meant you didn't have to pay capital gains tax on profits you reinvested. It was a smart piece of legislation that helped boost private-sector investment and gave me a third option. This coincided with me becoming convinced that the health-club business was what I wanted to get into, and so I formed a company called Bannatyne Health and Leisure Ltd in order to do just that. If I could sell my shares in QCH, I could reinvest the profit into the new company and make even more money.

QCH was sporadically approached with takeover and buy-out offers, and once I had decided to sell, I started to pay these offers some attention. Several of the offers came from companies wanting to buy my freeholds off me and then lease the premises back to me, which was the way much of the rest of the industry operated. As I've said before, I like to own freeholds and have complete control, so I wasn't interested in selling the freeholds unless I could sell the facilities at the same time.

In early 1997, a company called Principal Healthcare, which was owned by an American real-estate investment trust called Omega, made an approach to buy my freeholds. They were prepared to offer a good price to get a toehold in the UK care-home market and I felt the time was right for me to sell. As well as enjoying running a private company, QCH had racked up some expenses with advisers in the previous year, which would hit our profits and our share price. If I wanted to sell, I knew I should do it before that happened. Their offer was no more than the offer I'd rejected from John Moreton the year before, but as our share price was only £2.74, the £3.30 offered represented a significant boost to my wealth, so I agreed to it – but only if they simultaneously bought the facilities. So Principal Healthcare teamed up with a public company called Tamaris, who came on board to buy the facilities, and we pieced together a deal that valued the company at £46.3 million, of which just over half would go directly to me.

I called my lawyer and asked him for a quote to handle the sale and we agreed on a fixed fee of £25,000. I can't stress enough how important it is to agree fixed prices when agreeing deals with suppliers and contractors: I firmly believe it's one of the secrets of my success. I remember when we first approached the stock market there were some investors who doubted our valuation because they just couldn't believe we could build quality buildings at such low cost. The way I had done it had been through agreeing fixed fees with our builders in an industry where most projects run over time and over budget. I had even begun to insert penalty clauses into contracts to give contractors an added incentive to stick to the contract. I adopted a similar approach with all my contractors, and lawyers are no different. Why should a professional get paid more for being inefficient? It's crazy. On this occasion, we even agreed a very weighty penalty clause: if the deal didn't go through, he didn't get a penny.

It was a very complicated deal and it dragged on and on, so I tried to speed things up by imposing a deadline of 6 p.m. on the Friday. I told the buyers that if they didn't hit the deadline I would pull out. The truth was that I had planned to go to Lake Windermere that weekend to spend some time with my kids on the yacht, and I knew I'd have a better trip if the deal had been done.

When we finally sat round the table to do the deal, the lawyers took things very slowly – if we sold things in the wrong order we'd have had to pay a lot more tax. But as the meeting dragged on, it was clear that the deadline was going to be missed. The buyer's solicitors weren't on a fixed fee – I later found out that they spent £7 million on professional fees to buy QCH – and at every stage they found some reason to charge their client for an extra clause or subclause. I reminded them of the deadline and announced that I was leaving at six o'clock – with or without a deal. Obviously my lawyer wasn't very happy, as without a deal he would leave the room without a penny, so he, Joanne and Chris Rutter persuaded me to sign over power of attorney to them. They promised they would get the deal done while I went off water skiing with my kids.

This was the middle of July, so by the time I'd got to the Lake District and got out into the boat, there were still a couple of hours of daylight left. It were one of those warm, magical evenings where the water was completely calm and the sky was shades of orange and pink. For stretches of time, I'd completely lose myself in the skiing and forget about the lawyers back in Darlington, but as soon as I was back in the boat, I felt nervous – what if they didn't finalise it? What if I couldn't sell and the share price dropped? I only needed to take one look at my kids making the most of the warm summer evening to know that it didn't really matter – if the share price dropped enough, perhaps I could even buy back the rest of the company – but I would still rather have £26 million in the bank. The phone eventually rang at ten o'clock, when I was still in the boat – mobile phones are a great invention! – and Joanne told me they'd signed the final piece of paperwork. I don't know how other people would celebrate getting a cheque for £26 million, but I decided to carry on waterskiing until the sky went dark. After that, we went to a pub where the landlord let us in after hours and got very drunk.

A few days later I went downstairs in our house in Cleveland Avenue and picked up the post. To my surprise, one of the envelopes contained two cheques – one for £23 million, made out to me, and another for £3 million which I was putting into a trust for my children. I had expected that kind of money to be transferred directly into my account, but I didn't really mind: there's something quite wonderful about seeing a cheque for that amount of money made out to your own name. Obviously this wasn't something I was going to leave lying around, so as soon as the bank opened, I went into town and queued up for a cashier.

The woman behind the counter looked at me, looked at the cheque and then back at me again. The Darlington branch of NatWest clearly wasn't used to such big sums.

'I'm sorry, sir, but I don't think we can take this from you.'

'What?'

'I think it's too big for us. But I'll just check with my manager.'

In the end they had to get their head office involved and do some kind of elaborate transfer. I was in there for ages, but while they rushed around making a big deal about their very important customer, I just enjoyed the fact that, as soon as the funds cleared, I knew exactly how I would spend them.

TWENTY-THREE

How to lose a million
1997–99

It's in my nature to reward hard work and loyalty with promotion and responsibility.

Shortly after I'd sold QCH, I received the CV of a young accountant, called Nigel Armstrong, who was looking for work. He had spent his early career at one of the big accountancy firms, but had recently worked for another local entrepreneur. He said he wanted to be more hands-on and not just crunch numbers, so I invited him in for a chat.

He impressed me: he was a good northern lad with a no-nonsense approach to finance. Like Chris Rutter – who had stayed with QCH – he could sketch out a business model in a couple of minutes. He also seemed interested in creating wealth rather than squandering profits on his expense account. I offered him the position of financial controller. Nigel tells me now that when I offered him the job I also told him it was his big chance. It turns out I was right: Nigel is now my managing director and, nearly ten years on, he has share options worth millions of pounds. I always try to be good to my word.

Joanne has pointed out to me that my most successful members of staff – and she includes herself on this list – are managers I've nurtured. Very few outsiders have done well in my companies.

Perhaps it's because we have such a non-corporate culture that anyone with experience of big companies elsewhere finds it difficult to fit in, or maybe it's because it's in my nature to reward hard work and loyalty with promotion and responsibility. Either way, Nigel is another key member of my team, along with Irene, Joanne, Chris and Tony, all of whom have been instrumental in my career.

As I've mentioned before, I had to reinvest my profit from QCH or pay 40 per cent capital gains tax on it. I'm not averse to paying tax – and I never have been – but I saw the sense in the chancellor's new law, and believed that my money was better invested in new businesses, where it could create jobs, than in the Treasury's coffers. Just as Alchemy had needed to invest in Just Learning, I now had a deadline for spending £23 million, and one of the ways I could do this was by buying stock. I asked Nigel to set up a company for me which I could use to make investments. We optimistically called the company Maximum Return Ltd.

As part of my research into the health-club business, I had discovered a company operating women-only gyms in the north-east. Lady in Leisure seemed like an interesting proposition, so I started buying shares in it. Shortly after I'd committed cash, however, I discovered that it wasn't the great investment I'd initially thought it to have been. Some of the information I'd been given wasn't accurate and I became pissed off at the directors, who I felt couldn't run a bath, let alone a business. Other investors might have cut their losses, but my response was to buy up more shares: if I could get my hands on 10 per cent of the company, I'd have enough clout to force the board to make some changes. The more I looked into the company, the more of a state I realised it was in, but I also saw that there was a way it could be run much more profitably. I saw the £1 million I'd spent on that 10 per cent as the first stage of an eventual takeover.

Lady In Leisure was a small company – far too small to be listed on AIM, the Alternative Investment Market, a stock market for small companies with what is known as 'low market capitalisation', which basically means that the total value of their shares is normally less than the threshold needed for entry into the main Stock Market. Yet key members of the management team were running it as if it was a big player and spending money on unnecessary expenses like flash cars and plush offices. Even the listing on AIM was setting the company back £250,000 a year. My plan was to take it out of the stock market and operate it as an efficient private company.

As soon as a single person or company owns more than 3 per cent of a listed company, the board is obliged to make this shareholding public, so as I bought up more stock, the financial journalists started to call and ask me about my plans. I let a few stories slip, with the intention of putting more pressure on the board and the MD, while making my fellow shareholders think twice about the competence of the board.

UK law allows any shareholder with 10 per cent of the stock to call what's known as an 'extraordinary general meeting', so as soon as I reached that threshold I wrote to the shareholders and forced the board to call a meeting, at which I made it clear I was going to ask for the MD's resignation. This obviously caused a few ripples of concern across the board, so it wasn't a complete surprise when the chairman rang for a chat. So I invited him to my office and explained to him that I thought I knew how the company could be run better and that I should be given a chance to prove myself. I started talking to him about the specifics of the different clubs and the changes we could make. As we spoke, it slowly dawned on me that this 16-stone man had never actually been to any of his clubs.

'Well I can't,' he said. 'They're for women.'

I couldn't believe it!

'*I've* been to your clubs,' I told him. '*I* checked out my investments.'

'Oh.'

'Perhaps you should have a woman to chair the board then!'

He was embarrassed and tried to assert his authority. 'Look, Duncan,' he said, 'this meeting you've called could be very damaging. Perhaps we could reach a compromise.'

We discussed the options, and I agreed to withdraw my demand for an extraordinary meeting only if the chairman guaranteed that the MD, a guy called Graham Foster, resigned at the next AGM, which was in six months' time. As the MD, I felt he had to take responsibility for the shortcomings I had identified. When the Annual General Meeting came up, I was pleased to see that Foster's resignation was on the agenda as promised, but what I hadn't anticipated was that the board would refuse to accept it.

By now, because I had such a big stake in the company and a pretty good reputation, I was asked to join the board. Finally, I thought, I'll be able to make a difference, and so I gladly accepted their invitation. However, when I got to see more of the paperwork and observe the other directors at work, I wondered what I'd got myself into. The directors are responsible to the shareholders, but the board was so irresponsible that I feared we'd be open to criticism from our investors. In my view, the company was mismanaged, and this inevitably meant it was short of cash. To get more investment, the directors decided to return to AIM to raise a further £3 million. I looked at the placing document and thought the figures didn't add up, so within a week of joining the board, I resigned: staying could have seriously harmed my reputation.

To cut a long story short, within a year of that AGM, Lady In Leisure went bust and I lost the £1,040,000 I'd invested. Maximum Return Ltd certainly wasn't living up to its name! Losing the money wasn't a big issue for me, and in an odd way it felt good, as I'd been proved right. I'd known it was a badly run company, that the MD wasn't doing a good job and that it would go bust if someone didn't take it over.

About three years later, when I had already opened several of my own health clubs under the Bannatyne brand, the administrator who'd taken control of the assets of Lady In Leisure got in touch and asked if I was still interested in the company. Although I still thought it could survive as a franchise operation, I was happy to pass on the opportunity to get involved. By then I'd come to the conclusion that women-only gyms didn't have such a good future. They were necessary in the past when gyms were spit-and-sawdust affairs, but the new breed of health club I had started to operate catered just as well for women as it did for men. I also realised that Joanne and I weren't the only couple that enjoyed working out together. Not only does a women-only gym automatically exclude half the population, it also excludes the percentage of women who want to exercise with their boyfriends and husbands. It was also clear by this stage that the future was in big health-clubs with pools, and Lady In Leisure's premises were small and unsuitable for enlargement. Despite my earlier interest, I was happy not to get involved for a second time.

People in business often say that you learn more from your failures than you do from your successes, and I like to think you can learn from every situation, but it's difficult for me to see what I could have done differently on this occasion. What I was able to identify, though, was that Lady In Leisure was made more attractive to investors by the tax laws at the time, as they qualified for 60 per cent tax relief on their investment – 40 per cent on capital gains and 20 per cent on income. This effectively meant investors had a choice of giving their money to the Treasury or taking a punt on Lady in Leisure, and this created an investment opportunity where one didn't really exist. Lady in Leisure had floated on AIM with the intention of soaking up tax-efficient investment it wouldn't have deserved on the open market. If there is a lesson to be learned from Lady In Leisure, it's one for the legislators as much as for investors. Gordon Brown, I believe, closed that particular loophole a few years later.

TWENTY-FOUR

Business angel

1996–2003

Sometimes becoming rich isn't about opportunity, it's about desire.

In the late nineties, I had the opportunity to get involved in several other businesses, and after spending a long time dedicated to one company, I relished the chance to get my fingers into lots of pies. As I started to be offered non-executive positions in other people's companies, I realised that others had started to see me as a leader, as an example to be followed and someone to respect. Having acquired my business acumen the hard way, it was gratifying to be asked to lend my experience to new ventures. The experience I gained at this time as an 'angel investor' – someone who invests time and money in young companies – stood me in good stead for my work on *Dragons' Den* a few years later.

Although I felt I had proved myself personally in business, I wanted to prove that I could run other people's businesses as well as I had run my own. The first venture I was asked to get involved in was a Newcastle-based company called New Life Care Services Ltd. The investment company 3i approached me and asked if I'd like to become the non-executive chairman of this relatively new company, which they intended to invest in because it had a guaranteed income from the government. New Life Care Services offer accommodation to adults with learning difficulties and helped them to live independently – in return for roughly £600 per resident per week from the government. It was very flattering to be asked, and it was exactly the kind of business I thought I'd have something to offer, so I took a 10 per cent stake in the company, which set me back about £40,000, and became their chairman.

The company had been founded by four men who had all worked in the sector before. In the course of their work, they'd found out about the government money available and had been encouraged by those incentives to provide independent sheltered housing. On the one hand this was fantastic for the company because the directors knew and cared about the industry, but on the other, the fact that they were all carers by profession meant none of them had any experience of running a company, nor, I was about to find out, much aptitude for business. I would sit in board meetings with the four of them and, no matter what question I put to them, I'd get the same answer: 'I don't know.' It drove me nuts.

When I had made my investment, I had truly believed I was going to steer New Life Care Services along a similar course to that of QCH. I saw no reason why we couldn't expand as rapidly or be as successful: I thought my 10 per cent stake would be worth a million before long, and I believed that the four directors – John Knox, Jack Twizell, Colin Hanking and Bill Small – would all become multimillionaires.

I only ever saw the directors at board meetings, which happened every six months or so. When you have such infrequent contact, it takes a while to spot patterns of behaviour. Eighteen months in, I realised the company was barely bigger than it had been when I'd become chairman, despite the fact that they were turning a massive profit.

'Why don't you use the money to expand?' I asked them.

Despite the fact that three of them were older than me, I felt like a father figure gently encouraging them to make the most of themselves. But no matter how much I tried to persuade them, between them they owned 60 per cent of the company and so didn't have to take my advice if they didn't want to. None of them was prepared to take responsibility, and consequently none of them was taking control, making it impossible for the company to expand. The truth was they were quite happy running one of the homes each and didn't want to expand.

I still have the minutes of our board meetings and it's almost funny how often phrases like 'Duncan advised the company was not expanding quickly enough' appear. They would often tell me they were looking into new properties to acquire, but their opinion was that 'expansion would happen when the right property comes up'.

'You could build the right property,' I suggested a couple of times.

'Ooh,' they dithered, 'wouldn't that be very expensive?'

'But you're stockpiling profits. You can afford to, and then you'd make even more money.'

They didn't want to hear it, and I had to satisfy myself with taking a modest salary of £6,000 and a healthy dividend on my shares.

Without any expansion to advise them on, my role was almost surplus to requirements and it became clear that they resented paying me a salary, not to mention the charge 3i took each month. After six years of virtual stalemate I said to them, 'Look, it would be cheaper for you to get a loan to buy me and 3i out. Why don't you go and see the bank and get a loan?'

'Oh, I don't know,' said one.

'Neither do I,' said another.

'Aren't loans very expensive?'

'And what if interest rates go up?'

'Haven't you heard that it's possible to *fix* interest rates!' I said incredulously.

'Oh.'

They were clueless, which made them impossible to deal with, so eventually I wrote a business plan for them, showing them precisely how they could borrow the money and pay less in repayments each month than they were currently paying their investors. I even arranged the loan for them, and this enabled me to walk away with about £230,000, which was a very generous return on my initial £40,000 investment.

I'm still amazed that New Life Care Services didn't become a huge success in the way that QCH had done. Those four men had everything they needed to become fantastically wealthy – they had the backing of 3i, one of the best corporate investors; they had a chairman who had steered a similar company to great heights; they produced a massive profit *and* their income was pretty much guaranteed. I can't believe they didn't make millions out of it.

As far as I can tell, the reason why New Life Care Services wasn't a runaway financial success was because the directors didn't want it to be. They were happy running a small business with modest profits, and doing a good job with it. If they had taken my advice, they could all have retired by now with millions of pounds in the bank. Sometimes becoming rich isn't about opportunity, it's about desire, and these guys just didn't have it.

You can learn from every situation in business, and the thing I took away from New Life Care Services – apart from the profit, of course – was that you should be very wary of going into a venture with partners who don't share your ambition.

TWENTY-FIVE

Radio times
1996–2000

First: ask to see the accounts.

In the late nineties, just before I sold QCH, I got involved with a local radio station that provided me with another opportunity to learn about a new sector and put into practice what I'd learned in business.

It felt like a boom time in the media industry as the government was selling off radio frequencies to the highest bidder, and consequently the sector was getting a lot of speculative investment as the big media companies vied for supremacy. The attraction to me was the chance to prove my skills in a completely different field, so when a radio DJ called Mark Page – known to listeners of Radio 1 as 'Me Mark Page' – got in touch and asked if I'd like to be part of a consortium to bid for the local licence, I jumped at the chance. Unfortunately we lost out to a consortium run by Alan Noble, another prominent businessman in Darlington who runs Northgate, Britain's biggest van-hire company.

However, six months on, Alan – who is a good friend of mine – realised he didn't have the time to run the radio station as well as Northgate, so he gave me a call. He told me the station was 'under capitalised', which is a polite way of saying they needed more investment, and wondered if I might like a piece of the action. So I bought some shares and took up Alan's offer of a seat on the board.

I turned up for my first board meeting, keen to meet the team and excited to find out how things worked in a different sector. I certainly wasn't expecting Alan to announce his resignation, which went hand in hand with a recommendation that I take over the chairmanship! Although I was truly shocked, it felt great to be offered the role and I saw it as an acknowledgement of the success I'd made of QCH from a fellow self-made entrepreneur, so I accepted and jumped in at the deep end.

I soon realised that A1FM was just about the worst radio station in the world. If I put it on in the car, the kids screamed at me to turn it off; to put it politely, the music was awful, the advertising was infuriating and the presenters were annoying. I also discovered that Alan really hadn't had the time to put proper accounting procedures in place and that half of the twelve directors didn't know what the other half did. The fact that there were twelve directors should have been my first clue that the outfit was inefficient – no company that size needs so many directors all taking a salary for their minimal contribution. I saw an opportunity to make a difference and I took it.

The first thing I did was ask to see the accounts, but I was told that one of the directors would have to bring them in from home first.

'Why are they at home?' I asked.

'He always takes the disc home to add his own expenses,' the secretary told me.

I didn't have to ask why. I asked to see the directors' expenses claims, and when I started reading I didn't know whether I should laugh or cry. It turned out that the director who'd originally had the contract for supplying the computers charged a fee every time one of the computers needed attention, and that the director whose company had the contract for the maintenance of the building charged £40 every time a lightbulb needed changing! I asked the secretary who arranged for the expenses to be signed off and discovered that each director had his expenditure approved by just one other director. It was a case of 'you sign mine and I'll sign yours'. They also all had company cars, even though they only worked a couple of days a month.

One of the things that has always made my blood boil is when people take the piss, and the attitude of these directors meant there was no point sorting out the on-air output – even if we had a great radio station we'd never have a great company until the board was sorted out. It seemed to me that these guys simply liked the idea of being in the media and felt that being in a so-called glamorous industry was enough justification for living it up. However, you have to remember that I'm the guy who wouldn't let his nurses order paperclips, so I wasn't about to let these directors get away with it. I was going to knock some heads together – with considerable force.

I wrote to all the directors and told them I was about to introduce something called corporate governance; part of this, I told them, would involve all directors submitting their expenses to the entire board for approval. At this point, unsurprisingly, the proverbial shit hit the fan, and it was only a matter of days before the radio station's finance director stormed into my office at QCH and demanded to know who the hell I thought I was.

'The chairman,' I replied calmly.

'Well it's not going to happen,' he insisted furiously. 'I've known these people for years and I trust them. You can't just take over and start making changes like this.'

'OK,' I said, 'at the next board meeting, I'll propose the new system, you can vote against it and if you win I'll resign.'

He had come for a fight and I wasn't giving him one. I could see the rage that wanted to burst out of him.

'I'm not having this,' he fumed, throwing down his car keys like a kid in a tantrum. 'I resign!' Then he stormed out as quickly as he'd stormed in. One down, ten to go, I thought.

Word got around about our encounter, and by the time of the next board meeting, the ten remaining directors had been given countless spurious reasons to distrust me and I could see it in their eyes. The moment came for me to raise the matter of expenses.

'What I'm proposing is very simple,' I explained. 'Each of you will bring your expenses to the board for approval.'

After a few minutes of muttering and refusals, one of them bothered to ask me why.

'Well,' I said pointing at one of the directors, 'did you know that he gets forty pounds every time a lightbulb is changed?'

They looked blank.

I pointed to another director. 'Or that he goes to the pub at lunchtime every day and buys a round that he puts through on expenses?'

They had no idea what everyone else was claiming for and some of them were genuinely shocked.

'Now tell me,' I said, 'who's still got a problem with their expenses being approved.'

A few shifted uncomfortably in their seats, but after a long discussion the board accepted the new idea in principle. One of them still had an objection, however.

'Who's going to check your expenses?' he asked, thinking he'd caught me out.

'I won't put any expenses through.'

He was gobsmacked. I also offered to get my financial director, Chris Rutter, to do the radio station's accounts for £2,000 year, saving them the £18,000 they'd been paying to the finance director. They couldn't really argue with that, and I could see that I was persuading a couple of them that I knew what I was doing. After that meeting I had the authority to start turning the company around and stop it from haemorrhaging cash at such a critical rate.

Of course, the new regime wasn't to everyone's liking, and over the next few months a few of the directors resigned. As there was no need to replace them, we started to make considerable savings on the payroll. However, that wasn't enough to make the company profitable; to do that I had to recapitalise the company – i.e., issue new shares to get more money in – several times. Our major shareholder was Border Television, and the station's Articles of Association – documents drawn up when the company was founded, which set out how it's to be run – stated that the major shareholder had the right to buy the balance of new shares. Border assumed that this meant they would always have control, but what they didn't realise was that, during the recapitalisation, my stake had crept up above theirs when they declined to exercise their right to buy some of the new shares.

Simultaneously, I also made changes to the output of the radio station. Although I didn't know much about the media at that stage, I knew enough as a listener to know things had to change on air. I had some enormous battles with the MD, who insisted his music policy was working and that we had an 18 per cent audience share, which wasn't bad for a new station. The trouble was, I didn't believe him: I didn't know anyone who listened to A1FM. I was so convinced no one was listening that I wrote to all my employees in the Darlington area and asked them if they had heard of A1FM, if they listened to it and if they liked it. It wasn't especially scientific, but the results showed that just 2.1 per cent of the available audience tuned in. However, as I couldn't prove it, I couldn't use it as leverage to oust the MD.

Eventually the RAJAR figures – the industry's official audience figures – were published, showing that A1FM had an audience share of precisely 2.3 per cent. Obviously this was terrible news for the advertisers and our sales staff, but it was terrific news for me as it meant the MD resigned.

Although I didn't have the contacts in the media to replace him, I knew that every industry has its own trade magazine, so I put an ad in *Broadcast* for his replacement and got some pretty good applicants. One guy in particular really impressed me, and together we set about relaunching the station.

A1FM had such a terrible reputation with listeners that it seemed clear to me we could never be a success unless we rebranded. You don't need to be a media expert to know that. We employed a local

PR agency to help us generate some coverage in the papers, changed the playlists, got some new presenters and relaunched as Alpha FM. I had wanted to call it Crap FM as I thought we'd get loads of publicity, but the PR company – probably wisely – persuaded me out of it.

In the next couple of years, the relaunched Alpha FM became such a success that I decided we should put the company up for sale. However, when I mentioned this, Border TV turned round and said, 'We're the major shareholder and you can't do anything without our permission.'

'Actually,' I told them, '*you* can't do anything without *my* permission: *I'm* now the majority shareholder.'

They were stunned. They hadn't realised I'd bought so many shares, but once they'd got over their shock they agreed to look into the idea of finding a buyer. With so much competition between the big radio networks, it wasn't hard, and so less than three years after my first board meeting, I sold my shares for twice what I'd paid for them, having completely turned the station around. All the other shareholders, of course, had the option of selling at the same time at the same price.

I took enormous satisfaction from my work at Alpha. I had proved my business instincts were right, and that I didn't have to be the founder or the MD to push things through and make a success of a business. I was showing anyone who cared to take notice that I was good at what I did.

You would think that having saved the company and made a profit for the rest of the directors and shareholders, at some point someone would have taken me aside to say thank you, but I never got a single bottle of champagne or card in the post, never even a handshake of gratitude. Sometimes in life, it has to be enough for you to be proud of yourself, even if no one else notices.

TWENTY-SIX

Hotel Bannatyne
1996–

If you're looking for a reputable company, try the guy who's named the company after himself.

Although most of the £23 million I'd made from QCH was reinvested into Just Learning and a new company I formed called Bannatyne Health and Leisure, with the aim of opening some health clubs in the future, I was still looking for other ventures to invest money in. Whenever we had some spare time, Joanne and I would get in the car and drive around looking for opportunities. If a business was doing well, we'd try and work out why and see if we could learn from it, and if a business was on its knees, we'd come up with ideas about how to make it profitable. Other couples played golf together or went to garden centres, Joanne and I cruised for opportunity.

For years I'd driven past a mysterious building in Darlington that was all but hidden from the main road by a high wall. It looked half derelict and it was only the fairy lights you could just spot over the wall that made me think there was something going on inside.

My director of projects, Tony Bell, has lived in Darlington all his life, and he told me that the huge Georgian building used to be a Catholic girls school called the Immaculate Conception. This only added to my intrigue and one day, when Joanne and I were driving past, we decided to find out what lay beyond the big brick wall.

It turned out that the Immaculate Conception was a very impressive listed building that had been converted into a hotel. I knew instantly that the Grange couldn't be a very good hotel, otherwise I would have heard of it. Consequently, I wasn't surprised to find out that it was up for sale – the elderly woman who owned it was only getting two or three bookings a week.

Joanne had always liked the idea of opening a restaurant with rooms, and I could tell as we started looking round that this was a business she wanted to get involved with. I could also see the huge potential in the building – and the business – and another way of using up some of that £23 million.

We found out that the hotel was on the market with an agent in Carlisle, about 80 miles away, which went some way to explaining why it was seriously undervalued: they wanted offers in the region of £2–300,000 when it was clearly worth double that. Joanne and I talked it over and decided that we wanted to buy it, so the next day we went back to see the hotel's owner, Maureen Jackson, and were disappointed when she told us she'd already accepted an offer of £300,000, subject to planning permission, to turn it into a hospice.

I saw an opportunity to clinch the deal – I knew the planning officers well enough by now to know it was the kind of decision they'd take years to make, if they could reach a decision at all.

'Well, we'll pay you three hundred and fifty thousand,' I told her. 'Cash, of course. And we won't hold things up by seeking planning permission because we want to keep it as a hotel.'

I told her we could complete in a couple of months, so she called her solicitor and got him to draw up contracts and tell the other party the deal was off. A few hours later, though, the hotelier called to tell us that the other bidders had now upped their offer to match ours, and as she had originally accepted their offer, she felt she had to go with them.

So I offered her £400,000, which still represented an enormous bargain, and that was enough to get her to say yes again. But the next day, when Joanne and I went round to thank her for accepting our offer, she was very sheepish with us. After several minutes of awkward conversation, she confessed that the other party had made her an even better offer, but only on the condition that she didn't tell us the amount. It was getting silly, but by this time Joanne and I had really fallen in love with the idea of opening a hotel, and I knew that there were several big companies in Darlington – such as Alan Noble's Northgate and the biggest nursing agency in the country – whose clients would always need a good hotel. I just wanted to do the deal and get on with creating a great new company.

'Look,' I said, 'I want this hotel and I want the deal done quickly. I'll offer you six hundred thousand. I'm assuming that's a lot more that your other offer.'

It was a stunning offer and one she quite rightly couldn't resist. I was confident it was enough for the other bidders to withdraw permanently – in just a couple of days the asking price had doubled, so the chances were that I had thrown their plans into disarray. We shook on it, but while we were driving home to celebrate the phone rang.

'Hello, Duncan.'

It was a local businessman whose path I'd crossed a few times, and as it's probably too libellous to print what I really think if him, I'll call him Trevor.

'Hello, Trevor.'

'I believe you and I have got ourselves into a bidding war,' he revealed.

'I didn't realise you were the other bidder,' I said honestly.

'Did she tell you that we're buying it to turn it into a hospice?'

'She did mention it.'

'Now, Duncan, you wouldn't want to be known locally as the man that gazumped the hospice would you?'

'Actually, Trevor,' I told him, 'I think there's an old lady there about to retire, and I think she should get the best price for her hotel, don't you?'

By the end of our conversation, Trevor had agreed to withdraw from the bidding and Joanne and I got the hotel we wanted.

As I've said, this was a business Joanne really wanted to run, and as I was fully occupied with the new health-club business, not to mention the radio station and other projects, I was very happy for her to take responsibility for the hotel as managing director of Crème de la Crème Ltd. She had impressed me with her professionalism at QCH, and despite our relationship, I thought she would do a terrific job.

We knew the hotel would need a major renovation, so we closed it down for a year while the builders came in. As well as adding ensuite bathrooms – something of an emblem of my career! – to each of the thirteen rooms, they also had to take off every roof tile as the nails holding them in place were rusting. Although we thoroughly modernised the Grange, we were able to save and restore some spectacular original features, including two beautiful fireplaces. Unfortunately, I didn't pass on to Joanne my belief in the wisdom of getting a fixed price from contractors, and the bills started to mount.

I've often found that I perform better in business when I'm not emotionally involved. The more detached I've been, the better decisions I've made. With the Grange, I slowly realised that I had two problems: the first was that Joanne was emotionally involved with the idea of opening a perfect hotel; and the second problem was that I was emotionally involved with her. She was happy to overspend and I was reasonably powerless to stop her.

Nevertheless, at the end of the refit, the New Grange Hotel was beautiful – all we needed was some guests. Running a hotel isn't like running a care home. Instead of guests staying for years, it's rare for a hotel guest to stay longer than a few nights. Constantly filling the hotel was a problem, despite the fact that our chef had established a fantastic reputation for our restaurant, Maxine's.

Not long after we'd opened, I took a call from our receptionist.

'Mr Bannatyne?'

'Yes.'

'I thought you'd like to know that a Mr Bannatyne has just checked in.'

'*Bannatyne*? Really.'

'I've double-checked the spelling.'

'Tell him I'd like to meet him.'

Nairn and Donalda Bannatyne were visiting from Canada, and considering at the time it was estimated there were only 400-odd Bannatyne households in the world, the chances of them checking into my hotel were pretty slim. The odds that we would actually be related – we shared a great-grandfather, the rather fabulously named Ebenezer Bannatyne from the Isle of Bute – were even slimmer, though.

Distant relatives aside, there weren't enough customers to get a return on my investment. Joanne's dream of a Michelin-starred restaurant with rooms to rival Raymond Blanc's Le Manoir, proved to be just that: a dream. It certainly wasn't a business. I told her I thought we needed to rethink the business as there just weren't enough customers for such a classy establishment in Darlington: our guests wanted cheaper rooms and bigger portions. I told her it was time to downscale her ambitions, and to her credit she saw my point of view.

I realised that if I built an extension I could treble the number of rooms, and therefore income, without having to increase staffing costs. After all, a forty-room hotel still needs only one bar, one restaurant and one reception area. There would be an increase in our linen bill, but there wasn't really any other downside as far as I could see.

We have since extended a second time and the hotel now has sixty rooms, and we still have a waiting list for guests. During the week, business visitors pay a premium for the fact that we are the only upmarket hotel in the centre of Darlington, and at the weekends we have an excellent business catering for weddings, following our application for a licence to conduct ceremonies at the

Family moments. (Right) With Abigail and Hollie, my two eldest children.

(Left) Emily and Tom cuddling up; (below) Eve and Jenny behind the shades.

Celebrating with Joanne. After thirteen years together, I finally proposed to her in Barbados in the spring of 2006.

Relaxing on holiday in Cannes with the girls from UNICEF.

My villa in Cannes, bought with £3 million of the profit I made from selling Just Learning, is one of my few luxuries.

The conditions in Romania remain staggeringly poor. Since I first got involved in the country back in 1993, I have returned regularly to do what I can to help.

Two of the people who have helped me most in Romania. (Left) Ibi Unger, the hospice manageress who showed me what was required for Casa Bannatyne; (below left) John Moreton and I show off some of our finest moves, to the amusement of everyone else.

Before and after. (Above) The
dormitory in the hospice I saw
in Targu Mures, and (Left)
the bedroom in Casa Bannatyne.

The opening of
Casa Bannatyne.

Magnus MacFarlane-Barrow:
his wonderful charity work
has helped children
throughout the world.

A still from the drama *Girls' Club*. I quickly realised that my acting career was never going to be something that would go too far, but I enjoyed it while it lasted.

With a couple of other actors you might just have seen: (right) Sir Roger Moore and (below) Alicia Silverstone.

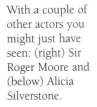

Talking to Richard Branson, who regularly organises parties for entrepreneurs.

Speaking at the Fast Track conference in 2006. I have been asked to do increasing numbers of motivational speeches, especially since I started appearing on *Dragons' Den*.

The line-up for the third series of *Dragons' Den*: Theo Paphitis, Peter Jones, Deborah Meaden, me and Richard Farleigh. The series has not only been a lot of fun, it has been great for my profile. (© BBC)

hotel. Compared to the rest of my businesses, the hotel was a very slow mover, and at times it was a battle to make it profitable. In the end, I think we succeeded because we didn't swerve from our intention to provide a quality service. Even our restaurant now has a waiting list for bookings most nights.

Following the success of *Dragons' Den*, we renamed it Hotel Bannatyne when we realised that my name was becoming a recognisable brand. For a man who has had his name spelt wrong all his life – if you want to get on my wrong side, just try calling me Ballantyne – it's very rewarding to see people are finally learning how to spell my name!

I've often been asked why I name my businesses after myself, and it's not just to teach the world to spell, nor is it because I have an outsized ego. Apart from the fact that it's becoming a valuable brand that no one can take away from me, it also inspires me to do my best. Like Donald Trump, I'm only ever going to put my name to something I believe in. Knowing that my brand, and my name, could be tarnished by bad publicity is a huge motivator to ensure that all my staff are professional, that all my businesses deliver and that all my customers are satisfied. The next time you're flicking through *Yellow Pages* looking for a reputable company, try the guy who's named the company after himself. The chances are he feels the same way I do.

Of course, the business that really made my name a brand was Bannatyne Fitness, so I think it's about time I talked about how you can establish a chain of sixty health clubs in a little over eight years.

TWENTY-SEVEN

Getting the health clubs up and running

1996–97

I never set out to be the cheapest, only the best.

Although I had been thinking about opening a health club since my skiing accident in February 1993, my commitments to QCH, Just Learning and other projects meant it took me until 1996 to do anything about it. The impetus to finally put my money where my mouth was actually came about by accident.

I had been at home negotiating to buy some land to build a nursery on at a site near Stockton called Ingleby Barwick, which touts itself as the largest housing development in Europe. I ordered an acre of land, but it was only when I put the phone down that I remembered that care homes took an acre whereas nurseries only need half an acre: I had bought too much land, and there was no way Ingleby needed two nurseries.

It was Joanne who suggested – while we were on Eurostar going to Paris on one of our many trips away – that I use the plot for a health club. 'You've been talking about it for long enough,' she reminded me. By the time we got to Paris, I'd realised that my mistake was actually a stroke of luck – where better to start a health club than in the middle of a huge new housing development, where there would be precious few other leisure facilities?

By early 1996 I was a member of two gyms, the gym I'd originally joined, the Parkmore Hotel and Leisure Club to exercise my knee, and a new purpose-built facility at Scotch Corner on the A1 which had opened the previous year. It was the Scotch Corner club where I'd counted the ceiling tiles, and it was the model I intended to recreate for my club.

In fact, I was so impressed with it that I took my architect to see it and we walked round the outside of the building, picking up clues as to what made it a good club, and taking a tour of the inside to see what elements we wanted to replicate. It wasn't perfect, but together my architect and I worked out how we could improve upon it to make ours the best club in the north-east.

I didn't do the kind of detailed research into the market that you might expect: I was so convinced by my original calculations of a 35 per cent plus return on capital per year that it gave me the faith to go ahead without systematically analysing the sector. I took a look at a David Lloyd Tennis Centre, as they had the best reputation in the business, and the thing I learned from David Lloyd was that offering tennis – although popular – is financially stupid. David Lloyd clubs have no more members than any of my clubs, nor do they get people travelling further to use them; yet their overheads are massive as they have to pay rates on a huge amount of land. The gym was the most profitable part of their business, and that was the part of their business I intended to replicate. I also decided that each of my clubs was to have a pool, as it was a clear way of signalling to potential members that we were offering a luxury product.

As I hadn't yet sold QCH, and as there was no guarantee that I would be able to sell it at that stage, I set about opening the first health club knowing that it might end up being my only one. However, if I did manage to sell the care homes, I planned to reinvest the profits and make sure Ingleby Barwick was the first of many.

We started building in early 1997 and put into practice

everything we'd learned constructing care homes and nurseries. I didn't realise it at the time, but I had actually become a property developer as much as a businessman, and getting the building process right had been a key part of my success. My director of projects, Tony Bell, helped me refine the way we dealt with contractors, and with him onboard I was confident of success. One of Tony's ideas had been to bring in something called 'cost save sharing' which incentivised contractors to be even more efficient. It worked like this: a builder would look at the architect's spec, and if he could suggest a way of doing something in a more cost-effective way – perhaps he knew about a new glazing system or concreting technique – then we would split the saving with him 50:50. So not only did we save on the build cost and develop a good relationship with our builders, who were in a no-lose situation, we were also able to roll the saving forward to our next health club.

By the time I sold QCH in the summer of 1997, the construction of the Ingleby Barwick site was well underway. At first the new company, which I called Bannatyne Health and Leisure, consisted of just me and Joanne working out of our dining room. But as we had become used to taking plenty of holidays – you've got to remember, I still had around £20 million in the bank and I was madly in love – I employed Joanne's sister Jacqueline as my PA to answer the phone while we were away. In fact, much of my work after the flotation was done from the beach in Barbados!

I was keen for Tony Bell to join me full time, but under the terms of the flotation he had to stay with QCH for three months. When he was contractually allowed to join us, he too worked out of my dining room, and I can't tell you how much fun it was to be part of a small team again, working in an industry where there wasn't some little Hitler in a council office controlling our progress. And as I had so much money in the bank, I didn't need to hawk my plans in front of junior bank officials in search of approval. Very early on, I knew I'd really enjoy being in the health-club industry.

Just about my only problem was working out what to call the

club. It hadn't been my intention to name it after myself, but the north-east had recently had a couple of clubs opened by shysters who ran off with members' joining fees, so I needed something reputable.

'Why not use your name?' Joanne suggested over breakfast one day.

'Well no one can spell it, for starters!'

But as we carried on talking, she persuaded me that her suggestion wasn't just flattery. I had a good personal reputation in the north-east as a provider of quality care: if I put my name to the club, potential members would be more likely to believe it would be a quality club with responsible management. But I still had a problem with it – sometimes people can't even pronounce it properly, let alone spell it, and it seemed daft to try and create a brand out of such a difficult name.

'What about McCue's,' I said to Joanne.

'People haven't heard of me,' she replied.

So that was it, we decided to call the club Bannatyne's and Joanne's hunch paid off: we were inundated with people wanting to join. In fact we had to close membership before we opened, as we couldn't be sure how many members we could cope with. Although we'd had to do a bit of advertising, it only involved putting leaflets through doors and inserting a flyer into the local free paper. The fact was that residents on the Ingleby estate were aspirational high earners who liked the fact that a quality facility was opening on their estate – it made Ingleby more desirable and they were enthusiastic in their support of 'their' club. We capped the initial membership at 600 for our launch in November 1997, but as soon as we were open and could assess how full we'd be at various times of the day and week, we let more members join until we reached our optimum – around 3,000 – following a £1 million extension in our second year.

I discovered with the first club how useful a health club's joining fee could be, both from my point of view and from the members'. Firstly, it's a huge motivator for someone if they've paid £200 or so up front, on top of their monthly payments, to stick with their membership. Joining fees also tend to put off the kinds of members who would abuse the facilities, so by joining a club with an up-front fee, members can be sure they're joining a quality establishment, and we rarely have to deal with difficult customers who have no respect for the equipment or other members. Aside from the injection of cash at the beginning of trading, the joining fee also has another benefit: it acts as a regulator of member numbers. If we've lost a few members – we have a turnover rate of around 30 per cent each year – we can reduce the joining fee for a limited time and use that as a marketing tool to encourage new members.

I made a decision very early on that our membership fees should reflect the fact that we offer a quality club with the best facilities and staff. I never – not for one second – thought we should compete on price. After we'd been open for about three months, a few people wanted to leave Spring's Health Club, our nearest rival in Teesside, and sign up to Bannatyne's, but they wanted to haggle over the price.

'We'd like to join you, but you're forty-two pounds a month, and Spring's is thirty-eight.'

'Well stay with Spring's then,' I'd say to them.

'But your club is better.'

'Well perhaps that's worth paying for then.'

I was never tempted to bargain with them: we were the best club in the area, so I wasn't ashamed to ask for more money than our rival. Interestingly, when I talk to members now they tell me they wouldn't want to be a member of a club that didn't charge a joining fee or have twelve-month contract. They know that both those things mean their club will be used by considerate members who take their fitness seriously. I never set out to be the cheapest, only the best.

By the late nineties of course, Britain had moved away from a cash culture to one entirely at ease with direct debits. At QCH in the early years, a fair percentage of our income had been in cash, but with the health clubs, about 87 per cent of our income came straight from members' bank accounts into ours. That removed a huge opportunity for staff to put their hand in the till, which is always a risk for companies that deal with lots of cash.

Not that we had many problems with staff. We simply advertised in the local paper and interviewed the best candidates. The manager from the Parkmore gym I'd joined applied, as he wanted the challenge of running a bigger club, and I was only too happy to give him the job managing Bannatyne's. However, as we started to gear up and open several clubs, it became clear that the country had a finite supply of qualified gym instructors and suitable managers. For that reason we started a comprehensive in-house training scheme, which invited every employee, no matter what his or her position was, to apply for training that would lead to promotion. It's a cheap and effective way of retaining and motivating staff, and it saves on recruitment costs.

TWENTY-EIGHT

Borrow fast, build faster
1997–2003

The best club is always the one that
responds to its members' needs.

I was so convinced the health-club business was the right industry for me – apart from anything else, after running care homes it was nice to have a business that wasn't twenty-four hours, which meant the phone never rang with problems in the middle of the night – that I invested a total of £16 million in cash into Bannatyne Health and Leisure. At a build cost of around £4 million per club, that would buy me four clubs. But four wasn't enough! Just as I had done at QCH, I started buying up land and planning an extremely rapid expansion. If I split the remaining £12 million I had left after we opened Ingleby, and used £1 million as a down payment on a club, I could borrow the difference and open as many as twelve clubs instead of four. At one point I had seven plots of land with clubs at various stages of completion being built on them, some of which I hadn't arranged finance for. It was a bit of a headache for my newly promoted financial controller, Nigel Armstrong. One of his first tasks was to secure the financing for clubs I wanted to build on those seven plots of land. He went to see the bank managers and heard the same stories I'd heard when I'd started QCH. When I told Nigel not to worry about it, I think he doubted my sanity.

'You mean you've been in this position before and you didn't try to avoid it?'

'Oh no, this is a terrific business, why wouldn't you want to expand quickly?'

It didn't help that I had also told him to 'only pay the screamers'. Money was so tight that unless someone was screaming at us to pay their bill, they didn't get their money until our cash flow had improved.

Of course, there are a few risks associated with rapid expansion, in addition to committing yourself to builders without having secured the financing. There's a chance that you'll focus so hard on expansion that you won't pay attention to things happening elsewhere in the sector. And as with everything, if you rush, you might be tempted to cut corners and end up employing bad staff because you didn't have time to recruit properly. However, all of these possibilities were outweighed by the opportunity, and I quickly brought Nigel round to my way of thinking. To his credit, he also did a terrific job of explaining my strategy to the banks.

I also relied heavily on Tony in those days. I trusted him completely, so when Michael Fallon told us about a site in Essex that we should take a look at, I asked Tony to visit it for me. I would have gone myself, but Joanne and I had reservations at the Sandy Lane Hotel in Barbados. The site was called Chafford Hundred – interestingly, it too claims to be the biggest housing development in Europe – and Michael thought it was a huge opportunity for the company. However, the land was about £400,000 per acre, which was nearly twice what we'd paid for anything in the north. It was also being offered in plots of six acres, but as I had a deadline to reinvest the money I'd made from QCH, I wasn't put off by the price tag. If I had a concern, it was that we weren't yet entirely sure about the rules of rolling out a chain of health clubs. Tony and I agreed that we'd be taking a risk. However, he liked the plot and could see it had huge potential.

'I trust you to make the right decision,' I told him while sipping a cocktail on the beach.

So he bought the land, and not only did we build our second Bannatyne's club on it, we also built a day-care centre at Chafford, too. The rest of the plot lay vacant for a few years and we used it as a 'landbank', preferring to have our money in the soil than in the vaults. In due course, we found a very good use for the spare land, but I'd be getting ahead of myself if I told you about that now.

The Chafford Hundred club was my first venture in the south-east, and we noticed a significant cultural shift between our members in the north and those in Essex. I realised that people who live in the south-east suffer from something I call 'time rage'. In the north, it's customary to spend a maximum of twenty minutes a day getting to and from work, but in the commuter belt around London, some people travel for up to two hours each way. This shrinks their day and they have to cram in their leisure time, so we'd get members who would want their children to use the pool while they took an aerobics class. They were ruled by the clock and if a pilates class overran, we'd get irate customers. It seemed clear to me that people in the south-east might earn more, but they have a lower quality of life.

Of course, not only is land more expensive in the south, houses are too, and that meant a high proportion of residents of Chafford Hundred commuted into London to earn big salaries in the City to cover their mortgages. While that meant plenty of locals had the money to pay for gym membership, it also meant it was harder for us to find staff locally who could afford to work in the leisure sector, where salaries don't compete with the City. In the north, we'd found a regular supply of women who were happy to earn a bit of extra money cleaning for a few hours a day; in Essex, we had a much higher turnover of staff on the housekeeping side of things.

I've since found that it's not just a south-east problem – we have similar problems with our city centre clubs in Manchester and Edinburgh – and I've never found a great solution to the problem.

We've just had to accept that in affluent areas we'll have less of a problem finding and keeping members and a harder time holding on to good staff.

Building better clubs

Our next few clubs were all back on home territory in the north, and as each club was built, we modified the construction to accommodate the lessons we'd learned with each of the previous clubs. I wanted to build the most efficient clubs in the industry, and to do that we kept a tally of who used our clubs when. If, for example, we had cars queuing up to park when we still had treadmills free, we concluded that we needed a bigger car park. If all our lockers were full but the aerobics classes weren't, then we knew we needed bigger changing rooms. We established a matrix into which we fed information about the habits of our members, and this enabled us to refine our clubs until they were damn near perfect.

I also learned more about the construction process in those years and worked out new ways to save money on the build costs. Firstly, as you establish yourself in the industry, you meet people who are specialist Jacuzzi suppliers or sprung floor experts. We learned from everyone we met, and because we were opening so many clubs, we were in a strong negotiating position with all our suppliers.

Additionally, I realised that a fair percentage of our build cost was accounted for by things like corridors and stairwells, i.e., bits of the building that don't generate income. So I got Tony to calculate the percentage of the building that was dead space, financially speaking, and if it was 26 per cent, I'd tell him to go back to the architect and find a way of getting it down to 20 per cent. Not only did this save on the construction of unnecessary walls, it made the architects think critically about the overall design, and I always found that the second draft contained a lot of minor improvements.

One of our big innovations in terms of architecture was to

combine our reception and lounge area. In the early clubs we employed staff to manage our lounge, where we sold teas, coffees, juices and lunches. By combining the two areas, it meant the same staff could do both jobs and we saved on our wage bill as well as construction costs.

We also responded to changes in the industry: for instance, when we started nobody offered spinning classes, in which participants work out on exercise bikes. When spinning started to become popular around 2000, most clubs crammed their aerobics studios with bikes that were dragged into position at the start of a spinning class. We were among the first to build dedicated spinning rooms, where the bikes are permanently in position, and we invested in fantastic light and sound systems to help keep energy levels high.

That wasn't the only way we responded to our members' needs. To this day I have a photo of myself in every club with my email address on it, and I invite people to get in touch with me directly if they have any problems. Several years ago, a female member wrote to me because she'd been intimidated by another woman's eight-year-old son in the changing rooms. Obviously he was too young to change himself, but he was too old to be using the women's changing room, so we introduced family changing areas with big cubicles and private showers where parents can take care of their kids without irritating other members. The key thing is, no matter how good our clubs are, the best club is always the one that responds to, and fulfils, its members' needs.

I knew from using gyms myself that filling the place up at 6.30 p.m. on a Monday is a doddle – even bad gyms are full then. The secret to a successful health-club business is not to have an expensive facility lying practically empty during the day. Many gyms offer an off-peak membership to combat this, but they often end up selling cut-price membership to people who would pay the full price if the cheaper option wasn't available. We decided to actively try to recruit the biggest section of the community that doesn't work – people who are retired – and make them welcome at Bannatyne's.

As someone who was going through the big 5-0 myself at that point, I didn't think our target market of active retired people would be flattered with anything labelled 'over fifties'. We also didn't want to discourage younger users from visiting us during the day, so we came up with our 'Young at Heart' programme.

Young At Heart has been an outstanding success for Bannatyne's – if you come in after a class at lunchtime you can't get a seat in our lounges. Young at Heart was designed around being sociable and having a healthy lifestyle rather than attaining a certain level of fitness. So if you're a YAH member, you get a free cup of tea or coffee after every class, and we also give you day passes so you can bring friends in to try us out. We've also found that our YAH members are incredibly loyal and far less likely to jump ship if another gym opens nearby, and because they come for the social aspect as much as the fitness, they attend more regularly.

There is another benefit, too: without wishing to generalise, our older members are much nicer to deal with, and we rarely have payment issues with them. From time to time a member will try to cancel their sub halfway through their contract, despite the fact that they have to sign their membership documents *five* times beside a warning in block capitals that they're signing up for a minimum of a year.

It's a regular criticism of the gym industry that we insist on payment each month, regardless of whether you use the facilities. Perhaps I should explain why we work that way. Firstly, we're a club, not a shop, and we exist for the benefit of our members. I believe our members' needs are best served by having a well-maintained building with motivated staff who have job security. Some of our members might like to take a payment holiday over the summer if they go away for six weeks, but we still have a pool to heat, rates to pay and staff to look after.

Occasionally we'll get a member who threatens to go to the local paper and tell people we offer a rubbish service if we don't let them out of their contract. If they try that, I'm quite happy to let them go to the paper while simultaneously serving them with a county court notice for non-payment. I currently employ two people whose full-time job it is to chase and prosecute non-payers. It's not just about revenue protection, it's about treating all our members equally and making sure everyone gets a fair deal.

Sometimes non-payers will insist that they weren't told about the twelve-month contract when they signed up, even though it's a central part of our staff training. Over the years, we have developed the perfect way of introducing new members to the club – the tour of the facilities has to happen in a certain order, and only then should members be told about our pricing structure and terms. But just in case any of our staff miss out any part of the introduction, we employ mystery shoppers who wear hidden cameras while pretending to be potential members. It's incredibly rare – in fact, I can't remember a single time it's happened – that I've had a tape from a mystery shopper and they've not been told about the twelve-month contract.

I've been asked a few times by other business leaders about the morality of employing mystery shoppers to spy on staff, and I tell them that I really don't have a problem with it. I would if we didn't tell our staff that we use mystery shoppers, but they are all told when they join that they'll never know when they're dealing with one, and if they don't like it, they don't have to work for us. The benefit to the company of mystery shoppers is significant. When I get the tapes, I can get all sorts of insights into how each of my clubs is operating – is it clean? is it full? how high is morale? – on top of assessing the enthusiasm and skills of the individual employee who's taking the shopper round the club. It's also a way of talent-spotting staff who might be suitable for promotion.

I believe we have a very good relationship with our employees, and I always get the impression that they like working for us. We pay slightly above the average for the industry, which helps attract the best staff, although we don't pay anything above the statutory minimum for maternity, paternity or sick pay – that said, I have often made very generous allowances for loyal members of staff in regards to things like bereavement leave. And just as I don't let members ruin a great club for everybody else, nor do I let staff take the piss and affect the morale of their colleagues. I've often seen in other organisations how staff bitch about fellow employees who are always surfing the web, or making outrageous expenses claims and getting away with it. In the past we've taken employees to court who have run up £250 of personal calls on their company phone, and I wouldn't hesitate to do it again. It said in their contract that they couldn't make personal calls, and if they didn't like it, they shouldn't have joined the company. These days, we don't give out company phones any more: I ask employees to bring me in their phone bill with their business calls highlighted, and we then reimburse them for legitimate expenses. It really isn't about the money, though, it's about the principle, and the same injustice I felt when I was competing with ice-cream sellers who were fiddling the dole forces me to protect my employees who stick to the terms of their contract. Anyone who thinks that's unnecessarily tough can go and work for somebody else.

And in case anyone thinks I'm penny pinching, my senior staff are all rewarded with generous bonuses if their clubs hit their targets. I don't do this just to motivate them; I do it so they can share in the company's success, as I think that's only right. If they hit all their targets, they can earn as much as 50 per cent of their salary in a lump sum, which I understand is an incredibly generous bonus in any industry outside of the City. My directors also benefit from a share-option scheme that will see them become millionaires one day.

TWENTY-NINE

Running a tight ship
1997–

I made the decision to have an impressive balance sheet rather than an impressive foyer.

I couldn't continue to grow such a rapidly expanding company out of my house, and it became clear I would need a proper office for the admin and support staff who took care of our growing payroll and membership needs.

In the late nineties, I lived at 55 Cleveland Avenue in Darlington, and I would occasionally get post for a small business round the corner at 55 Cleveland Terrace. I built up a pretty good relationship with the owners, and when they decided to sell up, I was the first to hear about it. I bought their building and freehold for £150,000, and a couple of years later I bought the house next door for another £150,000 and knocked through.

Having the office a couple of minutes walk from my home was fantastic. It meant Joanne and I could pop home whenever we wanted to be alone, and when our first child, Emily, was born in July 1999, it meant we could be very flexible with our childcare arrangements. It also had a cheeky tax advantage: if you only use a car for business it's wholly tax deductible, so I bought a rather flash Bentley and always kept it parked at the office to offset my tax.

A few years later, in 2003, we started to outgrow the office in Cleveland Terrace, so I looked for something bigger. It turned out that I wasn't the only developer who'd had problems with the Darlington planning office, and after several years of trying to get permission to convert their old headquarters, the electricity board had given up and was looking for a quick sale. The old Power House was right next to our club on Haughton Road, so I was interested in it because not only was it cheap and I could go for a workout whenever I wanted, it also had plenty of parking.

Ironically, I was able to afford their £750,000 price tag, because I had finally had a bit of luck with the Darlington planning office. They agreed that our Cleveland Terrace office was incongruous in a residential setting and granted us planning permission to demolish the building and build a block of flats. We sold the land – which had cost me £300,000 in total – for £850,000, purely because the planning permission had made it more valuable. The developer who bought the land hasn't yet sold the flats, but when he does he'll make a lot more than he paid for the land. Seeing this, I started thinking that residential property was something to consider, so I started Bannatyne Housing. I realised that much of my expertise is the same as a property developer's and that a lot of my wealth has been created by land deals, so residential property seemed the obvious next move for me. You may remember that when Tony did the deal to buy the land for the Chafford Hundred club he bought more land than we needed. When Deputy Prime Minister John Prescott announced that 200,000 new homes needed to be built in the south-east, Tony was able to get the planning permission on our land converted to include residential use. We're now planning to build several new homes there following the success of our first housing project in Dumfries.

When we finally moved into the Power House, an uninspiring 1920s brick-built municipal building, we realised why we'd always got a warm feeling when we'd looked round it – the electricity board had left the radiators on for ten years because the electricity hadn't cost them a thing! The Power House is actually far too big for our needs, and like the previous owners I wouldn't mind if I could knock it down and build something that would better benefit the people of Darlington, but the planning office has rejected everything I've ever proposed. One day I believe our HQ and the car park and warehouse behind it will be a prime site, so I've left it to my children in my will in the hope that it will rocket in value soon after the current planning officer retires.

Visitors are often surprised when they visit my office as there's no grand entrance, no huge reception area – in fact if you hadn't been here before you'd think you were in the wrong place until you got inside. Many of the rooms, like the warehouse round the back, are completely empty, and I've never bothered remodelling the place. For a large organisation, we have quite modest overheads, with only a handful of admin and executive staff overseeing the whole company.

Unlike some of my flashier contemporaries, I don't see the point in paying for a fancy office when you can have fancier profits if you base yourself somewhere modest. I made the decision to have an impressive balance sheet rather than an impressive foyer when I first visited the brokers who floated QCH. I remember walking into their glass and steel towerblock in the City, where hundreds of square feet were given over to lift lobbies and reception lounges, and thinking what a waste of money it all was. 'One of these days,' I said to myself, 'there's going to be a pensions crisis if this is how financial institutions waste money.' I resolved then never to compromise the integrity of any of my businesses with such unnecessary waste.

One of the biggest benefits of saving on the behind-the-scenes offices is that I have more cash to spend on what matters: expansion. Pretty soon we had clubs as far apart as Eastbourne and Dunfermline and it became impossible for Nigel – who had by now been promoted to managing director – and me to co-ordinate their efficient management from our Darlington HQ, so we started appointing regional managers to support our existing clubs and develop new ones. Some of these regional managers came from outside the company, but many of our best club managers were ready for a new challenge and were well placed to pass on their experience to other clubs.

I consider myself very good at delegating, and an expert at working out who would respond well to greater challenges. One of the managers I promoted was a guy I'll call Jason, who had been with the company for many years and who had an excellent track record. I put him in charge of a region I rarely visited as I completely trusted him to get on with the job, and for the first couple of years he was outstanding.

But a few years ago my detailed monitoring system alerted me to the fact that his region was starting to underperform. Each set of accounts was worse than the last, and I got the impression that our club managers were operating without much help from him, so I called him in for a meeting at which he reassured me that each of his clubs had difficulties for very specific local reasons and that they'd all be performing well again soon. However, there was something different about him at that meeting and I wondered if he was covering up for a major difficulty.

By analysing the accounts and progress reports, as well as his expenses, I worked out that he was spending an awful lot of time at one particular club. This wouldn't have been too big a problem had it not been for the fact that this club was still under construction, so all there was to manage at that stage was a portakabin! I also noticed from his accounts that we were paying for an awful lot of advertising in the local paper to promote the unopened club. When I asked him about it he said he had a long-term strategy to create interest among potential members, so I asked to see the innovative adverts I was paying for, and when he handed me the paper I couldn't believe it: the ads were like something for a local curry house in the 1970s. The more I questioned him about his work, the more defensive he became.

I had no idea what to think. Was he secretly planning to work for a rival? Did he have some personal problem he was keeping from me that prevented him from doing his job? I needed to find out, and so I hired a private detective to follow him. It didn't take long for the detective to report back to me, and Jason's expenses claims backed up everything the detective said.

Jason had been observed in this one particular town, night after night, having dinner with the same woman who appeared on his expenses claims as a client. The detective discovered that the woman in question sold advertising space for the local paper, which meant that normally it would be *her* paying to entertain him, since he was a loyal advertiser. If it wasn't immediately obvious that they were having an affair, it became perfectly clear when Jason's wife called the office to see if we knew where he was as he hadn't been home for weeks.

I felt I had little choice but to confront him: his personal life was his business, but only if it didn't affect mine. He told me I couldn't prove anything, so I asked to see his company laptop.

'It's in my other car,' he lied.

'You're on company business today, why isn't it with you?'

He made some lame excuse, and as he was talking I noticed that next to the files he'd dumped on the table was a set of car keys. I snatched them.

'So you can honestly tell me that if I go down to the car park, I won't find your laptop on the back seat?'

'No, Duncan.' He looked nervous.

'Well let's just see about that.'

Of course, the laptop was there, and sure enough his emails proved he was having an affair, and that meant his expenses claims and fuel bills driving to that incredibly vital Portakabin were all fraudulent. I also discovered a series of emails relating to our earlier meeting in which he boldly slagged off the chairman, i.e., me. I wasn't having it and immediately initiated a disciplinary procedure that ended in his dismissal.

In the months that followed, Jason took up much of the

company's time as he prepared to take us to an industrial tribunal for unfair dismissal. It was a costly affair and I felt sure he had calculated it would be cheaper for me to pay him off than go to court. However, money wasn't an issue for me and I called his bluff, so he too spent time, and no doubt money, preparing a case instead of looking for a new job.

In the end it never went to court. Jason withdrew his claim just two days before the date for our hearing. He had finally got a job offer from another chain of health clubs and realised that an industrial tribunal was not a good thing to have on his CV. Especially if he'd lost, which I am confident he would have done.

One of the reasons I run such efficient companies is that I strip out any unnecessary layers of management. In the company hierarchy there are club managers, then five or six regional managers, then Nigel and Tony, then me. This means it's very rare for the right hand not to know what the left hand is doing. There's also no duplication of responsibilities or work, and it's always clear who's expected to do what. It also makes for interesting days in the office for Nigel and me, as when we start in the morning we don't know if our strategy meetings will be interrupted by a minor issue from one of our clubs. While this can be distracting for Nigel, it means he's very close to the ground and has a good idea of what's happening at the coal face.

It also helps that Nigel and Tony complement each other so well. Tony's more of a by-the-book operator who knows what the standard industry response would be in any given situation. Nigel's much more like me, although less risk tolerant, and I often leave them alone in a room together to play devil's advocate to determine which direction the company should take. I'll ask Nigel to take the side of Bannatyne Fitness and work out if a move would be good for us or not, and simultaneously ask Tony to act for Bannatyne Housing and see what the impact would be for that part of the operation. Together they can brainstorm some pretty remarkable options.

Curiously, Tony tells me that he thinks my success has in some part been down to the fact that I often ignore his advice. His reasoning is that he has been trained – as a quantity surveyor – to give the standard response to a problem, which he thinks makes his response identical to 90 per cent of the operators in our industry. That trained response will usually mean certainty and modest profits, whereas my response is more of a maverick one: my way could be more likely to lead to failure, but so far I've successfully followed my hunches and by making moves that 90 per cent of other operators don't consider, I've found new territory to exploit. It also makes it very difficult for rivals to predict what I will do next. In fact, Tony says it's practically impossible even for *him* to predict what I'll do next.

In the early years of the new century, we were growing so fast it seemed plausible that we would be attractive to the market if we decided to raise further funds from the City. I looked at the health club chains that had floated and noticed that those with 'fitness' in their name were valued more highly than those with 'health' in their title. It was probably a coincidence, but just in case, I saw no reason not to change my company's name to Bannatyne Fitness.

By 2001, we had established a very efficient template for the construction of our clubs, and we had also worked out a set of strict criteria to decide where and when to open a new club. Between 2001 and 2004, we opened twenty-three clubs, and to cope with that rate of expansion you need to be sure of two things. The first one is money, and after I sold Just Learning Ltd in 2001 I put £18–20 million in the bank just at the time that Bannatyne Fitness had reached its maximum lending levels with the banks. If I had put the new money into existing clubs with existing loans, my cash could ultimately have been taken by the banks if we ever defaulted on any of the loans. There seemed no point in putting the money at risk in that way, so I formed a few new companies – Bannatyne Fitness 2, 3, 4 and 5 – and split the money between them, thereby using it as security against several new loans to fund the expansion.

Of course, this had the added benefit of making the banks compete for my business, which meant we got some very good deals.

The second thing you need is to be absolutely confident about is your business model. Obviously I'm not going to give away the secret of our success to our rivals for the price of this book, but I don't mind telling you our outline for success.

The first step is to look for an area that either has no health club or doesn't have enough health clubs for its size of population. The key thing we've discovered is that very few people are prepared to drive for more than ten minutes to get to the gym, so we do a drive-time analysis and see how many people live within ten minutes of our proposed site. If it's more than 40,000, then we do a more detailed examination of the population, using things like census and marketing data to establish what percentage of the population are affluent enough to afford our membership.

I was recently surprised when a health club on Leith Docks in Edinburgh came up for sale. Leith is a huge up-and-coming market with loads of young professionals – just the kind of people who pay to use quality gyms, so I was curious to know why its owners had put it up for sale. It's always worthwhile to work out what your competitors are getting right – and wrong – so I did a bit of investigation. As soon as I looked at the map, I realised what the problem was and that no one could ever make maximum money with that gym: it suffered from what I call half-moon syndrome.

Let me explain: it was right on the waterfront, which meant that if you drew a circle, representing the ten-minute drive time, around the club, half the potential members were fish. Leith only offered a half moon, so for that particular club to start making money it needed to move inland. If Bannatyne Fitness has one golden rule, it's the ten-minute one. You could apply it to almost any business: there are certain things that customers will travel far and wide for, and some that they won't. No matter what field you're in, you'll have your own drive-time calculations to make, and there'll never be any point in opening up shop where there aren't enough customers to make your business pay.

Talking of making it pay, I have established that it costs between £3–4 million to develop a club to our standards, and I look for a profit from most clubs of around £1 million a year. That's a 25–33 per cent return on my investment, which is also my benchmark for investments on *Dragons' Den*. Roughly speaking, that means a payback period of four years, which to some people seems quite slow, but I don't see it that way. If I put £4 million into a business that produces a profit of £1 million a year, that's a far better return than I'd have got from the bank.

However, at 5a.m. on 10 August 2006, my team, after working incredibly long hours, managed to acquire twenty-four health clubs from the Hilton Hotel Group for £92 million. We are now working feverishly to integrate these clubs into our business, and believe the enlarged group is much more valuable than the two separate entities.

The future for Bannatyne Fitness

In 2004 we opened three new clubs, and in 2005 that dropped to just two. The market is getting closer and closer to saturation, and although you can still find towns without a health club, there's usually a reason why. What often happens in industries approaching saturation is that the major players indulge in a spot of cannibalism, and we've certainly also had a few approaches from rivals wanting to take us over.

Part of our strategy for the immediate future is to make the most of assets we already own. We've identified that at our Durham and Norwich clubs we have more land than the clubs require. As these are parts of the country we know well, we know that it's often difficult to get a hotel room in both towns. We therefore decided that there was a market for a low-cost executive hotel in both these locations, along the lines of a Travelodge. And, of course, we have one massive advantage over our rivals in this sector: you'll be able to stay with us and, for no extra cost, use the health club next door.

The proximity of the health clubs also allows us to build very basic hotels, as the club reception can double as a check-in for the hotel and guests can use the club lounge for breakfast, all of which means the new hotel business will need remarkably few additional staff. The model couldn't be more different from my first foray into the hotel business with the Grange, nearly a decade ago. Smart moves like this mean I'm aware that bigger operators are circling us, hoping to make a well-timed bid to buy me out.

According to the *Sunday Times* Rich List, Bannatyne Fitness was worth around £120 million in early 2006. I was offered exactly that amount by a competitor, but I turned it down as I felt their offer undervalued the company, which is now worth even more after our acquisition. Obviously, I also have the option of doing what I did with QCH and floating on the Stock Exchange. Although it would be quite nice to get my hands on the cash, I'm not in any hurry. If I did sell, I would only want to start another business, so I may as well stick with one I love.

I'm not sure I've really conveyed that so far: it's not just the money, or the deal-making, I enjoy – I really love coming into the office and working with some of the best people I've ever met in my life. I love walking into one of my clubs and catching up with the staff or having a training session with an instructor; I love eating in our lounges; and I certainly love seeing lots of beautiful young aerobics instructors wearing a T-shirt that says 'Bannatyne' over their left breast.

We'll continue to expand as and when we find a site that meets our criteria, and I'll look into buying other operators just as they'll look into buying me.

Of course, there's a very good reason why I haven't been driving my team nuts with constant demands for more clubs in the past few years: I've been a bit busy doing this TV show called *Dragons' Den*. Perhaps you've heard of it?

THIRTY

Casa Bannatyne
2002–

*A deadline is a great motivator, and
without that projects can lose their way.*

John Moreton's 7 a.m. phone call the morning after I'd returned
from Romania to find out if I was all right was just one of many
coincidences that have happened in relation to my work in
Romania. John has been so moved by the stories I've told him that
he now funds several projects there himself, and Romania has
become yet another thing we have in common. As a committed
Christian, John tells me the coincidences are a sign from God. There
have now been so many of these coincidences, or signs as he puts it,
that there have been days when I've agreed with him. On one
particular occasion I was left in no doubt. It happened in a town
called Targu Mures.

I became involved with a project there after I met a remarkable
man called Magnus MacFarlane-Barrow, who runs a charity called
Scottish International Relief. Magnus started his charitable work by
driving donated second-hand goods to communities in Bosnia
destroyed in the war. He thought he would only make one trip to
Bosnia, but when he got home to Dalmally in Argyll, he found more
goods had been donated, so he went back. He then took a year off
work to keep making the trips, and eventually decided to form a
registered charity, working out of the shed in his dad's garden. He

works tirelessly, pays himself a tiny wage and is thoroughly dedicated to his projects.

I was introduced to Magnus by the athlete Steve Cram, a prominent figure in the north-east, who I met at a Labour party dinner. Steve had been the Master of Ceremonies at the event, so I'd spent a lot of the evening talking to his wife. She told me they had been raising funds for an orphanage in Romania operated by Scottish International Relief through their charity COCO (Comrades of Children Overseas). She was so passionate about Magnus and his work that I decided to give him a call and see how I could help.

In April 2002, Magnus took me and Steve to Targa Mures, an industrial town with a population of about 100,000 in Transylvania, where he was trying to re-house children living in disgusting, dehumanising circumstances in a big concrete Communist-era institute. It seemed impossible that even thirteen years after Ceausescu's assassination, so little had changed: away from the media spotlight, parts of Romania were still waiting for help. The people were so poor and hungry that if we ate at a café with tables outside the children would try and steal the food off our plates. Magnus had already bought and renovated a house, called Iona House, in the town where ten children had been re-housed: his ambition was to get the rest out. Magnus told me that he wanted to build another hospice in the grounds of Iona House so that the children could stay together. I asked him if he had any idea how much it would cost to build such a house.

'About £110,000,' he said. 'Do you think you could do some fundraising to help?'

I thought for a moment about how smiling and hopeful the children were in Iona House compared to the children in the institute, where they were scared even of being hugged. And I thought about how long it can take to raise funds.

'I'll give you the money,' I said. I knew that if I put up around £80,000, Magnus could claim the difference back from the tax man under Gift Aid rules.

I told him there was just one condition to me making the donation: I wanted the new house ready for Christmas. It was a short deadline, but those children were suffering, and I'd also found that most people respond well to a challenge. A deadline is a great motivator, and without that projects can lose their way. Magnus accepted my offer.

With no time to lose, he arranged for us to meet the construction team before I returned to the UK. I didn't say anything in the meeting, but as soon as we had some privacy, I told Magnus that although I thought the builder and foreman were terrific, I reckoned the architect was an idiot. Magnus, who is too nice to ever say anything bad about anyone said, 'Yes, I thought maybe he wasn't quite what we needed.'

I took the plans back to England with me so the architect I use for the health clubs, Mark Thompson, could have a look at them. When I got home, I phoned Steve Cram to tell him how I'd got on.

'Don't give them to your architect,' he said. 'I've got a friend who'll do it for free.'

A few days later, the phone rang and another one of my Romanian coincidences happened.

'Hi, Duncan.' It was Mark Thompson. 'Listen, Steve Cram's just handed me some plans that have got your name on them . . .'

And that wasn't all. Mark had a friend from college who was working in Romania.

'Whereabouts?' I asked.

'Targa Mures.'

This was just another of the Romanian coincidences that makes me think it's fate that I should spend time there. Within a week his friend had visited the site and they redesigned the building between them over the phone. The hospice was ready by Christmas and I went out for the opening. The manageress, a wonderful woman called Ibi Unger, who gave up a well-paid job as an accountant to work with the children, drove a minibus and picked up the kids from the institute. In the eight months since I'd last been there, several of them had died and there were now only fourteen children left. However, the new house, which Magnus had called Casa Bannatyne, could take only ten. The four children who were left were so severely disabled that they needed specialist help, so Steve Cram and COCO raised the funds to build Rozi's House, next to Casa Bannatyne, as a specialist centre for severely disabled kids.

The children hadn't known why they were being taken away from the institute, and Ibi told me they cried all the way there. As soon as they got there, however, their behaviour changed: it was as if they had suddenly been given a childhood instead of a life sentence. We decided that as Iona House and Casa Bannatyne both had ten beds, and as we had ten boys and ten girls, Casa Bannatyne would become the girls' house and Iona the boys' home.

One of the girls had developed mental-health problems in the institute and kept banging her head against the wall. A German woman, who took every summer off to care for the children, had got to know her and had brought a crash helmet from home for her. Another little girl had been orphaned twice: after her birth parents died she had been adopted, but when she was diagnosed with HIV she had been abandoned and ended up in the institute. Others had simply been abandoned because their parents could not afford to keep them. The poverty levels were so great that if you had five children, the chances were all of them would die. However, if you abandoned three of them, there was a chance you'd have enough money to raise the other two.

This situation was a legacy of Ceausescu's ban on abortion and contraception and his decree in the sixties that all women under forty-five should produce five children. One of these abandoned children was Ioanna, a thirteen-year-old girl with HIV who looked no more than eight because she had been so malnourished all her life. Like most of the kids with HIV, she almost certainly contracted it in the institute via an injection: no one had told the staff not to use the same needle on every child.

I arrived with my rucksack as the preparations for the opening party were underway. There was a big banner across the front of the house, and several local dignitaries had turned up, including the mayor and Miss Transylvania. At the party I met the staff, who were all local people trained to do the job and getting a decent wage. I also met some remarkable people who have devoted their time to projects like Casa Bannatyne. As well as the German woman, there was an American couple who had been so moved by TV images of the orphanages that they had spent the last three years in Targa Mures doing charitable work. I also met Sister Marta, a Romanian nun.

Sister Marta didn't speak any English, and as I don't speak her language, she would say something in French to someone, who translated into another language before someone could tell me in English what she meant. Yet, somehow, most of the time, we didn't need the help of the translator. Somehow, we understood what each other was saying. If John Moreton were writing this, he would probably tell you that Sister Marta was my guardian angel – there was definitely a spiritual connection of some sort.

I watched the children playing and remembered a previous trip when children at an institute had cried at the suggestion of the party because none of them knew what a party was. We started playing games and the children seemed unrecognisable from the kids I'd met back in April. A few hugs and some love and attention had transformed them. One of the most moving, and humbling, aspects of life I've witnessed in Romania is how the children harbour no bitterness: they are so grateful for their chance for a better life, and seize it so whole-heartedly, that there's just no room left for recriminations.

From time to time everyone involved in charity work like this breaks down in tears. I cry easily, but even those who don't will break down at some point. The tears are always a private thing, and when they come you find a place where you can be alone and sob. There's a little look we've learned to give each other, a tiny nod that recognises what's happening but doesn't bring attention to it.

For me the tears came at about ten o'clock that night.

I went outside and found a quiet place at the side of the house. I couldn't stop the tears, my face was wet, my nose began to run and I was a mess. I had no choice but to let the tears flow; and they just kept pouring out of me and wouldn't stop. After many minutes I began to get the feeling that I wasn't alone.

It was there and then that God said hello.

I felt that I had been consumed by this presence, that something had completely shrouded and taken hold of me. It was unmistakable: I knew who had come and I also knew why. It wasn't a spiritual thing, it was a Christian thing, and I felt I was being told, 'You've arrived, join the faith, be a Christian, this is it.' It was profound, and I stood there, stunned, considering the offer and thinking about what it would mean. I knew I wanted to keep on building up my businesses and I wanted to keep making money, and I also knew I wanted to carry on doing all the things I wasn't proud of – I knew I was never going to be this totally Christian guy going to church on Sundays.

So I said, 'No, I'm not ready.'

And God said, 'OK,' and disappeared.

The next day, we took the kids for a daytrip in the minibus to a nearby lake. These were kids who had spent virtually all their lives in one room in an institute. To see them playing and mucking about was one of the most rewarding moments of my life. I thought about my own children, who I'd taught to swim over a period of months, and was amazed when Ibi told me that little Ioanna was such a strong swimmer. I wondered where she'd learned to swim.

On the way back to the hospice, we stopped at a stall by the roadside which sold trinkets, and Ioanna – who spoke no English – pointed to a necklace with a tiny black plastic pendant. 'For you,' she motioned. She had big sad eyes and a mop of black hair, but she had such a cheery smile that I couldn't refuse, so I bought it. It only cost about 20p, but I've never taken it off.

The following night was my last night in Targu Mures for a while, so we had a bit of leaving party and for some reason I did something I never do: I stood up and made a speech.

'I just want to thank everyone for helping me to be part of this organisation,' I began. 'What everyone's done here is so fantastic and I want to take a piece of this away with me and I would like you all to do one thing for me. I want you all to buy me this necklace as a present, so that when people say to me, "Why, when you have all this money, do you wear some cheap little necklace?" I can say, "Because my friends in Romania bought it for me."'

They all thought it was funny, but chipped in a couple of ban – Romanian pennies – each, and the necklace has remained one of my most treasured possessions. This little necklace became even more precious to me when, exactly a month to the day after I bought it, Ibi called to tell me that Ioanna had died. She hadn't died of AIDS, though. That little girl, who was such a strong swimmer, had drowned on a trip to the local swimming pool. Sometimes the only scrap of reason you can find in a tragedy like that is that it reminds us we are still alive and helps us make the most of what we've got. I have never forgotten Ioanna, or the way she looked at me when I bought the necklace, or the fun she had playing at the lake that day. As long as I wear this necklace, Ioanna is still with me.

Children like Ioanna have made me committed to helping charities in Romania: I am in no doubt that my money has made a real difference to people's lives. I also know how important it is for charities to be able to plan projects for the long term, and to do that they need a regular, reliable income. So although I had made several one-off donations – including asking guests at my fiftieth birthday party to make donations to Unicef instead of buying me presents – I started a scheme to provide them with long-term funding. I asked members of my health clubs to make a voluntary donation of 25p a month on top of their membership to fund projects like Casa Bannatyne. I also tried to encourage other health-club operators to do the same, but they said their members weren't interested.

'That's funny,' I told them, 'because many of mine are happy to do so.'

That simple scheme now raises tens of thousands of pounds a year, which is the kind of money that goes a long way in Romania. It's enough to pay the salaries of several skilled workers who in turn can teach and train others, thereby helping Romania build its own future.

Towards the end of one of my trips to Targu Mures, Sister Marta and I stopped for a drink on the way back to the hospice. Even though we couldn't speak each other's language, I used sign language to buy her a couple of drinks, and when she wasn't looking I topped her glass up – I found out the next day that she had never been drunk in her life before! I felt a real connection to Sister Marta that I cannot put into words, and I know she felt it, too. On the morning of the last day of one of my trips to Targu Mures, she came to see me with the two interpreters we needed to communicate with words.

'Sister Marta says she wants to tell you something,' the translator said.

'What is it?'

Then, through three different languages, I got the following answer: 'Sister Marta wants you to know that she is going to pray for you every day for the rest of her life.'

I didn't know what to make of it, but I thanked her before saying goodbye.

Some months later, I was at the villa in France with Joanne and my two youngest, Emily and Tom, who'd been born in 2001 when I was fifty-two. Ibi Unger was also staying with us enjoying a well-earned break. We were having a wonderful family holiday until Emily told us that she'd hurt her ankle. Kids are always getting into scrapes, so we didn't worry about it too much. It always helps in these situations that Joanne is a nurse, and if she doesn't panic, neither do I. The following day though, Emily's knee was also hurting. We just assumed that she'd been walking funnily to

compensate for her ankle. On the next day, however, her *other* knee
started to hurt and we began to worry. We called ahead to our
doctor in England and made an appointment, and for the rest of the
holiday I carried Emily around.

The doctor diagnosed what Joanne had suspected: Emily had
juvenile arthritis. With the right drugs, we were told, it shouldn't
impact on her life too much and when she hits puberty the arthritis
will go. However, any damage the arthritis does to her joints will be
with her for life. Thankfully, the drugs have kept any damage to a
minimum, but the drugs are only part of her treatment as Emily also
needed physio. I used to get up early to give Emily a bath and
massage her legs before leaving for work, and because of this
treatment she was able to carry on at school when a lot of kids with
juvenile arthritis end up missing lessons.

About a week after we'd come home from France, I got an email
from Ibi in Romania asking how Emily was.

I typed back that she had been diagnosed with juvenile arthritis.

That's funny, she replied, I thought she would.

Ibi had been talking to Sister Marta, and Sister Marta had told her
that when she was a child, she had had juvenile arthritis.

Sometimes when life throws so many 'coincidences' at you, you
have to stop calling them that and find a better word for them.

THIRTY-ONE

From the sewers to the Palace
2002–05

It's easy to say what I put in, but it's impossible to say what I get out of it.

Since my first trip to Romania in 1996 the country has changed dramatically. It has been wonderful to see simple things like smiling children in clean clothes going to school, as I know what it took to affect such changes. When I visit now I'm amazed at the high standard of the hotels – even in a town like Targu Mures – and the influx of familiar high-street shops and products. The standard of living, education, housing and medical care has vastly improved, and it's easy to think that Romania is sorted now. It would be nice to think that every child had been rescued and was now being cared for in places like those run by Scottish International Relief, but stories still surface of forgotten institutes and forgotten children.

I took Hollie, my second eldest, with me one year so that she could see what her dad does when he goes away, but also to show her that there's still work to be done. For that same reason, I've also taken journalists with me to Romania a couple of times, so that we can keep shining a light on what are still some of the worst living conditions in Europe.

In 2002, the *Glasgow Herald* sent a photographer and, journalist with me, as I told them I could arrange for them to see a side of Romania no one wants to talk about any more. We would normally be escorted round institutions – some were the same old buildings, tarted up with a lick of paint, and some were brand new – but if we broke free from the party we'd often find neglected rooms where children were still tied to cots.

Angela Catlin, the photographer, and Lorna Martin, the reporter, were determined to get the full story and not just accept what the authorities told them.

I took them to the rubbish dump in Targu Mures where John Moreton and I had paid for some houses to be built for the Roma gypsies. Thanks to Ceausescu, the Roma had not been allowed to settle in Targu Mures, which he decreed an ethnically pure town, so they had been left to scavenge from the rubbish heap to make a living. We were chased off that rubbish tip by its manager, who didn't want the bad publicity, but Angela had a plan to go back at 6 a.m. the next day to get a photo.

'Oh sure, I'll come with you,' I offered, not really expecting her to be serious.

But the next morning, there she was, banging loudly on my door. I got dressed quickly and we took a taxi back to the dump. She was able to take a few photographs before the workers arrived and the manager again threatened us if we didn't leave. Angela wasn't going to be deterred, though, and she pointed to a nearby hill.

'If we go up there', she said, 'I'll get some shots of the entire site.'

So we climbed the hill and while she was working, the manager sent his JCBs to ram our taxi driver's car. He only just moved it out of the way in time, and it was enough for Angela to realise that maybe she had all the shots she needed.

Lorna was equally tenacious and had heard that many homeless children in Romania lived in the sewers because it was warmer than the streets. She wanted to go back to Glasgow with a report about what life was like for those kids in the sewers, so I told her I had some contacts who could help her get her story. I knew a girl in

Bucharest called Kristiana who had been a sewer kid herself and, thanks to the work of Unicef, she had got an education and now worked for the charity Parada. She said she would talk to the sewer children and get their permission.

Going into the sewers was dangerous, not because of the sewage or disease, but because of the lawlessness underground. Several of the kids were off their heads sniffing glue, which meant their behaviour could be anything from erratic to violent. And if they got physical, as many of them were HIV positive, the risk of blood contamination was a very real danger. If anything happened to us down there, no one could help. Our chaperone said it was too dangerous to go under the banner of Unicef, so I told her we would do it on our own.

We drove to the sewer and met some of the kids to get their approval before going down below. After talking to them, I asked Kristiana if it was safe: she just shrugged her shoulders. But Angela and Lorna wanted their story, and I had told them I would get it for them, so when the boys started taking off the manhole cover, I realised it was too late to back out. I looked down: there was just a ladder reaching down into the darkness.

'OK, Duncan,' Lorna said, 'you go first.'

Sometimes when you're showing off, especially to women, there's a moment when reality hits and the bravado goes. I realised I was absolutely terrified. I was wearing the oldest clothes I had – I never take anything new with me to Romania – and the slime on the walls was just millimetres from my jacket. As I carried on down the ladder the heat hit me, and as I was so nervous I started to sweat.

'Duncan! Hang on!' Angela shouted from above.

Thank fuck, I thought, she's realised it's too dangerous and is going to tell me to go back up.

'Here!' she shouted, 'Take one of my cameras.'

So I put a camera around my neck and carried on down the ladder. The deeper we went, the darker it got and the more frightened I became. When I reached the bottom, I could barely see a thing; I was just dimly aware of shapes moving in front of me.

'Shit,' I thought, 'If I get jumped now I'm dead.'

Kristiana followed behind me and lit a couple of candles so I could see that the wriggling shapes I'd seen were boys – twelve of them lying on the most filthy mattresses. All of them were just wearing underpants – filthy, dirty underpants – because the heat down there was incredible.

When Lorna and Angela joined us, we realised that one of the boys was in fact a girl. We'd mistaken her for a boy because she'd shaved her head and wore baggy clothes to make herself less attractive to the brokers who sold women into the sex trade. It also stopped her from getting nits and lice in her hair.

Lorna turned to me and said, 'I want to tell her story.'

We stayed down there for a couple of hours while Lorna interviewed her – oddly enough she spoke impeccable English – and Angela took a series of photos, one of which made the front page of the *Herald*. I'm very proud of the fact that I held the lights for that photo.

The girl's name was Kristina. From looking at her you'd think she was about fourteen, but she was actually twenty-two and had lived in the sewer for ten years with her boyfriend. She made a point of explaining that although she was the only girl, she slept with only one of them. It seemed odd at first to care about morals when her circumstances were so degrading, but on reflection it was the kind of information that brought her whole story to life.

Kristina was one of many young women I met in Romania who had gone into hospital to have a baby and left without it. They were told that the state was in a better position to take care of their children, and this was creating another generation of abandoned children. These women would say to me, 'I have baby, too,' and were very proud that they had had a child – presumably, this was still a hangover from Ceausescu's 'five baby' rule. But by the time Kristiana had her little boy, the authorities knew they couldn't cope with any more children and, in all likelihood – unbeknown to

Kristina – when she was in hospital she would probably have been sterilised. This was the story from just one sewer. Down manhole covers across Bucharest – and no doubt across Romania – there are hundreds of other children with similar stories to tell, and many of them are still there.

Angela, Lorna and I had a plane to catch, and we'd spent so long in the sewer that we didn't have time to change before going to the airport. I wanted to sit with them on the way back, so I asked if I could be downgraded to economy. However, the plane was full, though at least that meant I could use the business-class lounge where I picked up handfuls of complimentary sandwiches before rejoining the girls to wait for the flight.

When we got on the plane, one of the people sitting next to Angela and Lorna was very happy to swap seats with me, and as the three of us looked around at the other travellers in the cabin, we wondered if they could smell the sewers on us or see the lice crawling in our hair.

An honour

In April 2004, I was at home on my own when I went to collect the post from the mat, as I do every day I'm there. In among the usual junk mail and bills was a letter that read:

Dear Mr Bannatyne,
  The Prime Minister is minded to recommend you to the Queen to receive an OBE for services to business and charity . . .'

I couldn't believe it. I was absolutely astonished. I carried on reading and discovered that it was in recognition of my services to business and charity. But it was 'in confidence' and I couldn't tell anyone until an official announcement was made in June. This instantly made me think that I wouldn't get it. Perhaps it's got something to do with the way I was raised, but I've learned not to look forward to things. Even when Joanne says, 'Only another couple of days until we go on holiday, won't it be fantastic,' I find myself thinking, What if something happens? What if we don't go? So I hid the letter just in case anyone found it. But I was thrilled, and in the end I couldn't keep it to myself; after about three days I confided in Joanne.

You are only allowed to take three people with you to the palace, and I chose to take my mother and my two eldest daughters. It just so happened that the date the palace gave me – 26 October 2005 – was my mum's seventy-ninth birthday, so I booked flights for them all to come to London and rooms for us all at Claridges. My sister Anne had to come with my mum, as by then she was in a wheelchair and couldn't have made the journey alone. On the morning of the investiture, I told Anne to get dressed as if she was going to the palace to see if she would be let in, too.

We got a couple of cabs to the palace and got dropped outside, then we queued up with our passes. The guard checked our ID, and then realised that Anne didn't have a pass.

'Who are you?'

'I'm her nurse.'

'Very well then, enjoy your day.'

The investiture takes place in one of the function rooms at the palace that's guarded by soldiers with immaculate uniforms and shiny swords. It's quite a show, and because of mum's wheelchair, they all got front-row seats while I was taken off with the other recipients to a separate hall to be briefed on the etiquette of meeting the Queen. We were told that we would have to wait in line until we were ushered forward, and then when our names were called out, we were to walk forward and turn to face the Queen. We then had to bow and approach. Our cue to leave, we were told, was when she shook our hand. All the recipients then had pins put on their lapels so the Queen could just hang the medals on them rather than fussing about with pins.

When I stepped forward, I got the impression the Queen knew it was a big day for everybody there and didn't want to disappoint.

'How do you have time to combine business and charity?' she asked as she pinned the medal on.

'It's not that difficult ma'am,' I said. 'I get a lot of help from Unicef and have good people to run the business.'

She looked shocked and didn't know what to say, so she reached out to shake my hand. She has a very particular handshake that's friendly, but which also pushes you away!

That evening we all had a wonderful meal at Gordon Ramsay's restaurant in Claridges, and my mum and daughters told me how proud they were of me. I knew that, had my dad been alive, he would have been proud, too. It was a wonderful day.

I still visit Romania once a year, but I have also become involved in other projects elsewhere in the world, through Magnus and SIR. I went to have a meeting with him in Scotland to talk about future projects, and he picked me up from the airport saying he knew a great place to take me to lunch. We drove to a branch of the Loch Fyne restaurants, and as we approached I remembered the lunch John Moreton had bought me in the Strand, when I'd told him about Lorridana.

Over the course of lunch Magnus showed me some leaflets he'd had produced to help with fundraising in Africa. On the front of one of them, he'd used a photo from one of SIR's other projects. It was a very dark-skinned girl, but I knew she wasn't African.

'That little girl's Romanian,' I told him.

'Really?'

'That little girl is Lorridana. I know her.'

It felt like another sign. What are the chances that the two times in my life I eat in a Loch Fyne restaurant the same little girl becomes the focus of the conversation? I know it's probably just a coincidence, but it doesn't feel that way. It feels meant, and for that reason I'm now committed to a number of Magnus's projects.

One of my recent donations has paid for an orphanage to be built in Colombia for street children. I've also visited Malawi with Magnus, where the poverty is of an altogether different nature. There are people living in rural villages days away from hospitals or centres of government, and the projects SIR is aiding are small local services that make a real difference to people's lives. One of them is Mary's Meals, a tiny idea with a huge impact. Children are given lunch if they go to school – not only does this encourage attendance, but as hungry children can't concentrate, it also improves learning. Mary's Meals provides the food if the local community will volunteer to cook it. It's a ridiculously cheap programme – to feed a child for a year only costs about £5.

It really is a privilege to be involved with the charities I work with, and meeting people like Sister Marta, Ibi, Magnus and Kristiana is a constant reminder of how lucky I am. It's easy to say what I put in, but it's impossible to say what I get out of it. In an odd way, I am now both more impatient and patient at the same time: I am impatient with people who complain about their easy lives, and I am more patient with people who face real difficulties. I may have had my heart broken by some of the things I've seen, but ultimately I am happier for being involved and for knowing that some of my money has made a profound difference to a few people's lives.

THIRTY-TWO

An actor's life for me?
2002–05

---

*I was desperate to find a new way
of expressing myself.*

In 2002, I took Joanne to a charity auction where she encouraged me to bid on one particular lot: a walk-on part in Guy Ritchie's film *Revolver.* I don't know why I thought it would be fun, but I did, and for some reason something about acting really appealed to me. It was a time in my life when everything was stable: Bannatyne Fitness was reaching a plateau, my family was large enough and I had more money than I could ever spend, so I think I was just looking for something else.

Joanne and I joked that Guy would recognise me as such a huge talent that he'd offer me a bigger part, but it was a joke that got out of hand and I began to think I might really like a new career. It took Joanne a while to realise that I'd stopped joking, and once she knew I was serious, I think she thought I'd gone mad.

'Duncan,' she'd say, 'you're a very successful businessman. A very well-known businessman at that. You can't just jack it all in and become an actor – that's crazy.'

'But the business pretty much runs itself,' I'd say, 'and it's not as if I would never be around. Nigel and Tony could call me whenever they needed something.'

After several similar conversations, she began to realise there was no changing my mind. I realise now that it was very difficult for Joanne to see me in a new light: ever since she'd known me I'd been single-minded, probably not that artistic, and dedicated to my career. But eventually she came to see that I had spent so long running the business I'd almost lost my identity to it and was desperate to find a new way of expressing myself. To show that she supported my decision, Joanne booked me into a month-long intensive drama course at the New York Academy of Acting, which, not so glamorously, was held at King's College in London.

This period of self-reflection led to Joanne and me reassessing our relationship, and although we've always remained good friends – and devoted parents to Tom and Emily – we decided that we weren't getting what we wanted out of the relationship. She has since told me that she thought I needed to sow some wild oats and break out of my mould: I'd had a life of duty to my family and businesses for so long that I needed to go a little wild, and she was prepared to let me go so I could do just that. We separated and came to an amicable financial settlement that gave her enough money to buy a home for the kids, with something left over to start a business of her own, a boutique she set up with her sister Jacqueline. I carried on living in our wonderful house in Darlington called The Lindens, but after a few months there on my own, I realised it was full of memories and put it on the market.

I enjoyed the course at the New York Academy so much that I signed up for summer school at RADA. It was one the most enjoyable things I've ever done. There were people on the course from all over the world who, like me, were doing something they'd secretly wanted to do for years; others were well established as actors in their own countries and there were a few who thought they were in *Fame*. None of them knew I was rich, and I told them I was staying on a friend's floor when in fact I was staying in a five-star hotel. Together, we did a bit of Shakespeare, a bit of modern drama and a lot of drinking in the student union bar.

Our tutor, an actor named Greg de Polnay, gave us plenty of

advice, and one of the things he taught us was that we stood a far greater chance of getting work if we lived in London. He explained that most productions happen in London, and as it's standard for production companies to send cars for the 'talent', if you didn't live in London, sending a car would be too expensive. So I did what any millionaire in search of an acting career would do: I bought a flat in London. It's little more than a bolt hole, but it's right next to Home House, a private members' club where I can get breakfast and use the gym.

I also bought a house round the corner from Joanne on the Wynyard housing development in the north-east. It's the kind of estate where you're quite likely to bump into a Newcastle United footballer in the video shop, but despite the high profile of many of my neighbours, my house is surprisingly modest. If *OK!* or *Hello!* ever want to do a shoot, they'd have to go to my place in Cannes.

Looking back, I can see that perhaps my interest in acting wasn't as much of a surprise to me as it was to many people who knew me at the time. As a kid, I had been a bit of a showman, putting on magic shows for the Boys' Brigade and, as an adult, some of my after-dinner speaking, not to mention some of my presentations to the City, had involved a fair bit of acting. I've been in several student films and had quite a few paid acting gigs, including a small part in the Kelly Brook film *School for Seduction*, a pilot for a soap called *Girls Club* set in the north-east, and playing 'the accused' in an episode of *55 Degrees North* on the BBC. I also had a part in a Unicef information film that I funded about child exploitation, which was shown all over the world at Unicef events. Robbie Williams, who is a Unicef ambassador, screened it at his legendary Knebworth gigs and I was invited along to one of them. Just after the film was shown, I got a text from my brother.

Just seen you in a film, he texted.

Where are you? I texted back.

Knebworth.

Whereabouts?

Right at the front.

With 250,000 people there it proved impossible for us to find each other, but it was nice that he had seen the film.

By far my biggest role was as a gangster who drowns in an episode of the BBC drama *Sea of Souls*, and it was a part I really had to fight for. 'I want to do this,' I told the director, 'because it's filming underwater. I have a real connection to the water. I can stay down there for hours at a time while you set up shots. No one else will drown as well as me.' It was an odd promise, but it got me the job.

By the time *Sea of Souls* – a drama about paranormal investigators from a Scottish university – was broadcast, I was already well known from two series of *Dragons' Den*. While most of the critics – rather worryingly, I guess – thought I was pretty convincing as an underworld crime boss, a few of them said it was distracting to see a Dragon as an actor. And that's part of the reason why my acting career was so short: my reality TV career became too high profile for casting directors to take me seriously.

I would have loved for my acting career to have amounted to something bigger, but I recognise that acting is something you have to dedicate yourself to, and even if I was prepared to do that, the fact is there aren't that many parts written for men my age. I recently got a postcard from my good friend Sir Roger Moore that said, 'If there's any good parts for an old man . . . let me know. I work cheap.' If he's having trouble, I thought that maybe I should concentrate on something else.

THIRTY-THREE

Enter the dragon
2004–

A wise man once told me that the only time you enjoy your own plane is the day you buy it and the day you sell it!

Over the past few years, British television has become obsessed with business programming in the way that property programmes took over the airwaves in the late nineties. *The Apprentice*, a spin-off of Donald Trump's show in the States, has been a big success for Amstrad boss Alan Sugar; *Make Me a Million* on Channel 4 made a star of my good friend Chris Gorman and other self-made millionaires Ivan Massow and Emma Harrison; even daytime TV has a successful makeover show called *Mind Your Own Business* that I took part in where failing companies are turned round with expert help. And then, of course, there's *Dragons' Den*, a show that's been so successful it's shown in schools to help teach entrepreneurialism.

The format for *Dragons' Den* came from Japan and is now shown around the world, proving that it's not just the Brits who are starting businesses in ever-increasing numbers. When I was first told about the format, I thought it would make terrific television: a budding entrepreneur looking for investment pitches his business idea to five 'dragons', who put up their own money in exchange for a percentage of the company. It's very simple, but it lays bare the horrors of the pitch for the entrepreneur and gives insights into how five extremely successful investors assess an opportunity. If I hadn't been asked to be a dragon, I would have watched it anyway.

I was approached by the producers, David Tibballs and Martyn Smith, as a friend of theirs had directed me when I'd acted in *Girls Club*. David and Martyn came to audition me at Home House in London. They wanted to explain that if I became a dragon, I really would be expected to put my own money into businesses: I told them I would be absolutely delighted if the show introduced me to new ways to make money. Obviously there would be a risk, but the potential rewards – both in terms of finances and profile – were sizeable. I explained to them that I had already put my own money into businesses like Alpha Radio and New Life Care Services and turned them around, and I was convinced I had something to offer new businesses in addition to my cash.

I liked them both and felt we could work together, and a few months later I got the call from the BBC to ask about my availability for recording. I was invited to TV Centre for a run-through so the producers could see how all the proposed dragons interacted and experiment with the format. Doug Richard, Peter Jones and Rachel Elnaugh were also there, as was a fifth dragon who didn't make it to the final version. I hadn't met any of them before and my first impressions were that they were all bright, astute and good fun.

There were five seats lined up and I think there was a moment when we thought there'd be some competition for the middle seat – I think everyone thought it was the best location at first, although I don't any more – but the producers had already worked out what order they wanted us to sit in. Once we were in position, they brought in our first victim.

I wish I could remember what their business proposition was, but all I can recall is that all of the dragons thought it was a hoax and that some junior member of the production team was filling in to see our reactions. What we discovered was that, left to our own devices, the dragons would butt in whenever they got the chance and talk over each other, so we established some rules and worked out that we would take it in turns to start the questioning.

It was difficult to get a sense on the day of how the show would come across on camera, but as I was learning things from the other dragons, I figured the viewers would be learning something, too. When I finally got the call to say that the show had been commissioned by the controller of BBC2 and that we were going into production, I had a real sense that my life was going to change: I knew it was a show that would get noticed.

Before filming could start, I needed to sign a contract with the BBC, and it was clear that we weren't going to be paid like supermodels. The BBC couldn't afford to pay our normal day rate, but as none of us were doing it for the fee, that didn't really matter. What did matter to me, though, was that none of the other dragons would get paid more than me, so my agent at the time, Phillip Chard, suggested inserting what's known as a 'favoured nations' clause preventing the BBC from paying anyone more than they paid me. One of the dragons – it would be indiscreet to name names – often claims to be paid more than the rest of us. I don't bother to disagree as I know it can't be true.

There was something else I wanted to do before I started filming: I wanted to get a bit of voice coaching, as I know my accent sometimes makes me hard to understand, especially as I speak so quickly. I asked my tutor from RADA, Greg de Polnay, if he would help me out. He identified that, like a lot of Scottish men, my problem is that I tend to drop consonants, so he coached me with some tongue twisters and gave me a few techniques to even up my speech. Although it helped, the crew still tell me they have problems with my accent in the editing suite.

We filmed the first series in late 2004 in Stoke Newington, north London. A car arrived at my London flat at seven o'clock in the morning and took me to what appeared to be an abandoned warehouse. As soon as I saw the girls with clipboards – for some reason they're always in attendance at every production – I knew I was in the right place. The room we were to film in was huge and I instantly realised how intimidating it would be for an entrepreneur to try to fill the space while five dragons scrutinised them from the far side. It was only when I got there that I found out my old friend Simon Woodroffe, the founder of Yo! Sushi and all things Yo, had come on board as the fifth dragon.

Meet the dragons

I had met Simon Woodroffe a few years previously at a brainstorming session organised by the then Education Secretary Charles Clarke to discuss ways of encouraging entrepreneurship. I'm pretty sure I had been invited because, in 1997, I'd pledged £10,000 a year for five years to the Labour party. Simon stood out at the meeting, not just because of his bright red jacket, but because of his demeanour, which I would describe as casually eccentric. I then bumped into him again at a party at Richard Branson's house, which he organises annually for the UK's 100 fastest-growing companies. Simon didn't recognise me, but as Simon had a camera crew following him round, I decided to get him talking anyway and find out why he was being filmed. By the end of the conversation I realised I really liked the guy, but I'd forgotten to ask why he had the cameras with him. It was only afterwards, when the director asked me to sign what's known as a release form, so they could use the footage of our conversation, that I found out.

They were making a series called *Mind of a Millionaire*, in which psychologists analysed the behaviour of self-made millionaires to see if we shared certain traits.

'I don't mind signing it,' I said to the director, 'but why are you filming him and not me?'

'Well who are you?' she asked. My MD, Nigel Armstrong, who had come with me to the party, filled her in on the details.

'Well why don't you give me your card, then, we might need another millionaire for the show.'

She later told me she had been so intrigued by my card, which just had my name and number on it, that she thought I would be a good addition to the line-up. During the course of *Mind of a Millionaire*, as well as getting to know Simon a bit better, we all took part in a series of experiments to see if the psychologists could separate us from nine-to-fivers by our actions, and I'm pleased to say I was singled out as a serial entrepreneur. By the time we started on *Dragons' Den* together I'd got to know Simon fairly well.

Like me, Simon left it fairly late in life to make his way in business – he was in his forties when he started Yo! Sushi after being involved in a handful of less successful ventures. He's such a positive person that it was always going to happen for him – he really is one of the nicest, friendliest entrepreneurs I've ever met, and I knew he'd bring a sense of fun to the show. Needless to say, we became good drinking buddies during filming.

I never found out why the producers wanted to put Doug in the middle chair. Maybe there was something about his sober appearance that they thought would anchor the show. Whatever their reasons, it turned out to suit his personality, which is a bit measured and middle of the road.

Doug is a Californian who runs a firm called Library House, which invests in hi-tech businesses, and I discovered within hours of working with him that he has an amazing ability to assess a business idea: he's a terrific analyst. It took me a little while to realise that he found it difficult to say something in ten words if he could use a hundred – the complete opposite to me. He was incredibly impressive, but I also got the impression that he wasn't a typical SMEM, an acronym I've coined for Self-Made Entrepreneur Millionaires. Maybe it's just the way he dresses, which is pretty conservative, but I still think there's something of the bank manager about Doug.

I think Doug and I complemented each other well on the panel. We had made our fortunes in completely different fields in completely different ways, and because of that we often had our own investment criteria and assessed opportunities from divergent angles. I recognised he was someone I could learn from. Doug didn't take part in the third series, but we've stayed in touch and meet for the odd dinner.

Rachel Elnaugh was introduced to me as the founder and majority shareholder of Red Letter Days, a unique gift company with a valuation at the time of around £20 million. There's been some speculation – especially since her company went into administration in 2005 – that she was the token woman, but it was never like that. Her background is accountancy and I considered her a very astute and clever woman, who made an excellent contribution to the show. I didn't know much about Red Letter Days at the time, although I was dimly aware of a story in the papers about how she'd spent a large amount on a national advertising campaign, which she hadn't been able to recoup in revenue. Of course, I made it my business to find out as much as I could about all the other dragons' businesses once it was clear we'd be working together for a while.

That said, I've never really worked out how fellow dragon Peter Jones's company makes its money, but then his field is technology, which is something I freely admit is not my strongest subject. What I understood very well, however, was that his company had an incredibly high turnover of about £250 million, albeit with a very low profit margin. In a few years' time, I should imagine he'll be worth more than the rest of us put together, thanks to a deal he's done with ITV to produce and star in TV shows like *The Inventor*. He had an amazing ability to find the pun and brought something really different to the line-up.

I also met Evan Davis on the first day of filming. As well as being the host for *Dragons' Den*, Evan is the BBC's highly respected economics editor. He's not how I imagined the BBC's economics editor to be – sober, serious and dull – he's incredibly know-ledgeable, and when you hear him talk about global economics he's unbelievably impressive. I also happen to think he's terrific on *Dragons' Den*, effortlessly explaining jargon and interpreting the dynamics of individual pitches.

In the second series of *Dragons' Den* – which went out within a few months of the first series because it had proved so popular – Simon Woodroffe was replaced by Theo Paphitis. I was disappointed that Simon didn't come back for series two because he brought something different to the mix, and he was a great peacemaker if tensions ran high. He didn't come back because, like all of us, he found himself with plenty of lucrative offers to do after-dinner speaking and was just too busy. He was also working on plans for a hotel – called Yotel, of course – as well as rolling out more sushi restaurants.

Theo couldn't have been more different from Simon. He aggressively pursued investments and really turned up the heat in the den. There was no doubt he was a brilliant addition to the show. His retail experience gives him real insight into how a product will be packaged and sold, and I've learned a lot from listening to him during the series. Without his arrival, I guess there was a chance that we would have rested on our laurels, but Theo made sure we stayed on our toes. He shook things up and invested in more businesses in one series than some of us managed in two.

I didn't know he would be the new dragon until the night before we started filming, when we all met for dinner, and I must confess I hadn't heard of him before. That night I went home and Googled him and found out that not only was he one of the country's best retailers, he was also chairman of Millwall Football Club. I liked Theo from the moment we met. He's an incredibly witty guy, very sharp and great company. I think he breathed new life into *Dragons' Den* and made us all realise that the show can be more successful with different dragons. It made me hope that they change the line-up for every series, as it helps keep things fresh and dynamic.

I understand that the BBC also interviewed a selection of women to replace Rachel for the second series, as rumours that her business was in trouble had started before filming began. However, Rachel convinced the producers her business was robust, and as it happened, none of the other women they auditioned quite fitted the bill. Of course, it wasn't just Rachel's business difficulties that made her a problematic choice for the second series: when we started filming she was eight months pregnant and could have left the show at any moment. As a back-up the BBC lined up a substitute, Australian millionaire Richard Farleigh, who came off the subs' bench for the third series. During the second series he patiently waited in the background for several days, just in case Rachel's waters broke.

At the time of writing, the third series of *Dragons' Den* hasn't been shown, but it's my hunch that when it airs, Richard will become incredibly popular. He made his fortune working for an investment bank, where he talent-spotted technology companies and prepared them for flotation. He had famously made enough money at thirty-four to retire to the tax haven of Monte Carlo, but he couldn't keep away, and has continued to invest in UK companies privately, including Home House, the club next to my London flat. He's an enormously likeable guy and good fun to have around. When we finished filming the second series, the schedule overran on the last day as the crew made sure they had all the shots they needed to edit the series together. As the afternoon dragged on, I noticed Richard looking at his watch a lot.

'Have you got to be somewhere?' I asked him.

'I live in Monte Carlo and I've got a plane to catch,' he explained.

'Where are you flying from?' I asked.

'Heathrow.'

'Forget about your flight,' I told him. 'I've got a private jet waiting for me at City Airport – I'll give you a lift as I'm going to my villa in Cannes.'

I should point out that it's not *my* plane. I've never seen the point of owning your own plane, or your own yacht for that matter. A wise man once told me that the only time you enjoy your own plane is the day you buy it and the day you sell it! I subscribe to NetJets to get me around Europe quickly, paying a flat fee of £85,000 a year in return for thirty flying hours.

When we got on the plane, Richard and I found it didn't take us long to polish of a bottle of wine. In fact, it didn't take us long to finish *two* bottles between us. And with a couple of vodka chasers, by the time we landed in France I was sure he would be an excellent dragon and a good mate. I've not been proved wrong and he and his family have since joined my family and me for dinner at my villa.

The third series also saw the arrival in the den of Deborah Meaden, following Rachel's withdrawal from the programme. I hadn't met Deborah until we started filming, as our paths had never crossed. She made her money in completely different fields – holiday parks, ceramics and fashion franchises and has proven she can turn her hand to different situations from taking over the family business to starting things from scratch. Personality-wise, she's incredibly down to earth, strong-willed and sensible, and she's great at cutting to the chase.

Changing the line-up keeps everyone on their toes – even the entrepreneurs who come to pitch to us. In the second series, it was very obvious that everyone who came before us had seen the show and knew what to expect. They'd also done their research on each of us and tried to second guess what we'd be interested in, so introducing new dragons makes it a bit more unpredictable. I think after three series it's clear the producers really know how to put a panel together. But then I would say that – they've asked me to take part in all three series!

The producers have also been great at making sure that a wide range of business opportunities keep coming into the den to keep the programme interesting. As I write, we've been filming series three and in the past few weeks we've seen everything from disposable toilet seat covers, to baseball cap retail outlets, to a new range of doggie clothing, to a seatbelt safety device and a hairdressing salon just for children. That kind of variety makes great TV. If the producers can keep finding such a good line-up of dragons, and such varied business proposals, then I think it's a format that could run for many years to come.

THIRTY-FOUR

Into the den
2004

---

*Angel investment is high risk,
as you're usually investing in untried
products or untried entrepreneurs.*

The first entrepreneur who appeared on screen in the first series was a guy called Graham Whitby. He wasn't actually the first person to pitch, as the shows are edited out of sequence, but I completely understand why the producers decided to start with him: he made terrific telly. He came up the stairs into the den and started pretty well.

'I'm Graham Whitby and I'm the managing director of the Baby Dream Machine and er . . . er . . . um . . .' and then he just lost it. The five of us sat there willing him to regain some composure.

'Er . . . let me start again. I'm a father of three . . . Oh dear . . . I will start again . . .'

Pitching for investment is stressful enough, but doing it in front of the cameras can be too much for some people. Evan has since told me that there's even something physiological about walking *up* the stairs into the den that makes a nervous heart beat harder, and you can see that strain on some of their faces.

It was clear that Graham wasn't going to be able to continue, so he was joined by his partner, a chubby-faced northerner called Barry

Haigh who uttered the immortal line: 'I'm Barry Haigh the inventor who invented this.' They were not an impressive pair, but the fact was we could all see that their invention had potential, so we coaxed the information out of them.

The Baby Dream Machine is a patented device that rocks a cot or pushchair in such a way that a baby is more than likely to fall asleep. All of the dragons at that time were parents and we'd all experienced nights when we'd all have loved to have had something to ensure a bit of peace and quiet. I think it's safe to say that we were all interested in investing in the idea, if not in them.

'You don't have to sell the product,' I told them. 'We all think it's a good idea: just tell us about the investment.'

They found this even harder than telling us about the product. I have found that the longer a pitcher talks about the problem their device solves, the less attractive the investment. Entrepreneurs are told to prepare a three-minute pitch for the dragons, and when someone spends two and a half minutes telling us how awful it is to have a wobbly table in a restaurant – do you remember the Stable Table? – the less time they have to tell us what we want to know: how good the investment is.

Barry and Graham took forever to talk about the money, and like all good yarns, theirs had an incredible punchline: they wanted £100,000 but only wanted to give away 5 per cent of the company! We thought they were joking. There are very few investors who would take 5 per cent, and none of the dragons were takers at that price.

'How can you justify giving away such a small amount of equity?' we asked.

Somehow they had calculated that in three or four years' time the company would be worth more than £600 million – that's practically the combined wealth of all the dragons put together – and none of us believed them. I don't know whether they were confused abut the difference between turnover and profit or about the size of the global market, but there's no way their company was going to be worth anything like that. At that point they became uninvestable and we all backed out.

Graham and Barry were the only people to come back for the second series of *Dragons' Den*, and on their second appearance they repeated many of their mistakes. First they showed us a video of their machine rocking a baby to sleep, which was a complete waste of time as we already knew the product worked. They had also significantly lowered their valuation for the second appearance, but it was still ludicrously high in my opinion. Although they had a great product, they were still unconvincing as entrepreneurs – there was something about their business that didn't add up, and yet again they left the den with nothing.

My concern with businesses like theirs is that, although they have a patent, it's the kind of opportunity that can easily be taken away by a rival. A patent only covers the mechanism of the Baby Dream Machine, not the idea of a machine that rocks babies to sleep. While they arsed around with unconvincing pitches, which were being watched by millions of viewers, let's not forget, the chances of someone else developing a rival product increased. And, of course, that's just what happened – between the first and second series, a similar device went on sale, and that significantly lowered their valuation in an investor's eyes.

I've never had a patent in my career, and when it became clear that several of the investment opportunities on *Dragons' Den* would involve new products, I did my homework and found out the implications of patent laws, discovering that they offer little protection from market forces. A good product isn't enough – you also need a good business plan and a determined leader.

Barry was certainly that, and after filming he and his wife came to visit me at my office in Darlington, still hopeful that they could turn my interest in their invention into interest in their business. As they sat across the desk from me, I realised that their figures were never going to add up. By this stage their money had practically run out and they were offering me 50 per cent of the company for £200,000.

It was the kind of offer that got my attention.

'OK, then,' I said, 'let's look at the figures.'

He started to tell me, but then drifted off on some tangent.

'The figures, Barry. Just tell me about the figures.'

Then his wife butted in to tell me more about the invention.

'Look, I know about the machine – I *like* the machine – I want to know about the *money*.'

At some point one of them managed to tell me that if I put the money in, I'd get 8 per cent of the royalties.

'I don't understand, if I own fifty per cent of the company, why do I only get eight per cent of the royalties?'

'You get fifty per cent of the profits, yes . . .' and then they went off on another tangent.

'Stop it. Just tell me about this eight per cent figure. I want to understand how it's calculated.'

Eventually, Barry confessed that to keep the company going he'd given away royalties in exchange for investment. The company owned only 16 per cent of the royalties, so my 50 per cent share in the business equated to 8 per cent of the company's most valuable asset.

His wife would get 20 per cent, another friend would get 25 per cent, and somewhere down at the bottom would be me. I'd own 50 per cent of the company, but only 8 per cent of the rights. I showed them the door.

How to get it wrong

The next investment opportunity shown on screen was Art Out There, a music festival organised by an arrogant young man called Gavin Drake. At first he seemed articulate and confident, but we soon downgraded our assessment to mouthy and cocky. His was a difficult concept for us to understand and the best we could come up with was that Art Out There was some kind of pop concert.

Gavin told us more than once that he had a contract with Pizza Express, presumably to do the catering at the proposed event on Clapham Common in south London. Peter asked to see the contract, which Gavin duly presented. After reading it, Peter announced 'That's no more a contract than my Aunt Sally!' Gavin basically had a letter from Pizza Express, which anyone could have got, saying that they would do the catering if he paid them to attend. Only once their takings reached a certain level would he share in their profits. He had a similarly useless letter from the licensing committee of the local council. I have never forgotten Gavin's ridiculous reply, 'I never said that contract was a contract.'

At one point Rachel tried to ask him a question, to which Gavin said, 'Just a minute,' and carried on talking to Peter. I could see Rachel stiffen in the chair next to me and I knew she wouldn't be happy being spoken to like that. One by one we all said 'I'm out' until only Rachel was left. Gavin turned to her expectantly.

'That was a long a minute,' she said quietly.

He didn't know what she was getting at.

'I tried to talk to you thirty minutes ago and you said, "Just a minute." I've been waiting for you to come back to me. I don't like you, you were rude to me and I don't like working with people who are rude. I'm out.'

With no one left, Gavin gathered up his papers and bounced down the stairs for his debriefing with Evan full of I'll-show-you bravado.

'Thank you for the criticism,' he said, 'it's been very helpful.'

It's amazing to me how many people leave the den feeling that the five of us are idiots and that we must be wrong in the head for passing on the opportunity of a lifetime. Some people are rude, others are evasive and some are just bonkers. One, I'm quite sure, was drunk. I'm often asked who has given the worst pitch on *Dragons' Den*, and although there have been several awful presentations, one stands out as the biggest loser. Some of the other dragons may remember her pitch differently, but this is how I remember Gayle Blanchflower and her crazy business idea.

Gayle told us she had spent £60,000 on the worldwide rights to cardboard beach furniture.

'What happens if it rains?' I asked.

She looked at me with what appeared to be pure hatred in her eyes.

'You don't go to the beach if it rains, stupid.'

I didn't much like being called stupid.

'So what happens if my little boy Tom comes out of the sea and sits on the chair?'

Again, she looked at me with a look that could pierce skin.

'Well tell him not to. Discipline your children.'

Funnily enough, she left the den without any investment.

Journalists often ask me if I'd feel foolish if one of the ideas I rejected on the show went on to become a big success. I can say categorically that I won't, and if my criticism has been the spur for someone to prove me wrong then I'll be very happy indeed. Angel investment is high risk, as you're usually investing in untried products or untried entrepreneurs, but with high risks you tend to get high returns, and if you invest early in the right company, you can make a substantial amount of money. It's not a method of investment everyone is comfortable with: some very wealthy people put their money into long-term bonds and are happy to tie them up for years. It's no coincidence that all the dragons are entrepreneurs themselves – we are very risk tolerant.

Angel investment is very fluid, and the conditions that make a company investible change by the month as markets and opportunities mature and alter. Investment isn't an exact science and it's likely that we'll all turn down a great opportunity at some point in the show, but what represents a bad opportunity for me might be perfect for another investor. However, as the five dragons usually have different investment criteria, the chances are that one of us would respond to a good product or company when pitched by a competent entrepreneur.

Peter, for example, is extremely knowledgeable about technology, and if you look at the companies he's invested in, you'll see that there's usually a technological side to them. Even Truly Madly Baby, the clothing company he put money into in the second series, was setting up as an online retailer. Like me, I think Peter would love to invest in someone who went on to become a millionaire because of the show. He likes the idea that anyone with a good idea can make it.

Doug also knows a lot about technology, but he seemed to have a wider set of criteria, and as a professional investor – it's what he does when he's not on TV – he was always very focused on looking for a quick return on his capital. I often heard him say that eight out of ten businesses he invested in would lose money, but the other two would make him rich. I think he had an eye out for a really big company to invest his money in.

Simon looks at investment opportunities differently. In Yo! he has an extremely valuable brand, and he was on the lookout for companies that he could add his Yo! magic to. Like the Virgin brand that adorns retail empires, train companies and airlines, Simon saw that he could add a bit of Yo! to a wide range of sectors. Sadly, no one who came into the den left with the Yo! stamp of approval.

It's fair to say that I never really got a firm idea of what Rachel's investment criteria were. She frequently said on camera that she would only invest in companies she understood, but I never understood her motives as they changed from day to day. Theo's criteria were much clearer, however: as a first-class retailer, he looks for products he can sell either through his own chains or other people's. He quickly grasps how something will be packaged, priced and displayed, regardless of what it is. Theo also wants to invest in people. If he believes in you, he's more likely to believe in your pitch.

In series three, Richard Farleigh shared some of Theo's instincts. Richard has been described in the press as 'Britain's most prolific investor in private companies', so he's clearly interested in a broad range of companies, and for him it also comes down to the people.

Outside of *Dragons' Den*, he'll usually meet potential partners several times before he invests, taking the time to get to know them. Richard differs from the rest of us in that he is also on the lookout for companies he can take towards a stock-market flotation. It's something he's done with several of his investments, and he understands brilliantly how the City will assess an opportunity and, consequently, it's an area where he can add a lot of value.

Deborah Meaden also wants to add value and is quite prepared to do this by getting her hands dirty. She's got the time to really get involved if she believes in a proposition, and she clearly loves running businesses. I've found it fascinating how each of us have responded to the pitches, and because we all look at propositions differently, there have been several occasions when my opinion of an investment has been changed by a question from one of the other dragons. I've learned so much from them: no matter how long you've been in business, or how successful you are, there are so many ways to make a business work that you never stop learning. Sitting next to the dragons for the past few years has been a real education.

And how to get it right . . .

The producers picked fantastic pitches to put in the first show, and there's one that still sticks in people's memories: Charles Ejogo, the Umbrolly man. I don't think I was the only dragon who thought Charles, a former management consultant, had presented a very intriguing business opportunity in a very impressive way. I think I can speak for all the dragons when I say we thought we were looking at a future millionaire. Charles told us, concisely and precisely, that he wanted to put umbrella vending machines on the London Underground. That on its own was a nice enough business idea, but the part of his plan that really got us interested was that his vending machines would have TV screens in them which could show adverts. And to make the deal even more appealing, he told us he already had a contract from London Underground. We were almost fighting for the chance to invest the £150,000 he wanted: the only negotiation was about the percentage of the company we would get.

Peter was the first to express an interest – he was sure the mobile phone companies he was involved with would pay to get their adverts on to the Underground and he offered to put up half the money for 22 per cent of the company. I matched his offer, thinking that between us we would make Charles a huge success story, and in doing so secure a reputation for *Dragons' Den* as a great forum for entrepreneurs.

But Charles had walked into the den only wanting to give away 20 per cent of his company. We reasoned with him that he was a young man and he had a great opportunity to work with two experienced entrepreneurs who would help him build up his company more quickly than he could do alone. With us, we told him, you'll be a multimillionaire within a couple of years, and when we sell Umbrolly for a huge profit, you can start another business and begin amassing some serious wealth. He was tempted, and as he realised his dream was within grasp, he started to sweat profusely. The tension was amazing.

He told us that 44 per cent was too high, so Doug entered the fray and said that he was prepared to put up the entire £150,000 and asked Charles to make him an offer on the percentage. Under pressure, and obviously keen to do a deal, Charles offered 35 per cent of the company. Doug shook his head.

Then Peter did something that really got *Dragons' Den* noticed and led to me getting a reputation as a tough operator. He offered to put in the £75,000 for a 20 per cent stake. Charles turned to me, fully expecting me to match Peter's offer, but the investment opportunity hadn't changed so I didn't see any reason to reduce my stake. Peter looked over at me to see if I was bluffing, but I wasn't.

'Are you sure I can't persuade you to change your offer,' Charles asked.

I shook my head.

So he did the deal for 42 per cent and the three of us shook hands. But as Charles went downstairs to talk to Evan, the microphones picked up Peter saying, 'I think I've been had.'

He was not a happy man and accused me of being a 'sly little shit' that he didn't want to do business with. What he should have said was, 'You got two per cent more than me, well done', and I would probably have offered to split it with him and take 21 per cent each. There will always be differing opinions on the rights and wrongs of that situation, but it was clear that even if we worked together Peter, and possibly Charles, could be demotivated, so I asked Charles to come back and see us. Unsurprisingly, he was happy for me to give him back that 2 per cent.

There are still people who think of me as the 22 per cent guy. It made terrific viewing and the day after the first edition went out, I had people come up to me in the street and telling me I should have held on to the extra 2 per cent. When I went out for a coffee on Marylebone High Street around the corner from my London flat, the guy who ran the coffee shop refused to take my money as he wanted some business advice instead. I guess I should have been amazed at the immediate recognition I got – after all this was a show about business on BBC2 – but it had been clear during filming that this was a programme people would talk about. When the entrepreneurs left the room, some of the production crew turned to us and said, 'Why didn't you invest in that?' Or 'Why on earth would you give your money to him?' I could tell from their questions that non-business people were going to engage with the show.

With so many competitive people on the panel, inevitably there can be some rivalry and bickering, and the fact is that, under the lights, it can be quite stressful for us as well as the people pitching, especially after a twelve-hour day filming. But when the cameras stop rolling, we become very sociable and often go out for a drink. If we weren't all so busy, we might even see a bit more of each other.

THIRTY-FIVE

When the cameras stop rolling

Investment is about putting money in and getting more money out. It's amazing how many people don't realise that.

Anyone who saw the update show that followed the entrepreneurs who'd entered the dragons' den will know that Peter and I didn't end up investing in Umbrolly after all. What the cameras don't show you is that after the pitch we spend a lot of time with the entrepreneur to make sure everything they've told us about our investment is true. With Charles Ejogo, it turned out that the situation wasn't quite as good as we had thought.

'Due diligence' is the legal process through which an investor assesses the potential investment. Everything from the structure of the company to the validity of the patent is scrutinised before we put our money in. It can be a lengthy process and may take six months or more to complete.

The first thing I asked Charles was to see his contract with London Underground. It was 183 pages long and it made for very interesting reading. Before agreeing to invest I had asked Charles if he would have to pay to put his machines in tube stations, and he had told me that he wouldn't. Yet the contract said that he would

266

have to pay £2,000 rent per year per machine – to be fair he probably misunderstood my question. What was worse was that the contract also said that when he had more than fifty machines he would have to pay a huge one-off fee of £1 million to Cadbury's, who have a preferential vending contract with London Underground. I was instantly less inclined to invest.

However, that wasn't the deal breaker. Further on in the contract it stated that only products inside the machine could be advertised on the external screen: there would be no revenue from mobile phone adverts as London Underground had signed a preferential advertising contract with Viacom. This had been the most lucrative part of the business Charles had presented to us, and so both Peter and I felt we couldn't invest. Peter tried to renegotiate the contract on Charles's behalf, but the pre-existing deals with Cadbury and Viacom made that impossible.

Charles's remains one of the best pitches we've had on *Dragons' Den* and I'm still convinced he will become a very successful businessman one day. If he ever gets the contract he originally told us he had, then my offer of investment still stands.

One of my other investments from the first series also ran into problems after the cameras stopped rolling. When jewellery designer Elizabeth Galton first came up the stairs wearing an exotic necklace, I thought she was cuckoo. I didn't think much of her outsized jewellery either, to be honest. Some people have told me they thought her necklace looked like a vagina, and I think it was Rachel who said it reminded her of a giant cockroach.

'Oh I've heard the cockroach thing before,' Elizabeth laughed.

Elizabeth laughed a lot during her presentation, and there was something so natural about the way she smiled as she talked about her work as a jewellery designer that I started to think she might be worth investing in. It's very important to like and trust the people you invest in, and Elizabeth was one of the nicest people to enter the den. Nevertheless, I couldn't see how such large pieces of jewellery would become popular.

'Oh, no,' she explained, 'these are just show pieces to make our name. The real business is in selling normal everyday jewellery.'

As a man who likes to wear good, well-made clothes, I appreciate the impact designers like Louis Vuitton and Giorgio Armani have on price tags. When I looked at Elizabeth's jewellery close up I could tell it was very well made, and I heard the other dragons around me agree. I thought she was a high-risk investment, but the chance of owning a percentage of a future designer label offered a very big reward, so I offered half of the £110,000 she was looking for. When Rachel offered to put up the other half, we all shook hands and looked forward to a long and fruitful collaboration.

A few weeks after filming, Rachel and I went to one of Elizabeth's shows together and our legal advisers started to prepare the documentation. We were getting close to signing when Elizabeth phoned me.

'I have a problem,' she said. 'A problem with Rachel.'

The two of them had fallen out over a piece of jewellery Rachel had worn in a photoshoot. Rachel claimed the necklace had been on loan, but Elizabeth insisted that Rachel had commissioned it and agreed to pay £3,800 for it.

I looked through the emails I'd been cc'd on and saw an email from Rachel's PA agreeing to the commission, so I told Rachel that I thought she ought to pay for it.

'But it wasn't very good,' Rachel protested.

'It was good enough for you to use in a photoshoot, which is the purpose for which it was commissioned, so I believe you should pay for it,' I told her.

After some negotiation, Rachel and Elizabeth agreed on a price of £2,000, but after a few more weeks Elizabeth told me that Rachel still hadn't paid her. So I told Elizabeth to send Rachel a letter asking to be paid the £2,000 within seven days, otherwise she would reserve the right to ask for the full £3,800 and take out a county court judgement against her. Rachel sent a cheque. Needless to say, she also withdrew her offer of investment.

Elizabeth then told me that she thought she could make the business work with just my £55,000, so I asked her to write me a business plan showing she could do it for less. While she was writing it, she completely ran out of money, so I invested £10,000 to keep her going. I hadn't finalised the investment agreement with her at this stage, but I'd had enough dealings with her to think I trusted her, so I transferred the £10,000 thinking, if I lose it I lose it. Before she came back to me with a new business plan, however, she called up and said that she'd met a New York merchant banker who wanted to invest the other £55,000. I told her to get him to put his money where his mouth was and put in £10,000 immediately, which he did, but when we got round to scrutinising the paperwork he wasn't happy with a clause that allowed Elizabeth to sell out at a certain level. As this was something I'd agreed to on camera, I didn't feel I could back out of it, so we continued to negotiate the deal.

It had been going on so long that the edition of *Dragons' Den* she'd appeared in had been repeated on television, and she phoned me up to tell me she'd had another offer from someone who'd just seen her on TV.

'They don't just want to take the merchant banker's share, though, they want to take your share, too,' she told me.

'Presumably they'll give me a huge return on my investment?' I asked

'How much are you looking for?'

I calculated that a 25 per cent return for six months' worth of investment would be about right.

And a week later she sent me a cheque for £12,500, representing my initial investment plus profit. Profit of £2,500 might not be much, but at the time of writing, I believe it's the only profit any dragon has actually crystallised on an investment made during the show so far. I'm really quite proud of that £2,500.

What I look for

The most common thing I get asked since *Dragons' Den* became a success is my criteria for investing. The thing I really want from an investment is a return on my capital. My target is 20–25 per cent per annum and many people who come into the den forget to tell us how and when we'll get our return. The secret to a good pitch is simple: know what you're going to say and say it concisely. Tell us what your product or idea is, tell us how you're going to sell that product, and tell us what the projected profit is. It also helps if you can tell us the exit strategy, i.e., the way in which we'll get our money out of the company in the future. Several pitchers have assumed that we'll be happy to put money into a business that they will then run for the rest of their careers. That's not what investment is about: it's about putting money in and getting more money out. It's amazing how many people don't realise that.

I'm probably more relaxed about the exit strategy than other investors, but it depends on the company. Most venture capitalists look to get their money out within three years in order to invest in something else, but if I like the product and the entrepreneurs, I can be flexible and would consider tying up my money for longer. However, it's important to have an exit strategy in mind – either the entrepreneur would buy back my share, or I'd sell it, or we'd float the company.

Aside from the return, I'm also looking for a business that I can add value to. By that I mean something that I can run more efficiently, as I did with Alpha FM, or where my contacts and expertise can grow the company faster than if I wasn't onboard. Something else that makes an investment attractive is if I'll learn something from it. And, of course, the other question I ask myself is, 'Will it be fun?' Nor am I in any mood to work with people I don't trust, and one of the biggest mistakes people make when they come on the show is not telling the truth.

If an entrepreneur tells us something that isn't quite the truth, we'll find out through the due diligence process, so there's no point overstating your case: it will only make you seem sly. I've never understood how some people stand before us expecting us to invest our own money when they won't give straightforward answers to simple questions like, 'How many of you sold?' or 'What's your profit?' Although the final show edits the pitches down to somewhere between five and fifteen minutes, entrepreneurs sometimes spend as much as two hours in front of us, and they have to stand up to pretty intense scrutiny. We're all looking to catch them out and make sure they're as worthy of the investment as they claim to be.

In the second series, the editors made much of Peter's declaration that he wasn't impressed when men couldn't be bothered to wear a suit and tie for their appearance on the show – a couple of newspapers rightly pointed out that in the first series, he actually invested in a couple of guys wearing open-necked shirts! I don't share that view, I don't care what people wear, but I'm not very impressed if people turn up late – it's simple courtesy.

Sometimes I look at the people in front of us and wonder why they don't do what I did at the beginning: get a loan. Obviously there are some people who don't have a track record with the banks and so can't get a loan, but when a woman came before us wearing nice clothes and expensive jewellery, I wanted to know why she was looking for investment.

'You look like you've got a mortgage on a nice house,' I said. 'Why don't you extend your mortgage and get the fifty thousand pounds you're looking for that way? If you did that, you'd still own a hundred per cent of the business.'

To put it simply, she didn't need us.

'But I don't want to take the risk,' she said.

That was my cue to say 'I'm out'. Why should we invest in her when she didn't believe in herself or her business enough to take a risk herself. Every investor is looking for belief, passion and dedication: I've got to believe you're in it for the long haul and that you'll fight with my money as if it was your own.

The other admission that puts off most investors – and I think I can say that includes all the dragons – is when we ask entrepreneurs what they'll use the investment for and they tell us it's for their salary. Perhaps it's because I remember going to car auctions when I'd finished at the bakery, or doing up bedsits when I'd just done a stock-take on the ice-cream vans: I had been prepared to do whatever it took to make the time and find the money to grow my businesses and I like to see entrepreneurs who are prepared to work as hard. While it's true that it's difficult to get a new business off the ground while you still have a job, if you really want to do it, you'll find a way. Unnecessary salaries are a huge drain on a young company's assets, and it's the quickest way of blowing your investment before you've had a chance to prove your business case.

Every investor wants to know what you'll do with their money, and the smart answers involve starting production, increasing output or a marketing push. The really dumb answer is that you want us to pay for you to leave your job. An entrepreneur needs to be hungry: it's often the very nature of the risk that reaps the rewards. I read recently that over half of Britain's self-made millionaires left school without any qualifications. This didn't surprise me: it's much easier to take a risk if you've got nothing to lose. Some of the more established people who come into the den have a tough choice to make between opportunity and comfort.

So, to sum up my advice, it would be to follow four simple rules:

1. <u>Give me a pitch I understand</u> Don't over-complicate things – tell me simply what you do, why your idea is better than your competitors, how people will buy your product or service and why you're the right person to lead your company.
2. <u>Be honest and open</u> Give me simple, straightforward answers to my questions. Don't hide behind jargon, impossible promises or pie-in-the-sky talk. If you come across as sly or deceitful, you'll

leave with nothing.

3. <u>Know your numbers</u> If you don't know how much your product costs to make, what it retails at, your profit margin, your investors' return on capital or how many competitors you have in any given market, then I'm not going to be convinced by you. I want hard figures based on plausible projections.

4. <u>Tell me the exit strategy</u> If I invest in you it will be a partnership: you get my money and input, and in return you give me a return on my capital. That's the deal, so I want to hear how and when I'll be taking my profits.

THIRTY-SIX

My life as a dragon

---

*A nationwide profile was
good for business.*

When the first series of *Dragons' Den* was aired in early 2005, I was single and free to enjoy the perks of fame, and that included a lot more than free coffees on Marylebone High Street.

When I'd been at RADA, I'd been given a lesson in how money instantly makes a man more attractive to women. I had told my fellow students that I was staying on a friend's couch, and as one of the oldest in the group, I had been utterly unremarkable to the other students. It was only when *Mind of a Millionaire* was screened in the middle of the course that a woman who had previously ignored me began to shower me with attention. After *Dragons' Den* I became a bit of a celebrity, and as I was famous for being rich, the attention from women was persistent. I wasn't the only dragon who experienced this – in fact, one woman dated Simon and me simultaneously, and told her story to the papers – and my life in London became a merry-go-round of parties and premieres. It was an incredibly enjoyable time. It wasn't as good, however, as getting back with Joanne, which happened when she brought the kids out to Cannes towards the end of 2005. Throughout our two years apart, we had always remained close and holidayed together with the children, and while our reunion didn't put an end to my partying, it did bring some much-needed emotional stability at a time when it would have been easy to let my ego run away with itself. That said, someone did tell me not to take it personally: even Quasimodo, he said, would have got laid if he'd been on telly!

I don't want to give the impression that I took part in *Dragons' Den* to get my leg over. Having had a high profile in the north-east for many years, and having become friends with local MPs like Michael Fallon and Graham Robb, who became my PR agent after Peter Mandelson took his Hartlepool seat in the 1992 election, I wanted to have a profile nationwide. I didn't want this out of vanity or a sense of self importance: I wanted it because it was good for business.

Whenever I was at a function in the north-east, people would come up to me, either because they'd read about me in the local paper or because we had a contact in common. I see no point in going to parties unless you're going to talk to people, and conversation flows far more freely if people have a reason to approach you. However, although my pledge to the Labour party in 1997 had resulted in a few invites to talk at events down south, I still felt largely invisible to the power base in the capital.

Before *Dragons' Den* I was just another businessman, and politicians wouldn't remember me from one meeting to the next. Since *Dragons' Den*, they know me by sight and seem far more interested in what I've got to say. Gordon Brown knows who I am – he definitely watches the show – and after he attended a talk I gave about how entrepreneurship should be taught in schools, I noticed an announcement of a new government initiative to teach entrepreneurship. I have no idea if it was inspired by my speech, but I do know that I'm now listened to when I talk about anti-smoking legislation in the workplace or whatever else it is that improves the way I run my businesses. That wouldn't have happened without the profile I've earned through *Dragons' Den*, and to a lesser extent the work I did on *Mind Your Own Business*.

It's no wonder, then, that I'm hoping my career in television will continue. I'm now regularly asked to appear on shows like *Richard & Judy*, *The Wright Stuff*, and *Richard Hammond's 5 O'Clock Show* as a pundit. I've also been asked to do a few sessions of showbiz poker. I got a bit of a surprise when I turned up for the filming of one game: one of the pro players taking part, Carlos Citrone, used to sell me gym equipment in the early days of Bannatyne Health and Leisure!

There are other side effects to fame, too. I was interviewed by a journalist called Elisabeth Bolshaw, and in the course of our conversation she mentioned that she was thinking of starting a magazine about entrepreneurialism. Because of *Dragons' Den* she thought I'd make the ideal partner, and as well as putting in a modest investment, having my name on the cover helped *The Sharp Edge* sell out the first issue three times over in some shops.

In 2006, I was asked to become the chairman of an exclusive members' club in London called M1NT where the members were also the shareholders. It was the kind of place that was often featured in the gossip columns and where celebrities hung out – I was flattered to be asked. It had been started by a very charismatic twenty-eight-year-old from Australia called Alistair Paton, and for a time I thought he might be a major player of the future, so I invested some money, took some shares and looked forward to enjoying VIP treatment in VIP company. Sadly, or stupidly, it didn't work out.

Alistair claimed to have had some problems with his landlord, Gordon Ramsay Holdings Ltd, and refused to pay his rent, despite my advice that he should keep up to date with his payments. After many months, Gordon Ramsay's company understandably locked the doors, and effectively closed the club down. I've now written off my investment, and deep down I know I'm partly responsible as I didn't do my homework. I've since got the records from Companies House and seen the list of shareholders – something anyone should do before they invest in a company – and realised that M1NT wasn't the investment, or the club, I'd been led to believe it was.

Only Fools on Horses

The strangest offer I've had as a result of my fame was to take up showjumping for Sport Relief. I received a phone call in April 2006 from the TV production company Endemol – the people who make *Big Brother* for Channel 4 – asking if I wanted to take part in *Only Fools on Horses*, a show that would raise money for charity by training twelve celebrities to showjump. The idea was that we'd compete, the public would vote to keep their favourite celebrity on the show and all the money raised would go to Sport Relief, the charity set up by Comic Relief and the BBC in 2004 to use the power and passion of sport to tackle poverty and help disadvantaged people in the UK and some of the world's poorest countries. Of course, I said yes. There was just one small problem: I'd never been on a horse in my life, let alone showjumped!

The following weekend I had a couple of riding lessons with a friend of mine called Lesley Perry who owns some beautiful horses at Stotford Crescent Stables in Hartlepool. I told her I had six weeks to get half decent before filming started and, over the course of thirty intensive hours, she taught me the basics and got me to a high enough standard to be accepted for the show. I spent a lot of time in those weeks learning why cowboys walk with such a swagger – riding a horse doesn't half take its toll on your you-know-whats. No one told me how much it would hurt.

We started training for the show at Waresley Park Stud near Bedford on 9 June, where I met my fellow contestants for the first time. They were *Changing Rooms'* Anna Ryder Richardson, *Superbikes* presenter Suzi Perry, Olympic gold medallist Sally Gunnell, Ruby Wax, *GMTV*'s Jenni Falconer, Matt Baker from *Blue Peter*, TV gardener Diarmuid Gavin, actors Paul Nicholas (the only person who was older than me), Felix Dexter and Matt Littler. If any of us came a cropper, *Pop Idol*'s Nicki Chapman, presenter Josie D'Arby and fellow entrepreneur Ivan Massow were on the subs' bench. I know it's a cliché, but every single one of them is great fun and I got on extremely well with everyone.

On the first morning, I went down for breakfast and found Anna Ryder Richardson and Sally Gunnell already at a table.

'Hello, Duncan,' said Anna.

I still find it slightly odd when people recognise me from the TV, especially when I recognise them from the telly, too.

'You haven't got your riding kit on.'

It was only then that I realised she was fully kitted out in jodhpurs and boots.

'I think I've been had. Someone from the production team told me we'd all be in the gear.' She took it very well and it got the day off to a good fun start.

The riding parts of our days at Waresley were very serious, though, as we were constantly reminded that horse riding can be dangerous. On that first day, Felix was thrown from his horse, which started bucking and charging and ended up running straight at me. I managed to bring my horse, Jumbo, to a halt, but the sight of the riderless horse made him panic and he reared up on his hind legs. I felt sure I was going to fall off, so I threw my arms around his neck and held on for dear life. Just as Jumbo calmed down, Felix's horse swerved and headed straight for the camera. Luckily the cameraman noticed what was happening and jumped out the way and over a fence before running for his life. When we got back to our hotel, we all had bruises to compare, but thankfully there was a fantastic – if brutal – physiotherapist with us, who kept us fit enough to ride.

After an initial stay at the Park Inn Hotel, we were all moved into a hotel that left a lot to be desired. Double Barrel didn't like her room.

'What's wrong with it?' I asked. 'Not enough MDF?'

Kieran, our runner, arranged for her to change rooms. As a hotelier myself, I'm always interested in how others run their hotels, so when the assistant manager showed Anna to her new room, I tagged along. I was impressed to see a no-smoking sign on the door, and then astonished to see an ashtray in her room.

'Why have you got an ashtray in a no-smoking room?' I asked the assistant manager.

'In case anyone wants to smoke,' he said seriously.

'That's diabolical,' I told him. 'When I check into a room I can smell if someone's been smoking.'

'Well how can we stop them smoking,' he asked.

'Two things. Firstly, most people are honest and will not smoke in a no-smoking room, and if you also provide smoking rooms, it shouldn't be a problem. Secondly, you put it in their contract that if they do smoke they'll be liable for the fumigators' fee and be charged for the twenty-four hours the room cannot be occupied.'

'Oh.'

There were a number of times when I thought things could be done so much better. When I went down for breakfast, I naturally sat at the biggest table so we could all eat together.

'Oh no, sir, you can't sit there.'

'Why not?'

'That table's for dinner guests.'

'It's seven o'clock, no one will be eating dinner for some considerable time.'

'Sorry, sir, it's company policy.'

When Joanne came to visit, they told me they couldn't give me a second key to the room. And when Kieran and I bought a drink at the bar and took it outside, we were told the tables were reserved for people using the restaurant.

'But no one from the restaurant is using them,' I protested.

'It's company policy.'

'But it's sweltering in there.'

'It's company policy.'

Hotel gripes aside, the training was absolutely amazing and we all had a fantastic time. Even though I was having fun, there was absolutely no way I was going to miss John Moreton's wife's fortieth birthday party. Fitting in a trip to their house near Southampton was going to be tough with our training schedule, so I chartered a helicopter to pick Joanne up from the north-east, land at Waresley and take us both to Southampton. The following day, the helicopter dropped me off before taking Joanne home.

Sadly, my time on the show was about to come to an end. I had been complaining to the trainers all week that Jumbo was too slow. I told them he was lazy and wouldn't do anything without a good kick, so they gave me Scooby. It wasn't long before I wished I'd kept my mouth shut. I was in the ring with Paul and Felix when I put Scooby into a canter. A little too late, I realised Paul was coming towards me on his horse, so I tickled Scooby with my left foot to tell him to move over to the right. Being a more sensitive horse, he thought my little tickle meant *turn* right. Unfortunately, there were some poles just to our right and Scooby had no choice but to jump them. As I was not in a jumping position, I lost my balance, which confused Scooby even more, and ended up coming off the back, landing with an enormous thud, and a little snap, on my arse and left arm.

I was instantly in a lot of pain and swore so badly the show's editors had trouble bleeping it out. The staff and nurses came over quickly and, while they were fussing around, Felix trotted up on Jumbo.

'Get off my fucking horse!' I told him, 'I want him back.'

'No chance,' he laughed, 'I love this horse, he barely moves, and when he does it's only to walk. I'm keeping him!'

I ended up on the floor in the green room where Jenni Falconer strategically placed ice packs around me. Matt Baker made me a sling from a luggage strap, which is the kind of thing you'd expect from a *Blue Peter* presenter. Double Barrel came and lay beside me and offered sympathy as the pain in my legs and back got worse. And as we lay there I realised I couldn't move my left arm. I was taken to a hospital forty minutes north of Bedford where an X-ray confirmed the worst: I'd fractured my radius bone. There was no way I would be doing any more riding. There was no point in going back to the hotel, so Endemol put me in a car that took me straight home to Joanne. I was so badly hurt that I had several different types of painkillers and it was clear I wouldn't be going into the office for a full day's work for some time. Never have I been more grateful that I'd learned the art of delegation.

I was incredibly disappointed not to be continuing with the show: I'd loved every minute of the training and was really looking forward to filming starting as the producers were going to put us altogether in the same house to live, *Big Brother*-style, for a fortnight as the viewers voted for their favourite. I received texts from everyone on the show saying how gutted they were that I wouldn't be able to continue. My kids were disappointed, too, they were really proud that their dad was doing something with some celebrities they'd heard of! I was also disappointed because Theo and Peter had pledged to give Sport Aid £12,500 each if I'd won, and it would have been lovely to see them get their cheque books out. Not that there's any serious rivalry between us. Well, not much...

There's a reason they call us dragons

When the first series aired, the five Dragons did a fair bit of publicity and occasionally inflammatory quotes would make their way into print. The *Daily Mail* reported Rachel as saying, 'With so many strong personalities, it wasn't long before things deteriorated. We were like five sticks of dynamite all put together in the den.' I don't remember things being that bad, but there were certainly occasions when we got cross with each other. Being in front of the cameras for ten hours a day will get to anyone eventually.

Over time, I noticed that Rachel had a particular habit of waiting till the rest of us had declared ourselves 'out' before stating her position on a potential investment. I think this was because after we say 'I'm out', we're meant to shut up and let those still interested in the investment use the time productively. But in Rachel's case, it gave her an opportunity to make an uninterrupted assessment of the business, and often this assessment was informed by the comments the rest of us had just made. We usually broke promptly for lunch at one o'clock, except when Rachel was the last dragon in. She once spoke for half an hour about something she had no interest in investing in, and meanwhile our lunch was getting cold.

'Come on, Rachel,' I said. 'You've got no intention of investing in these guys, why don't you let us all go and eat some lunch.'

And do you know what she did? She only went and invested, and I'm sure it was just to prove me wrong.

I wasn't the only one who noticed Rachel's waiting tactic, and one day we all – rather childishly, I'll admit – agreed not to declare ourselves out and wait and see what happened. The entrepreneur who was doing the pitch didn't really have the kind of business any of us were interested in, but nevertheless we managed to keep the questions going for an hour before Rachel piped up.

'I'm confused,' she said, 'Are you in or out? I can't tell.'

'Actually, we're waiting to hear what you think first.'

Throughout the course of three series, there have been some petty fallings out, but never anything that threatened our ability to work together. For example, there was one occasion during filming when Theo didn't like something I'd said and accused me of making a personal attack. It happened when we were considering a pitch from an inventor who'd made a new kind of light for conservatories. Theo announced that 'Mrs P would love one of those'.

Later on in the presentation, I said, 'Well, I haven't seen the inside of Theo's house, but I think those lights are ugly.'

Theo took this as me insulting his taste or perhaps his wife's, and he insisted I retract the remark, which I did immediately. It was an entirely innocent remark with no intention to embarrass or offend, nevertheless, that's the way it was interpreted. It's funny how tiny little comments like that can be the catalyst for a row when you're under pressure, and pressure soon builds up when you film into the night.

Of course, after a hard day under the lights, there were many nights when some or all of us would go out for a drink, and I do remember a couple of drink-fuelled confrontations that it would be inappropriate, and ungentlemanly, to repeat sober. On one occasion, though, something I said in confidence to another dragon ended up in the papers. It wasn't the most sensitive story in the world, but it was a reminder that there's a reason why they call us dragons!

The story, which appeared in late 2005, was that I hadn't been able to attend the launch of my new magazine, *The Sharp Edge*, because I was recovering from cosmetic surgery as the scars were too bad for me to go out. Now it happens that I *had* just had some work done, but the only person who knew about it was a fellow dragon. We'd been talking on the phone and I told him I wouldn't make the launch because I'd just had an operation.

'Has your surgery gone wrong then?' he joked.

'No . . .'

'What did you get done then? Did you get your nose fixed?

'Actually,' I told him, 'I've had some skin removed from around my eyes.'

And sure enough, that's the story that appeared in the paper the day after the magazine launch party.

I'm not ashamed of having had surgery and I don't mind who knows. I first had my eyes done about fifteen years ago, when I decided I didn't want to live with the hereditary Bannatyne bags any more. What I haven't done, which people often accuse me of, is dye my hair. I have absolutely no regrets about doing the work, and I know I'm not the only dragon who has taken care of their appearance with more than regular haircuts. If you compare the first series with the second series, you'll see that swapping Simon for Theo wasn't the only change.

THIRTY-SEVEN

The future

2006–

---

*You don't need to be ruthless
in business.*

It's been twenty-seven years since I sat on that beach in Jersey and decided to become a millionaire. In that time I've made money in industries as diverse as ice-cream vending, nursing homes, radio stations, hotels, health clubs and day-care nurseries. I've also won a few awards aside from the OBE, including the North Region Entrepreneur of the Year, Master Entrepreneur of the Year 2003 for the North Region and, in 2006, I was given an honorary Doctorate of Science from Glasgow University in recognition of my achievements. For a lad who left school with no qualifications, I've now got some pretty impressive letters after my name: Duncan Bannatyne, OBE DSc.

Although I'm more than satisfied with my success, I'm having way too much fun to stop. I'm now moving into new areas like house-building, casinos, bars and magazine publishing. In many ways, some of these activities are extensions of what I already do. The house-building, for instance, involves many of the things we do when we build a health club – buying land, getting planning permission, instructing architects and overseeing construction. Bar Bannatyne, in the centre of Newcastle, was a little experiment to see if we could leverage the relationship we have with the brewery we use for the hotel and the health clubs to better effect. It's now incredibly profitable and produces a 35 per cent return on capital each year. If I have the time, I'll look into opening some more bars in the near future.

Bannatyne's Casino in Newcastle, which opened in 2005, oddly shares some similarities with my care homes and day nurseries, in that I was encouraged to get into it on the back of a change in legislation. It also, of course, shares another similarity: there's a lot of bureaucracy. However, I wasn't the only one thinking a change in the law would be an opportunity, and Newcastle now has four casinos and I'm quite sure we can't all survive. It's a tough business, and although it makes money, I'm comforted by the fact that I own a very valuable freehold on the building. I may decide it would be more valuable as a block of flats – we'll see.

At home, things are changing, too. After thirteen years together, off and on, I proposed to Joanne while we were on holiday in Barbados in the spring of 2006. As I write, preparations for a very elaborate – not to mention expensive – wedding are going on around me. Having made Joanne wait for so long, I'm not going to stand in the way of her dream wedding.

I'm immensely proud to say that I've achieved everything without being ruthless. You don't need to be ruthless in business. All I ever did was buy land at a price other people wanted to sell it for, give builders a contract at a price they suggested, and then people used my services at a price I advertised them at. What's ruthless about that? I've also done a lot of my work in industries – nursing homes, day nurseries and health clubs – that have made life better for people. Business really, truly isn't about being ruthless. Single-minded, sure; but ruthless, no way.

Since I started in business, I've seen huge changes in the way Britons view money. Working-class men like my father would be very unlikely these days to say to their sons, as mine said to me, 'People like us don't start businesses.' Maybe that's Thatcher's legacy, I don't really know, but I think it's great for the country that I get emails from eleven- and twelve-year-olds, telling me that when they grow up they want to be entrepreneurs. *Dragons' Den* has made a huge difference to my life in the short term, but what's more important is the long-term impact the programme and this new spirit of enterprise have on the nation.

A few months ago, Simon Woodroffe invited me to a party for entrepreneurs which he was holding on a magnificent barge he has permanently moored on the Thames in London. He wanted to get some established entrepreneurs together with the new generation of business leaders. As well as Simon and myself, several other millionaires were there – including Gadget Shop founder Chris Gorman, property tycoon Gary McCausland, dotcom doyenne Julie Meyer, and the king of the ringtone, Alexander Amosu. The combined wealth of the people onboard was probably over £1 billion, and although the party didn't last long, I reckon several deals were done that night that would have made the participants even wealthier. SMEMs have a particular way of operating that's direct, efficient, purposeful and generous. SMEMs are very exciting people to be around.

Interestingly, of the twenty or so millionaires I spoke to that night, over half of them had either taken part in a TV show or were about to. Britain is now interested in business and entrepreneurialism like never before. For this reason, I'm incredibly optimistic about the future – there are young entrepreneurs out there who will make fortunes for themselves and along the way create businesses and jobs that will benefit the entire country.

Many of them were on Simon's boat that night. Oliver Bridge was just fifteen at the time, and had started his business – biggerfeet.com – because he'd had difficulty finding shoes to fit his size 15 feet. Twenty-one-year-old Alex Tew, who found fame in early 2006 with his milliondollarhomepage.com stunt, was also there and it's clear he plans to use his $1 million to make a bigger fortune that will secure his wealth for the rest of his life. As I spoke to them, I realised that I hadn't even heard of the word 'entrepreneur' when I was their age.

I just hope they have as much fun with their careers as I've had with mine, because whatever you do, and no matter how much money you make, it's not really worth it if you don't have fun. I love my life: I love being a dad, I love running my businesses, I love my houses, I love my speaking engagements and I love my TV career. I have such a great life that some days I have to pinch myself. Am I really that scruffy kid from Clydebank? Of course I am; and if I can do it, then anyone else can do it, too.

Index